MADAME TUSSAUD

Portrait of Madame Tussaud painted in 1845 by Paul Fischer,
court painter to George III and the Prince Regent

MADAME TUSSAUD
Waxworker Extraordinary

BY

Anita Leslie & Pauline Chapman

HUTCHINSON OF LONDON

Hutchinson & Co. (Publishers) Ltd
3 Fitzroy Square, London W1P 6JD

London Melbourne Sydney Auckland
Wellington Johannesburg and agencies
throughout the world

First published 1978
© Madame Tussaud's Limited 1978

Set in Monotype Fournier

Printed in Great Britain by The Anchor Press Ltd
and bound by Wm Brendon & Son Ltd
both of Tiptree, Essex

ISBN 0 09 133810 7

Contents

Appendices

List of illustrations

Acknowledgement

The authors express their thanks and gratitude for the patient help on numerous occasions of members of archive, library, and record office staffs in tracing, photocopying, and photographing material relating to Curtius and Madame Tussaud and their Exhibitions.

Foreword

A short time ago an eminent professor of history happened to ask us, 'But did Madame Tussaud really exist?' Being in the throes of sorting out the massive documentation we were slow to formulate an answer. Madame Tussaud's life was so long and varied and sometimes incredible that it had not always been easy to shake truth from the dust, but she not only existed – she made her mark.

Millions know, and have known, the name of Madame Tussaud, and yet it remains unlisted in the annals of women's achievement. To the crowds who flock to the Exhibition in Marylebone Road from all over the world, Madame Tussaud is a vague figure from the past, a woman somehow mixed up with the French Revolution who modelled guillotined heads and established a Chamber of Horrors in the wax exhibition which she brought to England decades ago.

These facts are true, but Madame Tussaud was more than a clever showwoman. Because she lived at the court of Versailles, and then knew most of the French revolutionaries quite intimately, she becomes an historical personage. In addition to this she takes a high place in any record of the world's most successful women. She was among the first great career women, for although she never talked of feminist emancipation she created her own business and built up her own prestige without help from any man. Being an indefatigable worker, a talented sculptress and a brilliant journalist in her own medium of wax, she showed a courageous independence, and when she died in 1850, in her ninetieth year, she left her two sons an Exhibition that continues to flourish today. This is her monument.

No less remarkable in his own way was Philippe Curtius, whom she called uncle. He was her tutor in wax modelling and founder of the Cabinet de Cire in Paris in the 1760s. Research reveals Curtius as a fascinating, if not always attractive, minor character of the pre-revolutionary and revolutionary periods; certainly he was a man of great talent and energy. Had he not died at the age of fifty-seven it is unlikely that London would ever have seen Madame Tussaud's. His comparatively early death changed the course of Marie's life.

This biography, based on the archivist's twelve years' research in French and English sources, and on material previously in Madame Tussaud's archives, traces the life of this remarkable woman, from her birth in Strasbourg in 1761 to her death in Victorian London. She had lived at the French court, witnessed one of the greatest upheavals in Europe, and worked in England from 1802 during the reigns of four monarchs. Few women have provided so much pleasure for so many, combining entertainment with visual education in a way that no one had done before. Few have toiled so long and so intensely, undaunted by obstacles and misfortunes. Her life-story cannot be compared with that of any other woman; she was an extraordinary person, unequalled in her own sphere.

The two hundred pages of this book have to be the answer to that history professor's casual question, 'But did Madame Tussaud really exist?'

Anita Leslie
Pauline Chapman

Record of Marie Grosholtz's baptism, 7 December 1761. *Register of old St Peter's Catholic Church, Strasbourg*

I

The beginnings

She would always be an enigma. Two hundred years later her character bewilders biographers. It is typical that for no known reason she claimed Berne as her birth-place, when she knew that she had been born not in Switzerland but in Alsace.* In the old church of St Peter, standing in what was then an almost medieval working-class district of Strasbourg, many thousands of babies have been christened, but none would become as famous as that tiny human morsel carried there on a winter's day, who would eventually bear the name of Madame Tussaud. Apparently it was not her young mother but the midwife who presented this baby at the church. A translation of the vicar's Latin record reads:

Today on 7 December 1761 I baptized the undersigned Anna Maria, daughter of Johannes Grosholtz of Frankfurt and of Anna Maria Walder of Strasbourg who is known locally. This is confirmed by the midwife of this Parish, Maria Barbara Müller, who according to the declaration of the Mother, stood by her during the pangs of birth and who has, according to the trust placed in her office, laid the child before us.

As godfather Johannes Trappler our Sexton, and as deputy godmother Anna Maria Logler, known in this Parish have signed with me in the absence of the father.

Patrinus Trappler
Matrina Logler
Obstretrix [midwife] Müllerin
Jansen, Vicar

* Her marriage contract of 1795 gives Strasbourg as her birth-place.

The baby's mother may have been too ill to attend the christening but she was certainly well known in the parish, for the records show that Anne Marie Walder had been baptized in this same church eighteen years before. She must have been a very young bride, for that shadowy soldier Joseph Grosholtz of Frankfurt passes through this story leaving faint imprint. There is not even written evidence of the dates of his birth or marriage. All that can be firmly assumed is that such a man existed and it is probable that the family stories about him are true. According to Madame Tussaud's account, Joseph Grosholtz was a minor hero of the Seven Years' War and chosen as ADC to General Count Dagobert de Würmser, commander of a squadron of Hussars fighting for Maria Theresa of Austria. During a battle which took place prior to the birth of his only child he was badly wounded, having his forehead laid bare and his jaw shot away, to be replaced by a silver plate. There is no mention of the name Grosholtz in army records of the time, but General de Würmser did raise two regiments in the Rhineland and fought several battles in which Grosholtz could have participated. The absent father mentioned in Marie's baptismal record had returned with terrible facial mutilations and died before her birth.* The story has to be left there. We may well wonder why a dashing ADC should have married an ordinary little working-class girl in Strasbourg whose only outstanding talent mentioned over the next forty years would be her Alsatian cooking – maybe Grosholtz was very fond of sauerkraut; more likely, his seventeen-year-old bride was extremely pretty.

Whatever the reason for this match, misted over by time, within a couple of years after Grosholtz's death his widow and her baby daughter had removed to Berne, and there, in circumstances which arouse curiosity but have to be left to the imagination, she became cook–housekeeper to an unusually interesting German-born doctor. It is fruitless to wonder where they met or how affectionate the relationship became. Nor should the serious biographer speculate – although it is entertaining to do so – as to possible meetings in Strasbourg between young Madame Grosholtz and Dr Curtius prior to the baby's birth. There is no firm evidence that little Anne Marie was sired by the man who was to bring her up and teach her to model, and make her his sole heir, nor for that matter is there any evidence that her legal father came home from the wars at the necessary

* *Madame Tussaud's Memoirs and Reminiscences of France*, ed. F. Hervé (London 1838).

moment. All that matters is that Anne Marie was *born*; and a very exceptional person she would prove to be.

Peering through the smokescreen of her later recollection it is hard to envisage the 'set-up' in that Berne house which was the background of baby Marie's earliest memories. Madame Grosholtz must have been a cosy, lovable person, but she was very young, just in her early twenties.

Philippe Guillaume Mathé Curtius was certainly attractive. This gentleman's somewhat curious story is well documented. He was born on 30 January 1737 into a family which at that time would be deemed *petite noblesse*. His baptism is recorded in the register of the parish church of Stockach, a little town near the northern end of Lake Constance (which then lay in the Holy Roman Empire and now lies in West Germany). Philippe's father, Christopher Frederick Curtius, was one of the Emperor's officials in the Landgrave of Nellenbourg, and his mother, *née* Marie Catherine Mauret, a gentlewoman.

When, in his twenties, Philippe acquired medical qualifications, which was not very usual for sons of the small nobility, he opened his practice in Berne. Either to illustrate lectures or for his own edification, he took to moulding wax replicas of anatomical organs, and then, succumbing to the fascination of modelling with warmed wax, he turned to portraiture. It was more amusing to reproduce faces than livers, and Curtius showed that he possessed considerable talent. Small wax busts and heads were much in vogue and soon Dr Curtius found it more profitable to model than to dose. Naturally his knowledge of anatomy helped. When the widow Grosholtz arrived to keep house, she found the doctor already running a small waxwork museum. He was inventive and energetic and he had discovered what he enjoyed doing.

In 1763 the great Prince de Conti came incognito to Switzerland, where his protégé Jean Jacques Rousseau had taken refuge after arousing the wrath of the 'Establishment' in France by publishing *Émile*. De Conti was leader of the princely opposition party in Paris and a thorn in the side of France's kings. It was probably after visiting Rousseau on his island in Lake Bienne that he happened to look into the waxwork museum in Berne. He was so impressed by the doctor's talent that he suggested a move to Paris where Curtius could enjoy his patronage. When the Prince offered to provide an apartment the doctor decided not to miss such a wonderful chance. Under the aegis of his noble patron he could not fail to make a fortune and, just as modelling seemed more fulfilling than pre-

B

scription-writing, so Paris seemed more exciting than Berne. Curtius took the biggest decision of his life. The coach carried him away out of the Swiss hills into the kingdom of France and Madame Grosholtz and her toddling daughter were left alone dusting the house in Berne.

For about two years Curtius seems to have left them there. Paris revealed a new world of fantastic wealth and glamour and the Prince de Conti proved as good as his word. He provided an apartment in the rue St Honoré where a former grand mansion, the Hôtel d'Allègre, had been divided into small workshops, galleries and residences for artists. The Prince himself was Grand Prior of the Order of Malta and had the right to live in the great palace of the Temple where he kept tremendous style. Having quarrelled with Madame de Pompadour and been banished from Versailles by Louis XV, de Conti had established an unconventional brilliant court of his own. Good-looking, irreligious, full of himself, de Conti was a man of culture, eccentric but seriously interested in science, literature and the arts, and he deliberately sought to surround himself with genius. Princes were not expected to create, but to inspect, judge and encourage others, and to guide bread into the mouths of hungry artists. Every court in Europe possessed a shimmering outer fringe of 'talented hangers-on'. To the magnificent receptions and fêtes which it pleased this Prince to organize came a wide range of men. Although an upholder of the monarchy, de Conti often disagreed with its policies. He was a powerful enemy, and Louis XV could be nervous of him. He had a liberal mind and supported the philosophers of the time; apart from Rousseau, he extended his patronage to Beaumarchais and Diderot. Plays and concerts were held at the palace; wit and talent were at a premium.

Dr Curtius took to this marvellous world like a duck to water. He attended the Prince's receptions, made friends and raked in orders. It was his delight to be invited to enter that famous Salon of Four Mirrors through which it was said that every famous man in Europe must eventually pass. Among the more interesting artistic records of the eighteenth century is an oil painting by the Prince's 'personal artist', Michel Ollivier, showing an infant prodigy seated at the harpsichord in this very room – the child being Mozart.

In such an atmosphere Dr Curtius settled down to enjoy life and to work hard. His reputation spread and soon commissions for portrait heads in wax were piling up. Maybe it was caution that caused him to delay sending for his housekeeper. He knew that it was all-important to establish his name, and with so many orders and frequent invitations to the semi-royal palace within the Temple walls, he was always engagingly occupied. Paris had become the centre of the civilized world and the Prince de Conti's private court the very core of Europe. Curtius met many of the most interesting men alive and some of them ordered a portrait in wax. He followed a methodical technique. The face of the sitter would be oiled and any facial hair flattened with pomade. Then a mask of plaster was applied and allowed to harden while quills were inserted into the nostrils allowing the 'patient' to breathe. Later, after the sitter had been well washed and otherwise restored to comfort, a clay squeeze would be taken from the mask. The good doctor then settled down to a careful reproduction of every feature from measurements, observation and detailed notes. Eventually a plaster mould could be taken from the clay portrait head and from this would be made the final wax cast. A very special expertise had to be developed to ensure the success of this process for it was never easy to pour and cool the wax. The finishing of the portrait, the facial colouring and insertion of hair demanded a skill which allowed Dr Curtius to regard himself as a true artist.

Naturally the young German wanted to earn a fortune as quickly as possible, and he soon learned that a profitable market existed for groups of little wax figures in erotic poses. This amusing sideline was far easier to produce than actual portraits and allowed more chance of artistic expression, for each licentious boudoir demanded a new suggestion. In time Curtius opened a second salon on the Boulevard St Martin where, as well as modelling in wax, he produced pictures in enamel. He also studied the techniques of bygone artists and became so knowledgeable that he was able to pick up old paintings and re-sell at a profit. The craft of exact wax reproduction helped to develop the 'eye', and in later times Curtius might have made his fortune as an art dealer.

Soon Curtius possessed a wide circle of friends, and knew most of the important politicians and literary men. Eventually he was granted the honour of modelling wax miniatures of Louis XV and then of his queen, Marie Leczinska, and of her father, the ex-King of Poland.* King Stanislas was delighted and he went into the street to find a stranger to view the portrait. His Majesty invited a passing soldier to enter the salon and give an opinion. The King wanted to see what impression the wax head would

---

* This wax miniature of the Queen survived until 1925 when it perished in the fire which destroyed the premises of Madame Tussaud's in London.

make. The soldier seemed astonished by its likeness to the man who brought him in, but then he noticed the orders and decorations which even ex-royalty wore on their attire. The poor man became embarrassed. So King Stanislas put him out of his misery by explaining. The King possessed what was called at the time a 'graciously condescending manner'.

In 1765 Curtius modelled an extremely beautiful girl of twenty-two – mistress of the notorious rascal Jean du Barry, whose brother she would wed when it became imperative that she assume the married status which allowed her to come to court. The reclining figure of lovely Jeanne du Barry, last mistress of Louis XV,* would travel to England long after the lady had lost her life on the guillotine, and Dr Curtius would model Madame du Barry once again in less elegant circumstances.

Perhaps Curtius occasionally visited Berne when the roads were clear of snow, but not until 1767 did he feel sufficiently rich and confident to permit his housekeeper and her little daughter to join him. Marie, as she was now called, was six years old when her mother packed up and they boarded a series of coaches to bring them to Paris – the great city, the centre of the world.

*This figure survives today as 'The Sleeping Beauty' at Madame Tussaud's. The long almond-shaped eyes and the delicate arched eyebrows and long neck give the same exquisite impression as her early portraits. According to John Theodore Tussaud, great-grandson of Madame Tussaud, the mechanism which made the Sleeping Beauty's chest rise and fall as if breathing was first installed by a Clerkenwell clockmaker about 1837. The clockwork, wound daily by hand, remained until around the turn of the century. The late Bernard Tussaud, son of John Theodore, recalled that at the turn of the century, when he was a small child, the clockwork became automatically rewound by an electrical device installed by an engineer called Jenkins.

2

Girlhood in Paris

It is difficult to envisage the Paris of 1767, the teeming streets and twisting cobblestoned alleys, the open sewers, the clamour, the exciting and disgusting sights. Even the main streets were so narrow that houses were protected from damage by *bornes* erected against the walls to fend off passing carts and vehicles. The population had been packed into sixteen *quartiers* within walls erected to prevent the smuggling of food and supplies into the city without payment of dues. The narrow, winding streets were so dirty that only the poor walked, and there were no footpaths. All rich or moderately well-off people travelled by carriage or by sedan-chair – the legs and feet of the carriers might be coated with filth as they bore their gilded burden through mud and sewage, but that did not worry the personage within. Only the stench of the streets troubled the 'persons of quality', and they were busy thinking up witticisms. The robust survived infections, the weaker died. Luckily for her, little Marie Grosholtz had iron health, for within Paris were 30 000 wells, most of which were contaminated by sewers and cemeteries. Voltaire describes the main city cemetery of the Innocents:

the poor, often dying of contagious diseases, are buried there pell mell. Dogs come to gnaw the bones; a dense vapour arises, it is pestilential in the heat of summer after the rains, and almost next door to this garbage heap are the Opéra, the Palais Royal, the royal Louvre. The filth of the privies is taken a league away, and for twelve hundred years the rotting bodies from which this filth was produced have been stacked in the same town. In vain does the example of so many European towns put Paris to the blush; it will never reform.

After the fresh air and clean streets of Berne, Marie may well have wondered where she could run and play. Probably she was sent to learn French in one of the convent schools which owned large gardens within the city walls. There she could enjoy the company of other children as well as pick up a new language and polite manners. When she returned home it would be to watch her mother managing the kitchen and to listen with interest to the names of famous people who flocked to the apartment. She regarded Dr Curtius with awe. He had become an important personage, of that the child was well aware; he knew 'everyone', he worked incessantly and must not be disturbed. But soon, how soon we have to guess, there came a day when that small figure entered the studio and watched the doctor at his tasks. Already he had a certain feeling for the little girl and told her to call him 'Uncle'. Marie was a lively, precocious child, much noticed by visitors who reacted with amusement to her replies, but there was more to Curtius's emotion than mere amusement could warrant. Whether he had had an affair with Madame Grosholtz or not, he recognized something of himself in this tiny observant person, and there must have been a curiously interesting moment when he first handed her a ball of clay to model and watched the little face puckered in concentration. 'You shall be my pupil,' said the great Dr Curtius, and Marie knew her first moment of pride. She resolved to be a diligent pupil; she would learn this art and do credit to her teacher. From that moment on Marie never really entertained any thought beyond the perfecting of her craft. Her bright little eyes missed nothing. All faces, all human quirks, all habits and ways of dressing and sitting and laughing, were grist to her mill.

Sometimes she went for drives in Curtius's carriage, and then she could take note of another kind of people – the poor. These never crossed the threshold of her abode, but nearby, in the district extending from the rue St Honoré to the place du Carrousel, there stretched an area of dismal stinking hovels from which crept beggars and children so ragged and thin that it was hardly possible to feel they belonged to her own human race. Yet the nastiness of their existence held a certain fascination. An anonymous writer describes the scene:

There was scarcely in all Paris a more seething or more picturesque slum . . . the hovels swarmed with bird-sellers, brokers, shabby wine shops, and in the waste ground jugglers, dentists, quacks and dog-gelders.

This was a world into which a nicely brought-up child did not step. She only saw these people from the carriage window, and yet they were real, as real as the ladies who arrived in gilded sedan-chairs for a wax likeness. They always smiled at her, spoke to her and made her feel that her conversation was charming. *That* was the world to which Marie felt she belonged – the indoor life of people in silken clothes with laughing faces. These were happy successful days.

The underside of Paris which Mrs Thrale noted in her letters to Dr Johnson did not have to be spoken of: 'There is a place called the Morgue where all dead bodies which have been found in the night, drowned, crushed or assassinated, are carried every morning to be owned and buried by their friends.'

In Curtius's busy household the years flew, and by the time she reached her teens, Marie had become an extremely good modeller. Curtius often entrusted her with the responsibility of taking plaster casts and occasionally of making portraits. She seemed to have that knack, so important to any artist, of arousing interest in the sitter and then catching fleeting facial expression. In days before the camera, that expression had to be memorized and then implanted on the finished version. Marie could do this. She cared nothing for formal education; she found instruction in people, not in books, and the gruelling training which Dr Curtius insisted was necessary – the knowledge of anatomy and casting and wax tinting would serve her well throughout her life. Putting pen to paper bored her and although she wrote a clear strong hand it is obvious that her talents were entirely visual – she glanced, she saw and she remembered. To do this was a very special endowment.

And there was another aspect to Marie's upbringing – she could hardly have failed to develop a facility for intelligent conversation at her teacher's table. Until the moment came for ladies to retire after dessert, Marie and her mother sat with the doctor's guests throughout all meals, and his circle was extremely varied. Marie found herself chatting not only to the famous but to the interesting – politicians, writers and artists thronged the house. An alert young girl must have learned both to listen and to speak among such men. But while they held forth over the dinner table, few realized the polite young girl was watching, cat-like, what life had depicted on their faces.

Among those who made a particularly vivid impression was the brilliant, dissolute Comte de Mirabeau. Ugly and pock-marked, with flashing dark eyes and a shock of black hair, he had spent years in a running battle with his father over debts and other men's wives. However often Monsieur le Vicomte shipped his debauched son off to distant military posts, he managed to reappear and once again inveigle people into lending him the money necessary for extravagant self-indulgence. Marie studied Mirabeau carefully; there was indeed something fascinating in the deep lines on that mobile expressive face. His drunken behaviour occasionally caused Curtius to ban him from the house. Yet when Mirabeau came back, contrite and charming, the doctor would relent, and that attractive devil sat at table once again.

Marie Grosholtz hardly realized her luck. Few children of artistic bent are permitted to begin training at the age of six. From the start of her life she was doing what she enjoyed and with the added stimulation of knowing she did it well. When Marie Antoinette's brother, the Emperor Joseph of Austria, came to Paris incognito as the Comte de Lichtenstein, he visited Curtius's salon. The layout of rooms in the house was complicated. To reach the studio the doctor had to walk his visitor through the dining room where the aroma of Madame Grosholtz's famed Alsatian cooking reached the royal nostrils. The Emperor sniffed and insisted on sitting down 'with the family' to tuck into the sauerkraut and to hold forth volubly as if delighted to find, at last, German-speaking people. We do not know if the Emperor found time to pose, but he bought a figure of Venus and several other small wax figures. Dr Curtius could, of course, discourse admirably in French, but it is doubtful if his housekeeper ever became fluent. Marie never lost her German accent.

By 1776 when the Prince de Conti died, in his sixtieth year – after much trying-on of his coffin which the Prince, temperamental to the last, complained was too narrow – Curtius had transferred to new premises in the Palais Royal. A letter written to him by his Mayence lawyer, Altenburg, gives the address as 'Au Palais Royal – Côté de l'Avenue de l'Opéra par la Cour Desfontaine'. Marie remembered Lafayette bringing Benjamin Franklin to the house, 'an agreeable companion with amiable manner and simplicity of appearance' was her verdict.*

In 1778, when Marie was seventeen years old, she was allowed to model a head of Jean Jacques Rousseau. Then, such was her skill and accuracy, Curtius entrusted her with the task of modelling Voltaire from life.

* Her portrait of Benjamin Franklin survives in Madame Tussaud's. Franklin, sent to Paris 'to transact the business of his country at the Court of France', had of course the object of obtaining political and financial assistance in forming a United States of America.

The great man had returned from years of exile in Geneva and had only months to live, but his wit and gaiety never diminished. Sometimes Rousseau, who half-hated him or was jealous, would come to sit for his portrait, and the two philosophers would argue together at Curtius's dinner table. Rousseau, teeming with excitable ideas, and a heartless brute to his own pathetic illegitimate children, never produced a *bon mot* that could equal those which poured so lightly from Voltaire. 'A curious people the English,' Voltaire would say, toying with Madame Grosholtz's delicious cooking. 'They have twenty-eight religious sects and only one fish sauce.'

Rousseau's long-winded indictment of the English nation would die upon his lips. No girl could remain uneducated in such company. After the old man had departed, Rousseau would storm on, crazily declaiming that eighty-four-year-old Voltaire was 'a knave and a rascal'. Marie realized that philosophers do not suffer each other gladly. She was sent to do Voltaire's portrait a few months before he died. After Voltaire weakened, Curtius was called to the old man's bedside where he sculpted a wax miniature of that strange, wonderful face.*

As the Salon de Cire became increasingly well known, few persons of note passed through Paris without looking in. Curtius, in self-defence perhaps, became something of a snob, and only found time for personal contact with the famous. Distinguished visitors would be picked from the throng to be shown around by the doctor and introduced to Marie as his pupil-niece. Alas, that the girl kept no diary and that her chief memories are of royalty, on the whole remarkable only for 'amiable manners'. Gustavus III of Sweden came to pose and here Curtius found a hard test, for the King resembled nothing so much as a hare, with one side of his face smaller than the other. The doctor stuck to his lop-sided measurements, for His Majesty did not wish for beautification. He purchased two small heads – one of the famous Mohawk chief known as Joseph Brant, who sided with the British in the American Indian revolutionary wars, and one of Struensee, a royal physician who was executed in Denmark for dabbling in politics.

Marie would be highly critical of the Tsarevich Paul, son of Catherine the Great; this royalty was *not* amiable – he had disagreeable manners, scrofula, and 'a very high cravat which did not sufficiently hide a suppur-

* This is the only one of Curtius's wax miniatures still in existence at Madame Tussaud's. The life-size portrait made by Marie is still in the Exhibition.

ating jaw'. However, his German consort behaved 'graciously'. Prince Henry of Prussia, brother of Frederick the Great, came to be modelled, and his coarse features and squint imposed a slight problem on a craftsman whose aim was absolute accuracy. The Spanish Prince of Asturias sat for his portrait and so did an eccentric Russian nobleman, Prince Radziwill, who was travelling around in exile. His long cortège of carriages was considerably hampered by carts carrying his basic fortune in the form of twelve pure gold statues of the Apostles. One had been melted down and converted into cash before Curtius arrived to inspect them, but he reckoned their weight would enable the Prince to live in splendour during a very long life.

The diary of Elkanah Watson, a young Puritan from New England who arrived in Paris with despatches for Dr Benjamin Franklin, records his visit to an 'exhibition of waxworks' in September 1779, and this could only be the Cabinet de Cire of Dr Curtius. Having commented disapprovingly on the area of the Palais Royal public gardens as 'a mass of moral corruption', he stopped on his way to the theatre to view the waxwork collection. Watson continued:

In entering the door a surly Century [*sic*] rather obstructed our passage – in passing I was surprised to observe this supposed Century to be artificial. The doorkeeper told me it was a Bostonian, tho' entirely foreign, as it resembles an old Swiss with whiskers. The variety of these works are too numerous to detail – the most striking however was that of the celebrated Voltaire who is closely engaged with a table full of books, papers, etc. before him, and his countenance expressed the very sensation of being a philosopher.

This is a sketch of the turbulent Paris in which Marie Grosholtz grew up. It was a scintillating if horrific world, always changing, always noisy. Since the age of six she had lived in a house of incessant chatter, studying the faces of the famous and those who wished to be famous. A tiny bird-like creature who excelled at her craft, Mademoiselle Grosholtz had become part of the scenery of the Palais Royal.

But an extraordinary change in her life was to occur. At the age of twenty she would suddenly be removed from the noise and clamour of Curtius's house to different, more splendid surroundings.

3

Eight years in the Palace
of Versailles

When Louis XV had died in 1774 the coach of his mistress Madame du Barry rolled for the last time out of the great courtyard of Versailles. His hard-working, virtuous grandson ascended the throne with beautiful Marie Antoinette as his young Queen. Louis XVI had two younger brothers and two small sisters – Clotilde, who was fourteen at the time of his coronation, and the ten-year-old Elizabeth. Both these girls, who carried the royal title of 'Madame' from infancy, were dearly loved by their sister-in-law Marie Antoinette. When small, the two motherless princesses remained under the care of the Comtesse de Marsan, Governess of the Children of France. Then, after their brother ascended the throne, their education was assisted by an erudite lady of high character. This personage, Madame Mackau, had herself been educated at St Cyr, the girls' school devised by Louis XIV and his 'wife', Madame de Maintenon, for aristocratic girls from the provinces whose families could not come to court, and whose piteously dreary lives – for no dowry meant no husband – were to be mitigated by study and occasional pats on the head by His Majesty. While the school lasted the teaching was excellent.

Madame Mackau found the elder princess, Clotilde, to be a happy equable child, but at the age of fourteen she had made her début into the sparkling court of Versailles, and at sixteen she became affianced to the eldest son of the King of Sardinia. Poor little Madame Elizabeth, sensitive and loving by nature, had found it painful enough to lose her only sister when she 'came out' at court. Later the knowledge that Clotilde must depart to become future queen of some distant land caused deep pain to the eleven-year-old Elizabeth. Marie Antoinette in letters to her mother, the Empress Maria Theresa of Austria, describes the child clinging to her sister's arms and being carried away half-fainting when the time of parting came. 'Gone for ever' – these grim words represented the reality of marriage for princesses in the eighteenth century.

Madame Mackau realized early on that her charge possessed a proud, passionate temperament, but although Elizabeth could show obstinacy, she was eager to be good. In the unnatural circumstances of her royal situation, in the loneliness forced on a little Princess, in the heartbreak of losing her sister, she clung frantically to that stern yet kind governess who had been disciplined in the harrowing experiment of St Cyr. Madame Mackau did not pretend that life was easy, but she recognized the nature of this young Princess and determined to guide her along that hard path where passion can be an asset – the path towards God.

Madame Elizabeth suffered a kind of nervous breakdown when her sister departed. As she had no young companions to turn to, only her governess could offer consolation. Under the influence of Madame Mackau the girl became extremely devout. After being dissuaded by Louis from following her aunt into a Carmelite convent, she took a nursing course and then her fervent interests turned to charitable works, helping the unfortunate, sending money to the poor. But how difficult it was for a sheltered princess to judge which were the most deserving cases!

In 1778, the year in which Marie Grosholtz was modelling Voltaire, Madame Elizabeth reached the age of fourteen, left the schoolroom, and 'came out'. By now she had developed into a quiet girl of studious inclination. As a fully fledged member of the Royal Family she must not appear to be bored or unhappy, so she kept busy. She was extremely musical, able to compose songs, and she embroidered. Such was Elizabeth's dexterity with the needle and so sharp her ear that her creative impulses may have been fulfilled. As a Princess of France she would always be good, obedient, devout and self-controlled. If her brother arranged a marriage, she would dutifully depart unprotesting. If suitors failed, she would allow no emotion to show. Three husbands were considered during the next few years – Joseph II of Austria (Marie Antoinette's brother), the heir to Portugal, and the Duc d'Aosta. Madame Elizabeth accepted these possible alliances coolly and showed indifference when they fell through. 'I prefer to remain at the foot of my brother's throne than to ascend any other', she said. Madame Mackau remained her companion – an understanding older woman – whom now she dared call friend.

Louis XVI and Elizabeth were very fond of each other. After Marie Antoinette gave birth to her first child, the Princesse Royale, he permitted his sister a separate establishment. The fifteen-year-old Elizabeth was asked to dispense with several of her ladies who were now relegated to the household of the new baby, but with 10 000 people in attendance at Versailles there could hardly have been a shortage of personnel. The young Princess was charmed with her new independence, but she still wished to spend most of her time in the company of Marie Antoinette at Trianon. Her only trouble lay in not having enough to do. An intelligent, fervent, well-educated girl could never completely satisfy the fire of what that percipient governess called a 'passionate temperament' in prayer and court receptions, music and embroidery. The courtiers called Madame Elizabeth 'sensible and prudent'. She was also idealistic.

Around 1780, accompanied by her ladies-in-waiting, the Princess paid a visit to the waxworks of Monsieur Curtius at the Palais Royal, and Marie Grosholtz was presented to her. Arising from her curtsy Marie looked straight into the Princess's face and saw reflected one that curiously resembled her own. Madame Elizabeth was fair, Marie was dark, but they had the same long narrow nose. This was a Bourbon characteristic and Marie would later make much of the possibility that somewhere, somehow, one of her unknown ancestors had in the past caught a royal eye.

It is likely that Madame Elizabeth was less intrigued by Marie's nose than by her liveliness and her artistry. Already the Princess had dabbled with the wax modelling then much in vogue. Wax fruit and flowers were as entertaining to work at as embroideries, and Madame Elizabeth went further – she moulded religious figures and little arms and legs as votive offerings for those who suffered deformity. Permanently twisted bones were frequent in days before the development of surgical skill. The perfection with which Marie could copy a human face intrigued the Princess, and she took a fancy to the girl. Would Marie give instruction? To her surprise Marie was appointed to be art tutor at Versailles, and off she went to reside at the palace. Her mother surely rubbed her hands with delight at such an honour, and Dr Curtius was never one to stand in the way of ambition. He must have missed his clever pupil, while glad to see her better herself.

Madame Elizabeth was sixteen years old at the time; Marie four years older. The girls became close friends, as close, that is, as rank permitted. If Marie missed the hectic theatrical atmosphere of her uncle's studio, she found that another world of absorbing interest opened out to one who joined the royal household. And Madame Elizabeth proved a delightful patron, who disliked the incessant envious bickering among courtiers. Marie was not able to share the Princess's religious feelings but she could give first-rate instruction.

Although so different in rank, a certain bond existed between the girls. Both had creative temperaments; both were earnest, and artistic. Marie had always strained herself to attain professional excellence, and the Princess found pleasure in making things with her own hands as well as helping the unfortunate. Wax-modelling proved a perfect therapy. Meanwhile King Louis made very fine furniture in his own workshop and Marie Antoinette amused herself painting water-colours.

Marie Grosholtz must have had beautiful manners or she could not have fitted in to life at Versailles. Madame Elizabeth certainly found her congenial, for the art tutor was allotted a room next to her own suite in the northern wing of the great château. Every morning early, when Marie Grosholtz peeped through her curtains, she could see that the first windows to be lit were those of the King. Louis rose at six o'clock when most of his courtiers lay sleeping, breakfasted on lemon juice and unbuttered toast, by candlelight. Then he went out for an hour and a half's walk in the countryside before returning for his official *petit lever* at eight o'clock.

The well-paved, tree-lined road leading from Paris to Versailles was lit at night by large oil lamps suspended over its centre so that carriages could travel at a good pace even in the dark. Unlike the narrow city streets, this wide, thronged road was not filthy or dangerous for foot travellers. At the age of twenty Marie must have rejoiced at the turn of events which gave her the chance to travel to and fro.

'Maman' listened, impressed, to stories of the court. How could she not be proud of this talented daughter? And Curtius related his own plans and adventures. As well as Benjamin Franklin and Lafayette, he knew and entertained others whose talk was all of liberty and individual freedom.

In 1781 Louis XVI had presented Madame Elizabeth with a property of her own. This was charming Montreuil on the outskirts of the town of Versailles. The house lay in its own small park with a farm attached. The King decreed that Madame Elizabeth might not spend the night there until she reached the age of twenty-four, but every morning she and her household drove out and there amidst the flower-beds and trees they could play at being country-folk. The days at Montreuil were pleasantly regulated. After long years of Madame Mackau's discipline, the Princess disliked muddle. Her charity work never became haphazard. Riding and walking was carefully organized and there were set hours for reading and for study. At Montreuil, where Madame Elizabeth imagined she could emulate the quiet life of a country château, Marie dined with the royal household at a long table. Before returning to the palace each evening prayers would be said and then, in an aura of piety, the ladies would troop out to the carriages and drive back.

The royal Princess and the diligent modeller grew from frail girls into unfrivolous, accomplished women. Neither of them appeared to be interested in marriage. For Madame Elizabeth only a dynastic arrangement was possible; humble Marie Grosholtz seemed equally indifferent to possible husbands.

For a princess it was difficult to become shrewd, but Marie was well able to advise on the cases most desperately in need of financial help. Marie never pretended to be devout but she was kind and considerate, and it is possible that she may have put in a good word for Thérèse le Vasseur, the wretched servant-girl who as Rousseau's mistress bore him several illegitimate children. Poor Thérèse had applied in vain to that monster who deliberately spawned children and left them in orphanages, but when she turned to the royal lady who detested Rousseau's views, her plea was answered. Marie knew the world. She could explain dire financial distress to this princess who tried to help the whole suffering world.

Sometimes Madame Elizabeth overspent, and she often anticipated her allowance. Once when short of funds she asked Marie to lend her money for a pathetic appeal. No trace has been found in Madame Elizabeth's household accounts of any salary for Marie Grosholtz, but it is likely that she was remunerated directly from the Princess's purse.

Because Versailles was so different to the bustling, noisy ferment of the Palais Royal, Marie must have changed during her eight years in the royal household. Madame Elizabeth's elder brothers, the Comte de Provence (eventually Louis XVIII) and the Comte d'Artois (later Charles X), occasionally visited Montreuil to see the sister of whom all were so fond. The Comte de Provence fancied the look of Marie Grosholtz, but she remained unflirtatious and responded not at all to compliments. Eventually, when passing her on a staircase, the Prince took what she considered a liberty and, perhaps before she realized what she was doing, Marie slapped his face. That evening the Count seemed in such discomforted mood that his sister desired to know the cause. Eventually the story came out. Although men had the upper hand in the eighteenth century, a virtuous younger sister could bestow a wigging when a lady of her household had been involved. And no doubt this is just what Madame Elizabeth did. The Comte de Provence never tried again.

The King and Queen often paid informal visits to Montreuil. It was their pleasure to relax and chat to the household. Marie had the chance to watch Louis and Marie Antoinette behaving as ordinary people and to study their children, who came as near to romping in this young aunt's garden as ever they would in their restricted little lives.

Except for Vigée Lebrun, no court painter had the chances to observe the Royal Family that fell to the art tutor. As the ladies seldom retired from the room while Louis talked to his sister, Marie could watch the King happy or downcast or angry. She could guess that money was being discussed when he cried out: 'Well, then, I am vexed on every side', and she could study the graceful Marie Antoinette and wonder if the constant sour criticism of the courtiers was justified. Louis was a kindly king and on occasion very determined. Only three years before he had, against a strong body of legal opinion, insisted on abolishing the right of an examining magistrate to torture. The date of this great step was 20 August 1780.*

When at Versailles, Marie dined alone in her room or else she joined the four lady's maids attendant on the Princess. These young women were carefully selected from what was known as the 'poor nobility' – the vintage which had supplied girls for Madame de Maintenant's school at St Cyr. Maybe the reason that none of them appeared to consider marriage

---

* To depict the characters of the King and Queen known to Marie Grosholz, it may here be relevant to state as fact that Louis consistently strove to impose decrees which were just and humane – far more humane than his ministers sometimes liked. For instance, when freeing the Jews from certain medieval tolls, he used language of surprising modernity, stressing his determination to end 'constraints which appear to degrade humanity'. Although exceedingly religious, the King was never bigoted like his Parlement. In 1787 he insisted on giving civil rights to his 70000 Protestants. Parlement protested and Louis used his royal authority: 'My will is that my Parlement shall proceed to the registering of this edict without delay. You will acount to me on Wednesday.' And Marie Antoinette never spoke that famous line, 'If they have no bread, let them eat cake.' It was the Spanish-born queen of Louis XIV who said that, eighteen years before Marie Antoinette's birth.

was because they knew very, very humble gentlemen would have to be found for them. Most humble gentlemen were busily looking for humble heiresses, and on the whole the single state appeared to these girls to be the better part of valour.

Occasionally Madame Elizabeth invited her art teacher to play a small part at some court function. Among the first receptions which Marie attended was one given for the Comte d'Estaing who had co-operated with the American colonists against England. In 1779 he had been in command when France captured the West Indian islands of St Vincent and Grenada. The entertainments of Marie Antoinette always had style and originality. On this occasion she and her ladies wore white satin hats decorated with pomegranates (*grenades*) to greet the victor of Grenada, and Marie was among the maids of honour who walked around with baskets of pomegranates which they distributed to the assembled company.

And so the years rolled by with Madame Elizabeth and her entourage riding, dancing, walking, praying, embroidering and attending to charity. And day after day, week after week, Marie watched the Queen and her children – saw Marie Antoinette prepared for court balls and for theatricals at the Trianon, in her green velvet riding dress, wearing a feathered hat; in her satin gowns with high powdered hair; in her jewels and in her country gowns – saw her sorrowful when her children ailed and joyous when they ran and played.*

Among the Queen's intimate friends who sometimes visited Madame Elizabeth was the Princesse de Lamballe. Marie found her exceptionally charming and modelled her lying on a sofa, a singularly suitable position for a lady prone to fainting fits. Another person modelled lying down was the delectable Madame Sartine (*née* St Amaranthe), daughter-in-law of the Minister. These great ladies would, like Madame du Barry (the third recumbent figure, modelled earlier by Curtius), meet their end in the Revolution.

In 1787, when Marie had spent seven years at Versailles, the Sultan of Mysore, Tippo Sahib, sent an embassy to France in the hope of stirring up war against the English. These Indians were taken to the Cabinet de Cire at the Palais Royal and naturally the realism of the waxworks riveted them. When therefore the party visited Versailles, the King and

---

* Marie's wax figures of Louis XVI, Marie Antoinette, their daughter and elder son were exhibited in the Trianon in 1790 and can be seen in Madame Tussaud's today.

Queen ordered some courtiers to remain unmoving in a glass case and, with the practical-joke humour peculiar to royalty, nearly died of laughter when the Indians were taken in and stared admiringly at these amazingly lifelike wax figures. Marie executed a group portraying the ambassadors and their sepoys in native costume and this was placed under a tent in the Grand Trianon. She also executed by command of the King a group of the Royal Family which Louis intended to present to the Sultan. Thus it was that Marie modelled Louis and Marie Antoinette from life with their daughter and elder son.

Although Madame Elizabeth professed no interest in politics, Marie glimpsed the ministers at court, and she could memorize features even when not requested to make a likeness – Turgot, the Comptroller-General of Finance, the Comte de Vergennes, Foreign Minister, and the wise, disillusioned Malesherbes, were men with whom she conversed. Future generations must sigh that she kept no diary. A young woman deft at catching the character in faces should have been able to record so much concerning men weaving the history of France.

Meanwhile the Palais Royal itself was being reconstructed by the Duc d'Orléans (its new arcades are those which remain today). In order to avoid bankruptcy the Duke turned the beautiful gardens into shops, cafés, gambling dens and brothels. The new buildings decreased the size of the gardens, which became more disreputable as they became smaller. Political clubs and reading rooms sprang up beneath the colonnades as well as art galleries and exhibitions. The entire area became a not very respectable place for rendezvous. Curtius flourished in such surroundings.

In the *Almanach du Voyageur à Paris* of 1786 two Salons de Cire are listed in Monsieur Curtius's name – the first one in the Palais Royal gardens, which was probably an excellent money-maker, and a second one in the Boulevard du Temple which lay in the theatrical district but was *plus snob*. Prince Henry of Prussia remarked, while sitting for Curtius in his original studio, that the Palais Royal had ceased to be either a palace or royal. Curtius flickered between two worlds – the royal one of grandeur and pomp and the increasingly restless one of political reformers. In the cafés beneath the new arcades of the Palais Royal, he made contacts which would be useful when the terrible 'deluge' began.

In Paris there existed two great fairs, that of St Germain and that of St Laurent which kept open as a kind of bazaar all the year round. Curtius, who had been solemnly brought up to be a fine gentleman, possessed a natural sense of theatre, and never missed an opportunity to show his works at both places. He noticed two particularly successful theatre managers, Nicolet and Audinot who, after making fortunes at the fairs, had moved to the Boulevard du Temple. Curtius followed them, opening a second salon nearby. Nicolet had obtained the right to placard his theatre 'Spectacle des Grands Danseurs du Roi', and Audinot ran 'Ambigu Comique', in which light comedy was acted out by children. Amidst these attractions stood the Circus of Philip Astley, brought to Paris at the request of Marie Antoinette, with its tiers of galleries and 200 of the new oil lamps which were replacing tallow candles. Curtius was not shy of participating in the theatrical world. It excited him, and as a hard-headed businessman he did not blanch at reaping a fortune amidst tumblers, tightrope walkers and other entertainers.

When Marie came from the green peace of Montreuil and the immense reception rooms of Versailles, she contributed to the exhibitions. Louis and Marie Antoinette did not object when Curtius set up his famous group of 'The Royal Family at Dinner'. They had to endure the publicity of eating in public anyhow. Any respectably dressed subject could go to Versailles, stroll the terraces, and crowd in to watch the royal meal as long as the men carried swords. Madame Elizabeth disliked eating in public as much as Marie Antoinette but there was no avoiding it – *noblesse oblige*. Because she found this particular duty so disagreeable, the Princess usually swallowed a substantial meal beforehand so that she need only toy with the food. Parisians who were unable to journey to Versailles could gape at the life-sized royal figures feasting in the Cabinet de Cire. 'Only two sous,' called the barker at the door. ' "The Royal Family at Dinner"! Two sous.'

Even more spectacular was the lurid section which Curtius opened in his Boulevard du Temple Exhibition, entitled 'Caverne des Grands Voleurs'. In these scenes, the portraits of famous miscreants were assembled under a blue light, and de Bachaumont writes in his *Mémoires Secretes* that on 11 May 1783,

As soon as Justice has dispatched someone Curtius models the head and puts him into the collection, so that something new is always being offered to the curious, and the sight is not expensive for it only costs two sous. The barker shouts, 'Come in, messieurs, come and see the great thieves.' On one occasion when the Marquis de Vilette was passing by he called out, 'What about the Prince de Guéménée and Madame la princesse? Are they there?' [He was referring to a haughty pair recently gone bankrupt.] 'No? Well your collection is not complete! I would have given six livres to see *that* set-up.

Such was the uninhibited fashion in which Curtius amassed a fortune. 'Justice's dispatch work' was a polite way of describing executions, and Curtius was not over-delicate. Did he model the thieves before or after? Probably after. When the Salons de Cire had earned sufficient capital, Curtius purchased a plot of land for 30 000 livres in the rue des Fossés du Temple, and built a house which he let to one Antoine Canlon and his wife for 3000 livres a year. The legal document concerning this purchase has survived.

While Curtius's prosperity increased and Marie worked conscientiously at Versailles, the troubles which would end in revolution gathered. Curtius, intoxicated by the excitement of politics, kept his ear very close to the ground. Marie heard revolutionary discussions when she went home but she would not dare repeat such talk. And somehow when she returned to her room in the great palace, when she fell into step with the staff of 15 000 persons now in the service of the royal household, she could not imagine that this pageantry could ever be changed. The rising roar of public indignation against the luxuries of the very rich seemed so unreal when she went to Montreuil with Madame Elizabeth for a quiet day and listened to the household prayers before driving back. And the King himself was liberal-minded, determined to make taxes more just and to abolish the unfair *corvées* (forced labour) imposed on the poorer classes But the rain floods of 1787 and the drought and harvest failure of 1788 caused hardship. In Paris the cost of bread doubled and unemployment rose. Hunger spread over land and city.

Who was to do what? The Assembly of Notables was convened to consider reforms proposed by Minister Calonne, but this Assembly consisted wholly of members of the privileged classes, whose only idea was to frustrate the King's efforts to make them pay taxes. They threw Calonne out of office and steadfastly opposed reform.

After disastrous freak hailstorms destroyed the corn crop, the winter of 1788–9 proved a hard one for France. In the spring Marie hardly felt surprised when her uncle asked her to request leave from Versailles and return to his own house in Paris. She explained the situation to Madame Elizabeth who took no offence and made no effort to detain her. That plump, charming, sad little Princess, now in her mid-twenties, was despite her 'rose and lily complexion' beginning to look middle-aged. The disasters of France appalled her, and she saw her beloved brother's faults clearly. She said: 'He is always afraid of being mistaken.' Far from chiding Marie for asking to be allowed to leave the royal service at such a moment, the Princess pressed Marie to take the furniture of her room, including two chairs signed by the famous cabinet-maker Jacob.* Madame Elizabeth could hardly have envisaged the mob breaking into the palace; she had no thought of saving objects. Generosity came naturally to her.

So it was that in the spring of 1789 Marie Grosholtz packed up her modelling tools and all the things she had brought with her from Paris eight years before. She curtsied, then kissed the hand of her dear mistress. Her belongings were loaded into a carriage and she drove back to Curtius's house in the Boulevard du Temple. It seemed more crowded than ever and with strange people of a kind she had never met before. It was natural that Philippe Curtius and men of liberal mind should be revolted by the bigotry of the *ancien régime*, but none appeared aware of the historic fact that the violent overthrow of a government results in terrible human suffering.

* These chairs are at Madame Tussaud's today.

4

Revolution

When did Philippe Curtius begin to change? While Marie had been living in the isolation of Versailles, he had been meeting the most radical men in Paris and their ideas excited him. He had made his name through the good offices of a great prince, but although the acrimonious de Conti had quarrelled with both Louis XV and Louis XVI, no seditious talk could ever have been heard at his table. When he died, Curtius, free of any need for patronage, chose his friends from the extreme left.

Marie had never lost touch with her Paris home, but until she returned to live with her excitable, politics-obsessed 'uncle' it is doubtful if she realized the extent to which the atmosphere had altered. She had been relieved perhaps, though very sad, to leave Madame Elizabeth and to escape that pious household. Now in the spring of 1789, back under Curtius's roof, she had to accustom herself to incessant arguments about the rights and wrongs of reform. Marie knew that the King had recently doubled the deputies in the Third Estate (which represented what in England was the House of Commons) and from the chaos had emerged the new Nationalist Party, but politics as such had not greatly interested her. Now she sat in astonished silence while 'Uncle' and his friends waxed exuberant. It was a relief when after dessert the ladies could retire! Maman still appeared to be thinking only of her cuisine, and her daughter realized it was wiser to hold her tongue.

Lafayette, head of the National Guard, Bailly, Mayor of Paris, and the Comte de Mirabeau frequently dropped in for dinner, and the Duc d'Orléans often turned up to prate of *égalité* until Curtius would have to lead him away, usually the worse for drink, to a tavern opposite. There, in the *Cadre Bleu*, the Duke could remain carousing far into the night. On one occasion he brought an English royal duke, 'Butcher Cumberland', to breakfast. This fearful fellow shared Orléans's tastes for debauchery, and Marie regarded both men with disapproval. She had a prim disposition and had often heard Madame Elizabeth refer to her uncle as 'a disgrace to the family'. Orléans showed her why his niece called him this. Louis had forbidden him to send his son to be educated in England (Eton), saying that princes of the blood belonged to France, but he could not stop him having a mistress, Madame de Genlis, whom Walpole called a 'hen Rousseau' and Talleyrand described neatly: 'In order to avoid the scandal of flirting, she consents immediately.' However, when Orléans was sober, Marie took his likeness and Curtius modelled a miniature wax head to match the one he had made of Louis XVI.

More to her taste was Mirabeau, growing ever more fiery; his gifts as an orator were put to incessant use. How horrified Marie must have been at this stage, as well as bewildered. Curtius surely must have warned her of possible dangers; he may have told her not to talk too much of her eight years at the court. Was Curtius himself nervous? Or was he merely ardent for change? Marie later said that although a fervent monarchist he knew it was essential to go along with the times. But this explanation was invidious even for a liberal-minded German.

Among the men who dined occasionally was the Abbé Sièyes of Chartres Cathedral whose pamphlet, *What is the Third Estate?*,* had in February caused consternation. The Abbé's small neat head made a nice contrast for caricaturists against the huge head of Danton, whose thunderous voice declaimed down the table, stilling the brilliancies of Mirabeau. Amidst the clamour Marie Grosholtz sat watching the different faces, wondering why they shouted with such passion.

During the election for the Estates General, Curtius, like all male taxpayers over the age of twenty-five, registered his vote. Mirabeau (regarded as a traitor to his class) was rejected by the nobility and elected for Aix-en-Provence as a commoner. The Abbé Sieyès was elected for Paris, and Marie diligently read through his pamphlet demanding the rejection of the nobility from government posts. Meanwhile, each electoral district drew up a list of grievances to be put forward when the Estates General met at Versailles.

* The gist of this pamphlet was: 'What is the Third Estate? – nothing. What should it be – everything.'

Curtius took advantage of the situation. His wax models of Orléans, Cumberland, the Abbé Sieyès and the greatest of Louis's ministers – Necker – were drawing crowds to the Cabinet de Cire, for the chattering throngs wanted to know exactly what men of the moment looked like. Necker brought his plump young daughter Germaine to the studio, where Marie noticed the lively wit of the lady who was later to become Madame de Staël.

When the Estates General convened at Versailles it invented a new name. The unwieldy government machine now called itself the National Assembly.* Among the Paris deputies were the Abbé Sieyès, Curtius's friend the astronomer Bailly, and a kindly doctor named Guillotin, inventor of a humane killer for criminals.

In early June Marie heard of the death of the little Dauphin, whom she had modelled. His heart-stricken parents retired to mourn in the palace at Marly. Marie often thought of the green garden at Montreuil where she had watched the royal children play. The younger son, just out of babyhood, now became Dauphin.

On 19 June, Necker put forward plans for reform and a few days later the King announced the limits he would accept. Unwisely, Louis spiked his proclamation with a threat of dissolving the Assembly. Defiance increased. Sieyès warned, 'You are not today what you were yesterday.' And Mirabeau dramatically cried out, 'We will not move from our seats unless forced by bayonets.'

The National Assembly now called itself the Constituent Assembly. But the government needed more than renaming. Louis XVI ordered six more regiments to surround Paris. Some of the troops got out of hand and two extra regiments, mostly German and Swiss, were ordered into the city. The poor grew yet hungrier, and hunger makes men fierce. Meanwhile the bourgeoisie grew alarmed, and the summer heat addled minds. Before an anxious Assembly, Mirabeau denounced the King's action and formal protests to the monarch were made.

The harassed Louis then made the mistake of exiling Necker, who was popular because of his policy of raising loans rather than spreading taxes. The situation became yet more dangerous. As the price of bread rose and

---

* The Third Estate became the National Assembly on 17 June 1789. Thereafter it periodically renamed itself the Constituent Assembly (on 7 July 1789), Legislative Assembly (on 1 October 1791), and National Convention (on 21 September 1792), until finally in 1795 it became the Directory under Bonaparte.

Marie Grosholtz in 1778. Lithograph by F. Hervé from a portrait which has not survived. *Madame Tussaud's Memoirs and Reminiscences of France*, ed. F. Hervé, 1838

12 July 1789. Camille Desmoulins borrowed Curtius's wax heads of Necker and the Duc d'Orléans for a protest march after Necker's dismissal from his post as Director-General of Finance. The first blood of the Revolution was shed when the Royal German Regiment fired on the mob parading the heads. The Bastille fell two days later. *Gouache by Lesueur in the Musée Carnavalet, Paris*

Promenade du Boulevard du Temple. A water-colour by Jacques François Swebach des Fontaines, dated 1788. Curtius's wax exhibition which included the 'Chambre des Grands Voleurs', forerunner of the Chamber of Horrors, was located at No. 20, Boulevard du Temple, and was one of numerous entertainments offered for the diversion of the fashionable strollers. *By courtesy of Christie's, London*

men flocked in from the countryside looking for work and food, the city's temper rose to fever-pitch. Many aristocratic families left France and many faced bankruptcy, but Curtius saw that he could continue charging entrance fees for his waxworks. In a way he became a darling of the mob. Alas, again, that Marie kept no diary during this extraordinary summer when Danton, Mirabeau, Marat and Robespierre were frequent dinner visitors. The news on 12 July of Necker's dismissal caused an angry mob to flock into the Palais Royal gardens, where orators on boxes held forth indignantly. Rumour spread that the Duc d'Orléans was also to be exiled. Someone shouted out, 'Let us carry the effigies through the streets', and Curtius, watching somewhat nervily, saw the mob approaching his Cabinet de Cire. He closed the outside gate, but as the crowd converged, chanting the names of Necker and Orléans, he handed out these busts. For a moment the crowds shouted for the full-length model of the King also, but Curtius persuaded them it would be too awkward to handle, and they swarmed away shouting, 'Bravo, Curtius, bravo.' The wax busts of Necker and Orléans were draped with crêpe and held aloft whilst being paraded through the streets.

A college professor, Beffroy de Reigny, has written his own account of that evening of 12 July, and it is curious to realize that ordinary people were still going about their business. De Reigny had given theatre tickets to some ladies of his acquaintance who set forth, wishing to be in good time, towards the Boulevard du Temple, at half past four. Soon after leaving they reappeared breathless at the professor's home saying that Necker had been dismissed, all theatres were closed and people were shutting up their houses before a rampaging mob. De Reigny walked out alone to see what was happening. Amidst people rushing frantically about their affairs he reached the Boulevard du Temple:

There I saw five or six thousand men marching along, quickly and not in any sort of order, some armed with guns, others with sabres, lances or pitchforks. They were triumphantly parading the busts of the Duc d'Orléans and M. Necker which they had demanded from M. Curtius. Two black standards bordered with white were carried on either side of these busts to show the sorrow caused by this loved Minister's fall. The mob was threatening to burn down any theatres which opened saying that French people should not be enjoying themselves at such a moment of misfortune.

De Reigny talked to a carpenter who was among the ringleaders. 'All we wanted was to show spirit and make them take away the soldiers. The one thing we promised was to take care of the busts. We'll return them intact,' said this man.

But it turned out otherwise. Curtius has written the story.* More troops were sent for and the first blood of the Revolution was shed when the Royal German Regiment opened fire. The man carrying the bust of Orléans was wounded by a bayonet thrust in the stomach and the man carrying Necker was killed by a dragoon in the place de Vendôme. Late that night a group of demonstrators returned the head of Orléans intact. Six days later that of Necker was brought back by a Swiss Guard with its hair burned and the wax face slashed. Curtius would write: 'I can therefore say to my credit, that the first action of the Revolution happened *chez moi*.'

Next day the local committee, intent on recruiting a National Guard to maintain order, asked Curtius to become district captain. He handed over all the arms in his possession and hired four 'intelligent fellows' to keep watch in continuous relays and report happenings hourly.

This precaution was not useless. I was alerted in time when some ruffians planned to burn down the Opéra and other theatres in the boulevard. They arrived between midnight and one in the morning. Their torches were all prepared, and without my vigilance they would have destroyed one of the finest quarters of Paris. Would it have been easy to stay the flames on that night of trouble and confusion!

I raised a troop of forty men and when we saw 600 incendiaries arrive with the intention of burning, I went out at the head of my troop and spoke to them. By good luck I convinced them. They gave up their wicked ideas and made off.

All through 13 July people swarmed around the Hôtel de Ville shouting for arms, and on the following day – that famous 14 July which has remained the French National Holiday – the crowds flocked to the Invalides crying out for weapons. There were not many available, so they went to the great medieval fortress of the Bastille shouting for arms with which to drive away brigands and the troops outside the gates.

From then on accounts differ. The Bastille contained only seven prisoners and was staffed by eighty decrepit military pensioners – *les Invalides* – and thirty Swiss Guards. The kindly hereditary governor, de Launay, came out to speak to the crowd who, while clamouring for arms, were crying, 'Long live the King'. De Launay promised not to fire and, after forbidding the assailants to enter the inner courtyard, he withdrew his

* Philippe Curtius, *Les Services du Sieur Curtius*. Bibliothèque Nationale, Paris, 1790.

men. When the mob rushed forward towards the great inner drawbridge, a single gun charged with grapeshot was fired and several fell. But as Elie, the 'conquering hero' who accepted the surrender, would write, 'The Bastille was not taken by force. It yielded before being attacked, on the promise I gave on the word of a French officer that no harm would be done to anyone.'

At this juncture Curtius arrived with his troop of National Guards, halted them in front of the house of Monsieur de Beaumarchais and went forward with a few men to reconnoitre. Later he claimed in his printed pamphlet to have been among the first into the Bastille, 'certainly in time to share the final dangers and the glory of a conquest that put a seal on our liberty'. It is doubtful if he would have worded his story thus had the revolutionary party not triumphed, but Curtius never knew false modesty, and he would eventually be among the 600 who received an engraved gun and badge from the National Assembly along with the right to use the title, *Vainqueur de la Bastille*.

What he actually did was useful enough. According to the eyewitness Pasquier who went there as a spectator with a pretty actress,

Resistance was non-existent. Only a few rifle shots were fired. . . . What I saw perfectly was the action of the soldiers lining the platforms of the towers, who raised the butts of their rifles in the air and expressed by all the usual means their desire to surrender.

Curtius marched a party of *prisonniers invalides* to the Hôtel de Ville, where, defending them from a menacing crowd, he begged the French Guard for protection. After sending home his own detachment he conducted the old men to *La Nouvelle France* where they could be given supper and allowed to sleep.

Meanwhile the Governor de Launay, who had surrendered the keys and been given a safe conduct, was dragged away to the place de Grèves and beheaded with Monsieur de Flesselles, the Provost of Merchants. Their heads were paraded on pikes. Not very logically the Bastille was set up as a symbol of past oppression.

Now comes an extraordinary story from Philip Astley, the English proprietor of Astley's Circus, which had its site beside the Cabinet de Cire. Philip Astley and his son were famous trick riders and, indeed, their equestrian shows in which Marie Antoinette delighted seem to have consisted of a form of dressage – their horses danced a minuet. Astley had in fact returned to London and set up his circus near Westminster Bridge, but he returned to Paris just before the fall of the Bastille. Like all the showmen of the period he seized on such dramas to attract audiences. Two months later, back in London, he put on display a National Guardsman's uniform along with two wax heads modelled from the decapitated Governor de Launay and Provost de Flesselles, who had been shot dead on his way to trial and later had his head hacked off. That is factual, and a newspaper extract dated 30 September 1789 rings true: 'Mr Astley has brought with him finely executed in wax by a celebrated artist in Paris the heads of Monsieur de Launay, late Governor of the Bastille, and M. de Flesselles, Provost of the Merchants of Paris with incontestable proofs of their being striking likenesses.'* Another unnamed paper advertises on 7 October 1789, 'At the Royal Grove, Westminster Bridge. The Siege of the Bastille with addition by Astley, Senior, since his return from Paris. Particularly a striking resemblance in wax of the heads of Monsieur de Launay and Monsieur de Flesselles, which Mr Astley has obtained at great expense.'

So Curtius, who *was* the greatest of wax modellers, managed to obtain death-masks and create likenesses of two innocent men who were killed savagely on the day he led his troop of Guardsmen to the Bastille! That is clear. But an extract from *The Greatest Show on Earth* by M. Willson Disher (London 1937), must be suspect. While no sources are given, Disher writes:

The Fall of the Bastille was mirrored at Sadler's Wells and the Royal Circus in stage spectacles. To surpass these Astley went to Paris in order to buy exhibits from Dr Curtius whose waxworks were near the Amphitheatre. . . . The doctor's niece – the future Madame Tussaud – had had the head of de Launay, governor of the Bastille, brought to her after it had paraded the streets on a pike; also the head of Provost Flesselles, which had been seized as a trophy after he had been shot dead on his way to trial. Astley bought the wax heads of de Launay and Flesselles she had moulded, as well as a few uniforms.†

It is very hard to believe that Marie would have *had the heads brought to her*. Far more likely that she and her mother spent this day waiting ner-

---

* 'Astley's Amphitheatre', vol. 1. British Library, London.

† The widow of Mr Willson Disher told Lady Chapman in 1971 that her husband never wrote such statements without firm evidence, but she was unable to quote his sources.

vously behind locked doors, maybe peeping out of the shuttered windows and calling into the street for news.

The reaction of Curtius is a different matter. In his new state of fervour he might well have been pleased to make copies of these two eminent persons whom ill-luck had made the first victims of the Revolution. It is also possible that he did not seek the heads but that the mob brought them to his house late that night and roared for death-masks. Whatever occurred, it must be remembered that Curtius was a man who had studied anatomy and dissected human bodies in the past, and he was accustomed to reproducing the faces of dead criminals. In a less squeamish age it would have seemed quite natural to finish a hard day's non-lucrative work by embellishing his collection in this way. These two wax heads were to travel to England and to India in 1795 with 'Curtius's Grand Cabinet of Curiosities'. As revealed later the curiosities were to become curiouser and curiouser!

Although he tried never to let an opportunity slip, Curtius could not have found much time for taking casts and modelling. On the day after the fall of the Bastille he had what he calls 'the good luck' to catch some men carrying off several barrels of gunpowder from the fortress to hide in a house in the faubourg Saint-Antoine. He made them take the barrels to his own district and then caught others stealing books and papers which he insisted should be deposited safely in the archives of the Petits-Pères Nazareth.

On the 17 July his company was ordered to the place de Grève to meet the King. 'It was the most important post,' he wrote, 'for there the crowds were thickest. I kept all under such good order that in spite of the numbers of people no accidents occurred.'

Soon after this Curtius resigned as captain of the National Guard so that he could get back to his own work, but at the end of August he was again called up and used to flush out brigands who were mixing with the 'good workmen' of Montmartre. 'This operation was accomplished with such intelligence that within two days fourteen thousand men had been paid, given pass-outs and conducted out of the city.' But nasty incidents increased.

In August the National Assembly ended a thousand years of feudal control and repudiated the *ancien régime*, while naming Louis XVI 'Restorer of France's liberties'. The ex-minister Foulon, who lived near to Curtius, was captured trying to flee the city and brought back, hanged and decapitated despite Lafayette's efforts to save him. Marie saw his head paraded on a pike, and although Curtius appeared to be in the forefront of those who supported liberty, equality and fraternity, she could hardly feel secure.

By September the food problem became acute. Despite a good harvest the general chaos of the countryside prevented grain being threshed and transport was completely disorganized. The flight of aristocratic families meant unemployment for all workers in luxury trades. People grew tense and fearful. Within three months of its inception the National Guard had 30 000 volunteers. Tax-paying citizens elected committees to issue decrees, but disorders were common.

On 5 October, M. Hulin, the local Commandant, put Curtius in charge of the Bastille with eight men under him. They had a difficult time with certain roughs, but these were 'brought to order by patience and firmness'. Meanwhile M. Hulin and his National Guardsmen were marching to Versailles. Next day the Royal Family were forcibly brought to Paris. The tale of this terrible, humiliating journey has often been recounted. It must be imagined through the eyes of Marie Grosholtz who had known Marie Antoinette and Louis personally. The people still looked to Louis their King as the leader of the new France, but they wanted him under their control. Six thousand women and a number of men dressed as women marched to Versailles led by Stanislas Maillard, one of the *Vainqueurs de la Bastille*, whose portrait was soon to be seen in Curtius's Cabinet de Cire. Lafayette and contingents of the National Guard followed, and late that evening Lafayette requested Louis to agree to return to his capital. The bewildered King refused to make an immediate decision. All night the crowds camped noisily outside the Château de Versailles. Towards dawn a party of demonstrators forced their way into the great courtyard and during a skirmish with the Royal Guard several of both sides were killed. When the hooligans chased up the staircase to the Queen's apartment, Marie Antoinette fled to the King's room where, aided by National Guardsmen who had arrived on the scene, the Royal Guard succeeded in regaining control.

With the mob shouting, 'To Paris! To Paris!' Lafayette appeared on the balcony with the King and Queen and the Dauphin. Louis now agreed to go, but he would return to the capital as a prisoner, not as a leader. That afternoon the royal carriages rolled out from the splendid gates and drove with 30 000 people shouting and singing along the wide avenue to

Paris. Marie Grosholtz may have felt her heart turn when she learnt that Madame Elizabeth was in the party; we cannot know. The Tuileries, which for years had been let out to pensioners in 'grace and favour' apartments, was hurriedly prepared. By nightfall the exhausted King and Queen, who had hardly slept for forty-eight hours, were installed in discomfort. 'It's very ugly,' commented the four-year-old Dauphin. Madame Elizabeth slept on a sofa. The others fell into unaired beds.

Meanwhile Curtius was preening himself:

On the 6th when the triumphant army was returning to Paris, I handed over my post to a _Vainqueur de la Bastille_ whose prudence and energy I knew, so that I could join my comrades [returning from Versailles]. When I reported my conduct to M. Hulin he embraced me and said 'Dear Comrade. You have rendered as great a service as if you had come with us to Versailles.'

The roar of the populace around the Tuileries did not subside. During the next few days Louis and Marie Antoinette repeatedly showed themselves from the ground-floor apartment which had been allotted to Madame Elizabeth. If Marie mingled with the crowd which shouted from the terraces and courtyards for Louis and Marie Antoinette to come out wearing the tricolour, she would have seen her Princess also wearing the cockade of red and blue for _la patrie_, and white for the Bourbons. Madame Elizabeth walked daily in the gardens with the young son of one of the Queen's women-in-waiting as bodyguard. But the Royal Family, forcibly recalled to their capital, had become the prisoners, not the representatives, of France. There is no record that Marie ever exchanged a word with her former mistress or sought to send her a message. She may have wished to and not dared.

In December 1789, when the Jacobin Club, originally formed for leading left-wing deputies, opened its doors to prominent revolutionaries, Curtius became a member along with Robespierre. The subscription of twenty-four livres excluded the poorer members of society, but debates within its portals concentrated on the immediate emergency, and argued the necessity of state control for all authority, for in the existing chaos it looked as if all classes might go hungry this winter.

Curtius was not only a good artist, he was also a showman with unerring sense of timing. People had wanted to see royalty gorgeously gowned and felons getting their deserts. Now they wanted to know what the new leaders looked like. Curtius knew the top revolutionaries personally. He induced them all to allow him to make wax portraits and sometimes to give their own clothes. Burning with curiosity, the vulgar public trooped into the Waxworks. The 'barker' at the door would change uniform according to the mood of the moment. At first he was dressed as a National Guardsman: later when the *Sans-Culottes* gained power he would be rigged up in their attire.

The exhibition in the Palais Royal closed down to concentrate on that in the Boulevard du Temple, and indeed Curtius's premises here became not only a centre of entertainment but a meeting place for revolutionaries.

In the summer, to draw attention to the part he had played in the so-called storming of the Bastille, Curtius published the pamphlet from which his own descriptions have been drawn. The author of *Les Services du Sieur Curtius, Vainqueur de la Bastille* certainly has no intention of hiding his light under a bushel. Perhaps he lauds his own merits in order to keep his household safe, but there is a kind of childish boastfulness in his phrases which makes it obvious that he believed in his own splendid deeds as detailed in twelve pages. He includes a few hints that he might have been awarded more than the engraved gun presented to each *Vainqueur* by the National Assembly, and the decoration awarded to all members of the corps charged with sorting out the 'brigands' and workmen in Montmartre the preceding August.* The pamphlet is in fact a mixture of boasts, whines and self-justification. Curtius's last paragraphs read:

Finally, on 21 April 1790, I was admitted to the *Vainqueurs de la Bastille*, at the general assembly of my brothers in arms in the presence of M.M. the Commissionaires selected by the City to examine the proofs of justification of each one's service.

I have enumerated those I rendered to *la Patrie*. I could but prove myself by sacrificing the time belonging to my work. This is a loss for an Artist. I should add that I inevitably had extraordinary expenses.

Undoubtedly I could claim financial recompense, but I have served my Country disinterestedly; only mercenary souls try to speculate on public doings and think of such as an object of lucre.

My zeal and my courage will never diminish; I take the civil oath to my Country. I swear to be faithful to the nation, to the law and to the king, until my last breath.

CURTIUS
Citoyen actif et éligible de Paris, Vainqueur de la Bastille

* The inscribed gun perished in the fire at Madame Tussaud's in 1925.

When the sixty districts of Paris were reduced to forty-eight *sections*, each *section* appointed its own committee to deal with food supply, business transactions and the desperate poor, and maintained its own company of National Guardsmen and Chasseurs. As Curtius was an old friend of Bailly, the astronomer who was Mayor of Paris from 1789 to 1791, he held considerable power in the new organization. Soon he was appointed captain of a local battalion of Chasseurs whose chief job was to prevent smuggling and to guard the city gates, seeing that dues were collected. In June 1790 Curtius signs himself with this new military title of 'Captain' when writing to one Monsieur Guillaume, Director of a Maison de Secours, whose portrait he had finished. He now wore the uniform of the Chasseurs – a hunting coat in green material, green tassels on the hat and laced boots instead of Guardsmen's gaiters. The only existing portrait of Curtius dates from this time. It was made by Gilles Chrétien, inventor of the 'Physiognotrace', a machine for taking silhouette pictures, and it shows Curtius in the uniform and bears his Bastille title.*

Meanwhile all Paris flocked to visit the Bastille while the fortress was demolished stone by stone by the people of Paris. Curtius wrote to the authorities asking for a certificate of authenticity for the stone he had procured, with the intention of presenting it to the National Assembly. He lost the certificate they sent him, and a surviving letter in Curtius's own handwriting concerns a second guarantee. Preserved in the Bibliothèque Historique de la Ville de Paris, it shows his clear deliberate handwriting.

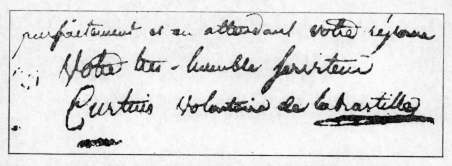

Curtius' signature as 'Volontaire de la Bastille', from a letter dated 16 February 1790, written to Palloy, the stone-mason, who made money by selling stones and fragments from the demolished Bastille. Curtius had lost the certificate of authenticity for a stone Palloy had sent him, and asked for another. *Bibliothèque Historique de la Ville de Paris*

* In the Bibliothèque Nationale, Paris.

D

Curtius and Marie had naturally been among the sightseers who thronged the old fortress as soon as it was liberated, and with them went Curtius's latest friend, the newly elected *député* for Artois. Robespierre, a well-dressed young man with flirtatious manners, caught Marie's arm when she slipped on a narrow stair leading to the dungeons, saying, 'Take care. It would be a pity if so young and pretty a patriot should break her neck in such a dismal place.' Marie was piquante but never really pretty, with that long nose and jutting jaw. She seems to have felt a little flicker of dislike, perhaps of fear. Yet why she could not tell. Robespierre fancied himself as an orator, and after a few friendly words with Curtius he placed himself on the wall and proceeded to harangue the crowd on the subject of despotism. It was almost impossible to explain the chill breeze which seemed to blow through his highly emotional rhetoric.

5

Start of the Terror

Chateaubriand describes the years 1789–90: 'In every corner of Paris there were literary gatherings, political societies, and places of entertainment; men who were one day to be famous mingling anonymously with the crowd.' And Dr Curtius mingled with them. When they thrust forward into the limelight, he quietly asked permission to do their portraits and found they were only too eager to be put 'on show'. Literary and political gatherings met at Curtius's house – the head of the National Guard; Bailly, the mayor; Barnave, co-founder of the Jacobin Club. Curtius could claim friendship with Lafayette, Mirabeau, the Abbé Sieyès, Marat, Danton and Robespierre, yet who could feel safe when they began to hate each other?

An extraordinary moment occurred for Marie in the turbulent summer of 1790, for the group of life-size models of the Royal Family, which she had made at Versailles, was rented out for show in the Petit Trianon.* The fantasy of this theatrical venture defies imagination. If, as was likely, Marie herself had to journey to Versailles to set up the figures, it must have been an eerie experience. The splendid rooms where Marie had watched the courtiers in their brocades and satins lay silent. The furniture had been removed – put into store or carted to the Tuileries; scaffolding had been erected in the great Gallery of Mirrors in an attempt to clean it – as if the King and Queen would be returning after a holiday. In the Petit Trianon, that seven-roomed pavilion designed for Madame de Pompadour where Marie Antoinette had organized private theatricals, often acting herself, all seemed unreal. The fate of the palace was uncertain, but

* These are the same portraits that can be seen in Madame Tussaud's today.

Versailles remained proud of its huge château, and sightseers flocked to gaze at the tableau of the former occupants set up in the rustic building where only two years before the Queen of France had been able to relax, saying, *'Là, je suis moi.'*

On 14 July 1790, the anniversary of the Bastille, a festival was organized in Paris attended by deputations from all over France. The Champs de Mars (in which the Eiffel Tower now stands) was then a deserted stretch of land useful for duelling. Thousands of workmen were employed to level the ground and make it suitable for the concourse. When it became evident they could not finish the task in time, the people of Paris laid down their jobs to lend a hand and Marie Grosholtz enthusiastically trundled a barrow with the best of them.

The celebrations included a long procession from the site of the Bastille across the Seine, using a bridge of boats to the Champs de Mars for a 'Ceremony of Federation'. It took three hours for the marchers to reach their destination. It poured with rain, but this could not dampen the festive spirit of the women, white-clad with tricolour sashes, the men with matching scarves, the singing choirs and deputations carrying banners. Carts carried figures of Voltaire and Rousseau, and on one cart stood the Goddess of Liberty herself, a personage described by Marie (who watched all this starry-eyed) as 'a lady of respectability and not as often erroneously stated a prostitute'. In view of the horrific tasks which Mademoiselle Grosholtz would later undertake without turning a hair, this punctilious insistence on morality is interesting. It shows what Marie thought mattered.

Any outing from the Tuileries must have been a relief to the Royal Family even if they sat there as mere puppets. A pavilion had been erected to shelter the King, the President of the Assembly and other officials. Marie Antoinette and her children stood with members of the court on an elevated balcony at the rear. Curtius strode forward with the *Vainqueurs de la Bastille* to lay the ribbons they had been awarded on the centre altar. Ceremonies started with a service conducted by Talleyrand, who was Bishop of Autun; Lafayette carried the King's commands and the form of constitutional oath which he laid on the altar. Louis stretched out his hands and pronounced his oath, while Marie Antoinette, watching from the balcony, embraced her little son and held him towards the people.

All seemed well. That night Paris was illuminated and there was dancing in the streets. Marie went out to the site of the Bastille and danced there, for it was not far from her home. The ghost of the decapitated governor who had merely sought to do his duty disturbed no one and his wax head made money for Dr Curtius.

After the Festival of Federation, tension slackened. It looked as if the Constituent Assembly, as it pleased to call itself, might succeed in constructing a new government on the ruins of the old autocracy. From Turin – where a group of *émigrés* was plotting counter-revolution with Louis's youngest brother, the Comte d'Artois – came a whiff of danger, but it was generally assumed that the French Revolution was over. Curtius had to steer a careful course among his friends in the Assembly, for they were ceaselessly bickering over leadership.

In November 1790 came trouble. A civic oath (forbidden by the Pope) was imposed on the clergy, and in December Mirabeau was defeated by Robespierre in a contest for leadership of the Jacobin Club. Although his brilliant, impassioned oratory had kept Mirabeau in the forefront, the revelation that in order to pay enormous, ever-accumulating debts, he had accepted a pension from the King, lost him favour.

Mirabeau was already a very sick man. He stood for constitutional monarchy, and now that liberal idealists were being ousted by proletarian dictators he could not have survived long politically. Marie did a portrait of him in wax a few months before he died of overwork and dissipation in April 1791.*

That spring Curtius was very pleased at being accepted in the Paris Salon. This established him among artists of note. The work he entered, No. 900 in the catalogue, was a coloured wax bust of the Dauphin. David, the celebrated painter, had three classical paintings in the same show as well as a drawing of the National Assembly taking its famous oath on the tennis court at Versailles. David was among the fervent revolutionaries who frequented Curtius's house. He took some interest in Marie and tried to persuade her to visit his own studio to see his pictures. She demurred, finding his manners 'rough' and the wen on his face repulsive. Although self-conscious about his own ugliness, he asked her to do his portrait in wax without improvement.

In June 1791 came the ill-starred flight of the King and his family from Paris. At Varennes they were recognized, captured, and forcibly returned to Paris. Hostile, silent crowds stood unsmiling around the Tuileries, and Marie Grosholtz became uneasy. She had always been charmed by Marie

* She brought this bust to England in 1802 but it has not survived.

Antoinette and she respected the King. They were unhappy prisoners.

Pétion and Barnave, the deputies sent to arrest the King and travel back to Paris in the royal coach, were both acquaintances of Curtius. Pétion has written his own boastful account of this heart-breaking return journey. Pleased as he was with himself, he expressed surprised admiration that Marie Antoinette showed such character, and being a fat conceited oaf he imagined that the saintly Madame Elizabeth, who listened politely to his talk, was falling in love with him. 'I think that had we been alone she would have fallen into my arms', he wrote. Marie sorrowed for the King and Queen who had been so good to her, and above all she wept for Madame Elizabeth. Even the fiery Curtius became pensive.

Lafayette and Bailly, who was still Mayor of Paris, tried to excuse the King's flight as 'abduction by counter-revolutionaries'. Against considerable opposition the Constituent Assembly on 15 July proclaimed Louis 'innocent'. Against this forgiving verdict a number of protests were organized during a hostile demonstration at the Champs de Mars. Some rioting occurred, and when the National Guard opened fire fifteen demonstrators were killed. Political opinions flared up like fireworks. Lafayette and Bailly were now cursed as reactionaries, and Curtius no longer boasted of his friendship with them.

The Jacobin Club split apart, the moderate section taking the name of *Feuillants*. Curtius remained with the original revolutionaries headed by Robespierre. It seems extraordinary that throughout these ominous months Paris continued her festive mood. Looking wildly around for something to assuage the mob, the Assembly took to theatrical pretensions and ordained a glorification of Voltaire. He was to be honoured in Roman style under the artistic direction of David, so a grand spectacle copying the deification of deceased Roman emperors was placed in the hands of frenzied theatrical organizers. Voltarian relics were laid for the night under heaps of laurels and roses on the site of the Bastille. As dawn broke, a deluge of rain flooded the streets and the organizers postponed the march for an hour, but, as it looked as if the rain would continue indefinitely, a start had to be made. In sodden robes the procession advanced grimly along the boulevards. A company of National Guardsmen came first, followed by political clubs, stonemasons in working clothes, stalwart women from the Paris markets, and bands of 'patriots'. All withstood their soaking bravely, and so did the spectators. One group carried a tattered flag captured during that imaginative storming of the Bastille, others carried a stone from the dungeons, and junk such as rusting armour dug from the ruins. The *pièce de résistance* took the form of a triumphal car drawn by a dozen horses. On it, forming a kind of upper storey, was a high couch on which lay a coloured wax effigy of Voltaire. Maybe Curtius himself made this under the direction of his friend David, but whoever was responsible had not reckoned with the elements. The image lay undraped to the waist in Roman fashion and although it started off as a fair likeness of Voltaire, the lashing rain washed away all colouring until only a hideous white cadaver remained.

All through this summer Louis XVI was still recognized as a constitutional monarch and often cheered by the crowds, but hopes of peacefully rebuilding a democratic France faded. In September a revised constitution was approved by the King, and a fresh Assembly with new deputies opened its first session. As the threat of war increased, some Frenchmen believed that bloodshed would clear the air. Emperor Leopold of the Holy Roman Empire and the King of Prussia deplored events in France and vaguely expressed a desire to help Louis, their fellow monarch, but they hesitated to actively interfere. England secretly rejoiced in France's chaos. Possibly the King and Queen might benefit by war; Lafayette and some generals thought that a limited campaign could stabilize the Revolution. Other left-wing deputies brightened at the possibility of spreading liberation throughout Europe by the sword. The moderates feared that war could but destroy the constitutional monarchy and wipe out the liberal-minded bourgeois class and, curiously enough, Robespierre and some others among Curtius's extremist friends shared this view.

It was a winter of armed chaotic dissent. Louis could see that the 9000 émigrés at Coblenz, led by his two brothers, constituted a very real danger to *him*, but they ignored his request that they return to France.

By the end of January 1792 the value of the paper money 100-livres assignat had depreciated to 63 livres, and shortage of foodstuffs meant long queues and angry attacks on shops. A new popular movement known as the *Sans-Culottes* gathered force. The *Sans-Culottes* wore trousers instead of knee-breeches, cut their hair short and disdained powdering it. They wore round hats or red bonnets instead of tricornes and shoes with laces instead of buckles. They demanded complete political democracy as well as economic reform. Curtius kept in line with popular views. As the movement grew, his doorman exchanged Guard National uniform for that of a *Sans-Culotte*.

Like everyone else in Paris, Curtius began to feel the financial pinch. Since 1789 he had been pursuing the matter of an inheritance in Mayence. This came through a deceased maternal uncle, but Curtius had an elder brother, Charles, who had disappeared fifteen years previously. He conducted a long correspondence with a lawyer and the French Legation in Mayence arguing that it was now reasonable to presume his brother dead so that he, Philippe Curtius, could claim the whole of his uncle's inheritance. In a letter dated 10 April 1789, the Secretary of the French Legation had replied that it was possible in the circumstances to allow the drawing of interest, but if he wanted to touch the capital he must not only produce legal proof that he was indeed Philippe Guillaume Mathé Curtius, brother of Charles Curtius and heir of Raban Maurer (who had been named a godparent at Philippe's baptism), but also a surety of similar value to the capital he wanted to lift. This was a precaution in case the long-lost brother ever reappeared. Charles was never heard of again, but the complicated correspondence concerning the matter survives in the archives of Madame Tussaud's. On 1 January 1792, when rumours and conspiracies were convulsing Paris, Curtius wrote to the Legation in Mayence explaining the delay of letters. 'The Revolution in France has prevented me contacting you. As I have sent several letters and never received a reply these were I suppose intercepted.' Having finally discovered someone willing to carry a letter to Mayence, Curtius enclosed the required documents, an extract recording his baptism, a life certificate and a letter from his Mayence lawyer, by now defunct. Curtius also states that if he is allowed to draw on the capital sum he will be able to provide the necessary securities if Charles should eventually turn up. Evidently the revolutionary Curtius was also a keen capitalist. As for proof that he is Charles's brother, 'the portion of the estate of my uncle that I have already received is sufficient authentic proof'. After his signature Curtius writes, '*Capitaine des Chasseurs*'.

There is evidence that Curtius held an official appointment from the National Assembly which took him to Mayence, but if so, he never called on the French Legation in person. The correspondence concerning his legal claim to Charles's half of the uncle's fortune continued throughout April, and apparently he failed to make headway although testily explaining that he was well known to the French Ambassador in Mayence.

As Paris grew ever more restless, Curtius signed his name with the less flamboyant title of 'Active and eligible citizen of Paris'. At this stage it was not always wise to appear military.

When Talleyrand had secured England's neutrality, General Dumouriez, the new Minister for Foreign Affairs, declared war on Austria. He was an intelligent adventurer, well known in Curtius's circle, and had preached the importance of striking at France's old enemy – the Austrian Empire, which was strongly opposing the Revolution. Soon Dumouriez transferred himself to the Ministry of War and then to the command of troops in the field. His campaign proved a failure. Robespierre and Marat turned on Lafayette, who had supported the war, but the people of Paris laid all the blame on the King.

When Louis dismissed his moderate Girondin ministers they joined the left-wing Jacobins in planning insurrection. The King vetoed two out of three decrees which the Girondins had sought to impose. He agreed to the disbanding of his personal guard, but not to the arrest and deportation to tropical Guinea of clergy who refused the civic oath, nor would he authorize the encampment of 20 000 *Fédérés* from all parts of France outside the gates of Paris.

It was chaos. As the *Sans-Culottes* mobilized to the strains of *Ça ira* a great demonstration was organized for 30 June. One of the leaders, a brewer named Santerre, was well known in the Curtius household, so the doctor must have been well aware of all that was being planned. Armed with pikes, and wearing the red bonnet of liberty, the *Sans-Culottes* marched to the Assembly and insisted on their petition being formally accepted. They smashed their way into the Tuileries Gardens and penetrated the palace where they induced Louis to don the red bonnet and drink a toast to the nation. When Prussia joined Austria in the war against France a state of emergency was declared. The provincial revolutionaries started to converge on Paris. Amongst these 'patriots' were extremists from Marseilles, singing what was to become the world's most rousing national anthem – the *Marseillaise*.

On 15 July the extremists demanded that the monarchy be suspended, and that a new National Convention be elected by universal suffrage. Then the *sections* of Paris revolted against municipal authority and Robespierre, the realist, hitherto an advocate of strictly legal methods, considering the situation uncontrollable, switched his policy. The *Sans-Culottes* and the Marseilles 'patriots' knew themselves in power.

Tension in Paris increased. On the night of 9 August the tocsin rang out and delegates from all the city *sections* arrived at the Hôtel de Ville, where a Revolutionary Commune took over municipal powers.

On 10 August the Tuileries were invaded for the second time. Louis XVI, with his wife and children and Madame Elizabeth, fled to the National Assembly, then nervously in session in the Riding School, who incarcerated them in the grim old Temple prison. The Swiss Guards opened fire on the demonstrators who were storming into the palace. After bitter fighting they were overpowered and massacred. The *Sans-Culottes* knew themselves completely victorious.

That night a terrible quietness settled upon the city. When dawn broke Marie crept out of Curtius's house to look for what she calls 'relations' in the Swiss Guard. This curious story in *Madame Tussaud's Memoirs*, dictated many years later, must have been an aberration of old age, for she had no brothers, or uncles, but the actual description of her outing rings true. She says that she went to the Tuileries with a woman whose National Guard husband was missing. They reached the gardens as the sun rose and a scorchingly hot day began. Silence prevailed. Not a breath of wind stirred the trees. Corpses were lying all over the gardens, some tossed into heaps on the gravel paths. The statues, although spattered with blood, appeared undamaged. The rioters would boast they had not harmed 'the country's works of art', but those who climbed them for safety were pricked down with pikes. Few people were about in that hot terrifying dawn when Marie and her friend began searching among the corpses for faces they might recognize. She worked furtively, knowing it would be dangerous to seem to be looking for anyone in particular. The search proved vain. She returned home sickened and despondent. The description of the Tuileries Gardens with the heaps of dead is so vivid that one feels she must have gone there, but who was she really looking for?

The invasion of the Tuileries shocked Europe. The French government asked Talleyrand to draw up a reasoned defence for such violence. The old fox did so in a document which cunningly laid the blame on Louis himself for betraying the new constitution and bribing politicians. Having justified the King's imprisonment, Talleyrand asked for, and received from Danton, a passport to England. On the day after his departure, the bloodbath known as the 'September Massacres' began. A mood of panic was being created by Marat's rantings. The war went badly for France, and when Austro-Prussian troops crossed her frontiers the Parisian deputies took stringent measures to secure the city's safety. Thousands of citizens enrolled daily for military service and an Extraordinary Tribunal was set up. House hunts began, suspects and priests who had refused to take the civic oath were arrested. Churches were no longer necessary. A civil registry of births, deaths and marriages was set up and new legislation permitted divorce. With much talk of freedom, the new rulers issued warrants and organized what were called 'domiciliary visits of inspection'.

Amidst this turmoil Marie Grosholtz could not but get frightened. She met the leading revolutionaries on the stairs, she sat with them at meals; their impassioned talk and their cold eyes froze her.

The September Massacres lasted for three days and 1400 people were butchered. The cruelty revealed by the masses terrified Paris. The *Sans-Culottes*, shouting that changes were too slow, forced their way into monasteries and convents and prisons, slaughtering the inmates indiscriminately. The killing began with an attack on six coaches of priests being conveyed to the Abbaye prison. Billaud-Varenne, a friend of Curtius, arrived on the scene wearing his official deputy's sash but he made no attempt to save the priests. Perhaps he did not dare. Marie had often heard him say, 'I hope they will spare poor Veto', meaning the King. Now she had to credit the story that when the *Sans-Culottes* moved on to attack the Carmelites, Billaud-Varenne cheered them on, 'Good people, do your duty and sacrifice your enemies.'

The brutality of the massacres of September 1792 marked the real beginning of the Terror which lasted for two years. Amidst the bloodshed Marie Grosholtz suffered a traumatic experience which is recorded in her memoirs and must be true, although no other parties have given an account of the incident. When the mob had driven the Royal Family to seek refuge with the National Assembly, the Princesse de Lamballe, superintendent of the Queen's household, and Madame de Tourzel, the children's governess, had been with them. When packed in one coach and sent to the Temple prison they found the keep unready. The Princesse de Lamballe and Madame de Tourzel were taken off to La Force prison on 19 August. Marie Antoinette's last words to the departing governess were 'If we do not meet again look after Madame de Lamballe. . . .'

A fortnight later, on the morning of 3 September, the Princesse was taken to the Revolutionary Tribune presided over by the monster Hébert, sadistic editor of the paper called *Le Père Duschene*. She was briefly questioned, then turned out of the prison into the street where heaps of corpses lay. 'Fie! How horrible . . .' exclaimed the Princesse. A banker named Charlat stepped forward to knock off her bonnet and the waiting gang set to work stabbing her to death. They then raped the dead body, sawed off her head and cut out her heart and genitals; the body was dragged away over the cobbles, and at a house which is now 113 Boulevard Beaumarchais the head was washed in a bucket and put on a pike, the heart stuck on a sabre and joke-moustaches made of sexual sections of the body. This pretty band then conceived the idea of torturing the Queen by holding her friend's head up in front of the prison window. The account given in *Madame Tussaud's Memoirs*, nearly fifty years later, and in which she refers to herself in the third person, is as follows:

Her head was immediately taken to Madame Tussaud, whose feelings can be easier conceived than described. The savage monsters stood over her whilst she, shrinking with horror, was compelled to take a cast from the features of the Princesse. Having known her virtues, and having been accustomed to seeing her beaming with all that cheerfulness and sweetness which are the heralds of 'Temper's unclouded ray' – to hear her accents teeming of kindness, always affording pleasure to her auditors, and then alas! to have the severed head of one so lovely between her trembling hands, was hard indeed to bear. The features, beauteous even in death, and the auburn tresses, although smeared with blood, still in parts were unpolluted by the ruthless touch of her assassins, and shone with all their natural richness and brilliance. Eager to retain a memento of the hapless Princesse, Madame Tussaud proceeded to perform her melancholy task, whilst surrounded by the brutal monsters whose hands were bathed in the blood of the Princesse.

What are we to make of this? Psychologically how was Marie affected? What were the real pressures on her? Fear of the blood-stained mob would be sufficient to make her acquiescent, but then comes that curious remark about being 'eager to retain a memento of the hapless Princesse'. What a memento! Whatever her reactions Marie never analysed them lucidly. We accept the statement that the head with its blood-stained auburn hair was still beautiful, for the Princesse de Lamballe, who had so often visited Madame Elizabeth, was beautiful, but what *were* the real feelings of Marie as she retreated to the workshop with the mould of that lovely face to prepare a waxen ghost for display? And she *must* have seen the genitalia on the other pike. Maybe she was too frightened to remonstrate. Meanwhile, the head on its pike was carried to the Temple, and Marie Antoinette heard the jeering mob beneath her tower. One of the prison commissioners entered to draw the curtains. 'They want you to appear at the window but we shall not allow it.'

The roar outside increased and other municipal officers appeared; they were pale and Marie Antoinette begged to be told the truth. A tall fellow explained, 'They want to hide from you the head of the Lamballe. . . .' The Queen fainted.

Did Marie's heart turn with horror when she heard the mob was carrying that blood-stained head to taunt her regal mistress? What could she have felt as she tinted the hair and painted the wax to exact colourings of the face she had known so well?

We can see that during the horrific years of 1792 and 1793 Marie became a secret person. She loved Dr Curtius, and although she saw him jumping on every political bandwagon, she suspected that his revolutionary fervour, once real, was being continued for safety's sake. She seems to have resolved to turn herself into one of her own emotionless effigies.

After the September Massacres, a sombre calm fell over Paris. On 21 September the newly elected Assembly, the third to sit since the start of the Revolution, took over. When the French armies achieved a victory at Valmy and the foreign foe were driven beyond the frontiers, the moderate section of the Convention gained a little power. Danton became Minister for Justice and Curtius's friend, Monsieur Roland, Minister for the Interior.

With the lessening of fear, a reaction against terrorism set in. Repressive surveillance eased and the suicide rate dropped. From houses overlooking the Temple prison people could see the Royal Family taking exercise on the battlements, and landlords found they could let out rooms with high windows most profitably. Marie herself went once, but a glimpse of Madame Elizabeth, whom she dared not attempt to contact, hurt more than she expected. She refused to go again and shut Versailles out of her mind.

At the end of November a wall safe opened in the Tuileries revealed documents of counter-revolutionary schemes. These proved that while alive Mirabeau, who had argued for a constitutional monarchy and also championed the Revolution, had during all this period received a pension from the King. He could not be executed but his remains were removed from the resting place of heroes in the Panthéon to a common cemetery. Marat now demanded that the King stand trial, although Robespierre and his cronies deemed a trial unnecessary since the fact that Louis was King automatically rendered him guilty.

On 20 January 1793 the National Assembly voted for Louis's death by a majority of five – the majority included his own cousin Philippe Egalité, Duc d'Orléans. The King was immediately informed of the sentence.* Marie heard that Louis was allowed to see his family privately before being taken from the Temple to the scaffold. The Abbé Edgeworth, who had been Madame Elizabeth's confessor at Versailles, was allowed to accompany him. Marie knew the Abbé and had modelled his head for the Exhibition. He was a man of firm principles who could not fail to strengthen the moral courage of that King who had worked hard and conscientiously for France.

While Curtius kept open house for revolutionary leaders Marie dared not say that she held the Abbé in esteem or that the monarch had always been kind to her.

On the day of the King's death the authorities ordered the closure of all shops and places of entertainment. The doors of Curtius's Cabinet de Cire remained locked. Curtius's friend, the brewer Santerre, rode on a big horse in front of Louis's carriage and thousands of men armed with guns and pikes marched behind the cortège. It was a misty day with rain falling, the silence broken only by the rolling of drums. The dignity of the King impressed onlookers but he was not allowed to address them.

After the execution, while an unlovely cheering mob danced a *Farandole* around the guillotine, Louis's remains were taken to the cemetery of the Madeleine. Somewhere, somehow, Marie took a mould of the King's severed head. She never revealed where this was done – but it must have been just before the burial that afternoon.†

Much later Marie would say that the National Assembly ordered the death-mask. But Marie never explained the extent to which Curtius may have brought pressure to bear on her. Did he force his pupil to such tasks? With that revolutionary uncle-professor she may have felt safe, but not all *that* safe. Hundreds of people were now paying with their lives for

---

* Dr Guillotin's invention had only recently come into general use. The first execution by means of the gadget had taken place in April 1792, when a 'mugger' called Nicolas Pelletier, caught running away with a wallet containing 800 livres, was beheaded in the place de Grève. An enormous crowd had turned up to see the new instrument at work.

† Few facilities were required for a death-mask. A carpet-bag could carry all that was needed. The features would be oiled, a little plaster mixed with water, then smoothed over the face (no need for quills in nostrils), and the mask removed when dry. The cast from this mould of Louis XVI can be seen in Madame Tussaud's.

some thoughtless act. Soon after the King's execution, a friend of Curtius named Monsieur Philipstal got into trouble through a technical mistake. He was a showman, running a kind of magic lantern known as the 'Phantasmagoria' which depicted moving likenesses of people on a screen. While Philipstal was giving a demonstration in a crowded hall, one of his employees inadvertently inserted an old slide of Louis XVI. On realizing his mistake, the man drew it up to remove it, but not before some hysterical loons in the audience started to shout that it had been done on purpose to depict the King rising to heaven. An uproar ensued, Philipstal was arrested and taken to prison. His wife tried frantically to get him released. In desperation she finally came to Curtius* and begged him to exert influence with the men he knew – Sieyès, Marat, Danton, even Robespierre, might listen to him. Curtius cautiously agreed to try; he was a realist and knew that bribes often got people out of trouble. Robespierre, the Incorruptible, was supposed to be above palm-greasing but Curtius decided it might be worth trying. He could explain that, after all, Philipstal was a very unimportant prisoner and his crime had obviously been a mistake. 'Your husband is rich and lives in grand style,' he explained. 'Three hundred louis might help.' Madame Philipstal willingly produced this sum to be passed to Robespierre as 'the gift of an admirer'. Curtius made his way to the great man's office and outlined his plea; he did not mention the money but simply left it lying on the table. Robespierre listened to the story impassively, then handed out an order for Philipstal's release. Curtius left the room without mentioning or even glancing at the silver on Robespierre's table. Not a word was spoken, nor was the money returned.

With trepidation Marie watched her uncle's relationship with this curious tyrant who was forcing his way to the top. She knew him to be a 'ladies' man', although pock-marked and unprepossessing. Robespierre had small sharp features and weak eyes hidden by green spectacles; he dressed beautifully and apparently had success with a number of women, although he did not consider marriage and kept no regular mistress. Marie noted his silk coats and frilled neck cloth, his powdered hair and buckled shoes, and thoroughly disliked and distrusted him. She believed all the tales about Robespierre sending inconvenient husbands and lovers to the

---

* Her arguments concerning Curtius's basic admiration for the monarchy are never very credible. Many years later in England Marie met the brother of Pierre de Paris who had stabbed to death a deputy who had voted for the King's execution. He spoke to her scornfull'y: You were a Republican.'

guillotine. One day when walking the boulevards with a lady he fancied, Robespierre heard her admire a certain house.

'Would you like to own it?'

'Indeed I should.'

'Then it shall be yours.'

The owner was denounced and executed and Robespierre's lady-love installed.

Marie had reason to believe this story, and she also believed that certain well-born ladies who had fallen on hard times and entertained gentlemen but refused Robespierre's advances were guillotined because of this. She herself had little sex-appeal and must have felt safe on this score. No one could have had an ear nearer to the ground than Marie Grosholtz.

A very different character was that strange, physically unsavoury lawyer Marat, who turned up so often at Curtius's house. Born of a Swiss mother and Sardinian father, he had started his career as a qualified doctor, obtaining his MD at St Andrews in Scotland; then after serving as physician to the Comte d'Artois's guards, he became deeply embroiled in politics. Deliberately dressing in filthy ragged clothes – as if for effect – he achieved a certain reputation in high society as an interesting eccentric and a 'card'. Pock-marked like many others, he also suffered from a hideous and painful skin disease, prurigo, which gave his person a nasty smell. His newspaper, *L'Ami du Peuple*, became notorious for its attacks on public figures in the Establishment of the day, and on all the moderates of the Assembly. Curtius first met him at the Jacobin Club, found him interesting, and often invited him to dinner where the Alsatian cooking appealed to Marat's palate. Once when he overdid invective in *L'Ami du Peuple* and called for France to be 'flooded in blood', Marat had to go on the run. He hid for a week in the Curtius house. Marie remembered him arriving with a carpet-bag containing a few necessities. A fastidious young woman, she recoiled at his repulsive appearance and odour, yet he emanated a kind of magnetism. During this visit he sat hidden all day in a dark corner scribbling by lamplight. Once Marat tapped her roughly on the shoulder: 'All aristocrats must be killed. You understand that?' She shivered and tried not to show her aversion. Marat thundered on: 'It is not for ourselves that I and my fellow labourers work, it is for you and your children. As for my generation, well – in all probability we shall not live to enjoy the fruits of our exertions.'

She felt uncomfortable in Marat's company, but sometimes she heard him bandying jokes at the dinner table with other members of the Jacobin Club. What had twisted him? When after a week of hiding he dared to depart, he suddenly revealed a charming smile: 'Thank you for being kind people,' he said and patted Marie's arm: 'She is a good child.' Marat was forced to go into hiding so often that he said his spirit had been 'soured' by subterranean existence.

The other revolutionary leader who frequented the Curtius house was Danton, the lawyer – a huge bull of a man, pock-marked too, yet attractive, mad about women yet happily married to an adoring wife. When he became Deputy Public Prosecutor to the Commune, Danton urged that continuing war against Austria was not the way to bring about a republic. ('What *is* a republic?' Robespierre had artlessly asked him not long before.) Then, as Minister of Justice and President of the Council, Danton became both Prime Minister and head of state. Danton was venal but human. Marat was not venal but inhuman. Robespierre was called 'incorruptible' but Marie knew better, and his human failings were tempered by an inhuman ferocity. Mirabeau, luckily for himself, was dead, and, as Saint-Beuve said: 'Mirabeau did not sell himself; he merely allowed people to pay him.'

As soon as Danton became virtual head of state he passed on to the district committees the decree embodying a general warrant to search the house of any suspect. Grudges were paid off and jealously triggered off many raids. Within ten days nearly 3000 arrests were made. While ordinary people cowered in their houses, sickened by the carts of corpses they met in the streets and frightened of being reported for not sufficiently applauding, there was much high-level talk of purging tyrants from the face of the earth.

It was Danton who had brought into being that Revolutionary Tribunal whose judgments were to be final and beyond the Court of Appeal. He had a lawyer's mind, but too late he realized how nicely he had laid the foundations of the Terror.

The year 1793, which saw the execution of the King and Queen, the outbreak of the war between England and France, and the rise of Robespierre, would freeze Marie Grosholtz into an impenetrable reticence which she never shed.

E

6

The Terror

The Revolution was the street, the triumph of the street, the dictatorship of the
street. Everyone out of doors, a whole people feverishly coming and going, a
whole city swarming, over-flowing with curiosity for the unbelievable new
things presented to its eyes. AMIOT-DUMONT,
Les Parisiens sous la Révolution,
Amiot-Dumont.

The sights of the street were not always very pretty. One Pierre Notelet
(whose letters to a brother-in-law were found a few years ago by a great-
grandson Jules Mazé) had only to lean out of his window at 404 rue St
Honoré (which always stank) to see the reactions of the crowds gathered
to watch the tumbrils rolling by to the guillotine. The smallest incidents,
he records, are the most revealing. When the Parliamentary opposition,
the Girondins, were disposed of, one cart passed containing the body of
Valazé, a deputy who had stabbed himself before the Tribunal. A child's
voice rang out: 'Maman come and see. They are bringing a dead man.
Will they cut off *his* head?' Another time Notelet heard a little dog
scolded for licking up blood that streamed from the scaffold. His mistress
wagged a finger and said: 'Naughty, naughty! Stop that.'

This was the Paris in which Marie had to live and work and take care
to give the right impression.

As food became scarce Curtius had the bright idea of buying a small
house, with its vegetable garden and a poultry yard, at Ivry-sur-Seine
outside Paris. They could travel down by hired carriage to escape the
tension of Paris, and Marie enjoyed feeding the chickens and supervising
the growing of vegetables. When they returned to the city their luggage

consisted of large hampers of fresh food, which, presumably, had to be well hidden from hungry neighbours. A breath of country air made all the difference to Marie. Curtius had become quite a rich man and his Exhibition was flourishing, but the Revolution affected everyone's pocket, and he could not afford to buy this house outright. He put down the first year's instalment at the government housing bureau.

By 1793 the successes of the Revolutionary armies had led to the annexation of Savoy, Nice and Belgium. England took alarm and became increasingly hostile when French troops occupied Belgium. Then France declared war on her and Holland. During February 300 000 Frenchmen were conscripted. Each department had to provide a contingent of bachelors and widowers aged between twenty and forty. As fathers of more than two children were for a time exempted, the status of paternity was industriously sought. Curtius found his male staff in the Cabinet de Cire sadly reduced and Marie noticed the streets of Paris becoming gradually devoid of men. Curtius was a bachelor, but over-age, and did not have to fear conscription. In any case he remained an officer in the National Guard.

Despite the hard work involved, there was a certain amount of fun to be had in the National Guard. As Jules Bertaut describes it: 'Each *section* wanted to have its own uniform, its own colours and its own special adornments – here the grenade and fur bonnet; there horsehair plumes falling from the head. What French heart would not beat at the thought of playing soldiers!'

The armies who marched against Holland were not playing at soldiers, but in Paris anecdotes abounded concerning the splendid classlessness of the National Guard.

'Keep in step. You're marching like a priest!' cried an officer to one of his troops.

'It's your fault, Captain. I'm wearing the shoes you made and they're horribly uncomfortable,' answered the soldier to his shoemaker superior.

Somewhat naturally, the elected government had little feeling of security. The revolt in the Vendée seemed impossible to control and the conscripted French armies fared badly. General Dumouriez led his troops successfully until he met defeat at Neerwinden. The National Assembly then summoned the General to explain this failure at the Bar of the House.

By this time Dumouriez had taken the government's measure. He interrogated the Minister and four Commissioners sent to interrogate *him*, then arrested them and handed over the lot to the enemy. He had a wild hope this party might be exchanged against Marie Antoinette and her two children. But the General and Orléans's son with him (General Egalité, the future King Louis-Philippe), realizing their heads were in danger, decided to defect. They packed their personal baggage and slipped across the lines to the Austrians.

When General Custine, who in 1792 had succeeded in penetrating Germany as far as Mayence and Frankfurt, came under suspicion and was denounced as a traitor, Curtius found his own name cropping up during Marat's interrogation. He had in fact stayed with Custine in Mayence, when on an official mission, and knew him quite well. Now certain letters were produced, in which Custine complained to the Duchesse de Liancourt that Curtius had ruined his, the General's, reputation in Paris society by speaking of him as a 'Patriot' (that is, a Republican). Curtius's alleged remark did not save Custine from arrest and ultimately from the guillotine, but his association with the General must have caused Curtius some uneasy moments. Later on Marie spread it around that her uncle had never completely recovered from an attempt to poison him made by the General during the mission to Mayence.

During all these dramas Marat and Danton continued to visit Curtius's house – to rage and to rant and to attack other members of the Assembly. It was Marat who, with his head wrapped in that famous bandanna kerchief which hid the itchy sores of his scalp, boasted he would bring in the Act which authorized the prosecution of 'deputies who might be suspected of conspiring with the enemies of liberty, equality and the Republican government'. A splendid froth of words soon to result in members of the Assembly sending each other to the guillotine in bewildering succession.

The atmosphere grew increasingly sinister and crazy. In the Vendée rising Royalist forces executed thousands of Republicans by firing squad, and whole villages were tortured while their avengers indulged in wholesale drownings. Meanwhile in Belgium the defecting General Dumouriez was able to brief the Austrians on weak points in the French defences, which was hardly encouraging for the next attack.

The real Terror began with the guillotining of three officers from Dumouriez's staff accompanied by an old woman tramp who had, when drunk, been heard to shout 'God save the King!' Because Danton pleaded the necessity of peace for France, Robespierre and Marat branded him a 'moderate' – which had become a most dangerous title. Then, in the desperate July of 1793, Robespierre succeeded Danton as 'dictator'. His skilful string-pulling brought about the defeat of that enormous, stormy man to whom he had written only a year previously when Danton's wife died in childbirth: 'If in the only kind of misfortune which can shake a spirit such as yours, the certain knowledge of possessing a tender and devoted friend can bring you any consolation, I offer that consolation to you. I love you more than ever and unto death.'

In mid-July 1793 men knocked at Curtius's door and Marie heard the extraordinary news of Marat's assassination. An unknown girl from Caen, Charlotte Corday, had broken into the room where he was sitting in his medicinal bath and stabbed him to death. The painter David asked the National Assembly to send Marie Grosholtz immediately to Marat's house where she was to take a cast of his dead face and make exact sketches of the scene so that he could reconstruct it later. How eerie it must have seemed to smooth the plaster over those haunted features and to recall the stinking little man crouched over a desk through long days of hiding. She found the task grisly: his dead face, with eyes rolled upward, was no less repulsive than his living one. From Marie's cast David painted the famous picture which now hangs in the Musées Royaux des Beaux-Arts de Belgique in Brussels.* Then, on the lines of a modern girl journalist, Marie was conducted to the Conciergerie prison to talk to Charlotte Corday and memorize her features. She found the twenty-five-year-old girl serenely contemplating death, believing that she had done her duty in freeing France of the man responsible for the September Massacres. Knowing that Marie would probably model her after death, she talked with calm and a certain exaltation. Marie felt a rare touch of emotion – for here was a noble creature amidst the ignoble dramas of the day. Charlotte Corday made a great impression on all who watched her driving to the guillotine. Notelet wrote to his brother-in-law:

All these people seemed to be waiting for a carnival procession. Suddenly a storm broke. Large drops of rain fell in the dust. The crowd became agitated, one could hear the *Carmagnole* being sung. Suddenly there were cries of 'There she is! There she is!' She was superb in a long red shift that clung to her body in the rain. One might have thought she was a statue her face was so calm. Behind the tumbril young girls were holding hands and dancing.

* The cast is in Madame Tussaud's in London The two were brought together at the Royal Academy exhibition of 1968 entitled, 'France in the Eighteenth Century'.

After the blade had fallen Charlotte's remains were conveyed in the usual cart to the cemetery of the Madeleine where Marie was waiting to take a cast of the face of that girl who had chatted in such easy friendly fashion a few days earlier. Of what stuff was Marie Grosholtz made? What were the pressures which drove her to the handling and reproduction of severed heads? The tableau showing Marat dead in his bath, looking his disgusting old self, and Charlotte Corday, looking her romantic self, drew enormous crowds. In fact, Marat, so smelly and unattractive in life, became a kind of cult in death. It was chic and wise to go to the Exhibition and stand there lamenting the murdered man. Robespierre took the opportunity of delivering one of his passionate, boring harangues. After staring at the tableau he walked to the main door and grandly addressed the passing world (the world was exceedingly frightened of this man and there were no titters). 'Citizens,' cried Robespierre, 'follow my example! Enter and see the image of our departed friend snatched from us by the assassin's hand, guided by the demon of aristocracy . . . let us fortify our minds with the resolution to avenge his death by extirpating his enemies who are ours and those of our country!'

Curtius appreciated this free publicity. For weeks people flocked in and the Cabinet de Cire made twenty-five livres a day.

That autumn, cold fear stalked the streets and deputies increasingly looked askance at each other. Montané, President of the Revolutionary Tribunal, was arrested while the Tribunal was actually in session and accused of having tried to save Charlotte Corday from execution. For the first time in history postal censorship was invented, and to keep the guillotine supplied with sufficient victims, all letters were opened and read by Robespierre's *Cabinet Noir*. Charges could be based on muddled phrases. Soon Robespierre boasted more power than had ever been wielded by Danton. He had at his disposal the Law Concerning Suspect Persons stipulating that 'those persons shall be regarded as suspect who, though they have done nothing against liberty, have also done nothing for it'. This made everyone vulnerable. It is difficult to discern a single important character who at some stage was not charged with extortion or treason. This may not have been the first time in history that a band of ignoble ruffians gained power, but never had there been so much grand talk about setting the world to rights as when Fouquier-Tinville, the Public Prose-cutor, roared for the death sentence.

In September, Danton, in whose clear legal mind the Committee of

Public Safety had originated, saw that institution turning into a sickening travesty of his intention. The Terror was destroying France herself. After a feverish illness Danton asked permission of the President of the Assembly to convalesce at his country estate. While he was driving southwards with his family in a post-chaise, Marie Antoinette, whom he had hoped to defend and free (if this did not endanger himself), was brought to trial and condemned. Misery at being separated from her children and the knowledge that her seven-year-old son was being perverted sexually had reduced the once lovely queen to a grey-haired skeleton, so blind that she could hardly find her way across the courtroom. Hébert, who had manufactured a charge of incest between the Queen and her small son, enjoyed seeing her condemned to death, and could not know how gratefully this tortured woman accepted the end. Yet Marie Antoinette sorrowed to leave her children. In the letter she wrote to Madame Elizabeth in the early morning of 16 October 1793, she began:

It is to you, my sister, that I am writing for the last time. I have been sentenced to death, but not to a death that is shameful, but to be reunited with your brother. Like him, innocent, I hope to display the same firmness as he did in his last moments. I am calm as one is with a clear conscience. I deeply regret having to leave behind my poor children. You knew that I lived only for them, and for you, my dear good sister. . . .

This letter was handed to the Public Prosecutor and never seen by Madame Elizabeth. Notelet gave one man's impression of this day:

There was a large crowd for the Queen and many people who were pretending to laugh wanted to weep. In the street I heard a mother say to her daughter, 'Above all don't cry when you see her; you will get us guillotined.' The tumbril looked like a dung cart; it bumped over the cobbles and you could hear it crack as though it would break. Poor Marie Antoinette was as though insensible but had kept her air of grandeur.

Marie Grosholtz went to a friend's house to make a sketch of this historic moment. Placed in a window overlooking the route to the scaffold, Marie waited, pencil in hand – but as the open cart approached she felt herself blacking out. She was completely unconscious as the Queen passed by. It was the pencil of David which sketched the pathos and splendour in a few lines. He did not mean to immortalize her, but it is a sketch which wrings the heart. By not allowing herself to retreat into insanity Marie Antoinette would give all women a model of how to die. Marie Grosholtz never revealed where she took the mask of the Queen's severed head, nor has she stated if Curtius stood by her. There is a possibility that the guards carried the head to the studio, but the cemetery is the more likely place.

It was Dr Curtius who later took a death-mask of Madame du Barry, and we have an exact description of how this occurred. The portrait of the delectable mistress of Louis XV had in the past proved one of his great draws. Curtius had, at her own behest, modelled Jeanne du Barry lying on a sofa, and when in voluptuous middle age she went hysterically to the scaffold, Curtius wanted her for his Exhibition. So he went to the cemetery of the Madeleine to await the cart arriving with the day's load of guillotined remains. He was what might be called quite a fly business-man. A few bribes had to be passed, and in the cold winter dusk Curtius stood waiting for the cart. He sorted through the grisly cargo and for-tunately the face of Madame du Barry proved recognizable. The doctor smoothed out her contorted features with skilled and practised fingers, he oiled the once lovely features and applied the plaster. Then he handed back the head to be tossed with the others into the common grave.* Marie did not attend this proceeding, although later on she modelled several severed heads in similar circumstances without turning a hair. So many people known to Marie were being executed that she must have become accustomed to the constant news of guillotining, if not to the actual sight of the tumbrils. Every kind of excuse was used to keep the executioner busy. When one of the Republic's better soldiers, General Houchard, thought fit to give his exhausted men a rest he was hustled back to Paris and beheaded. Philippe Egalité, Duc d'Orléans, went the same way; then came Bailly, Mayor of Paris, who had been Curtius's early friend. Barnave, co-founder of the Jacobin Club, went the same way, as did General Custine, already men-tioned, for his military failures. The Christian era had been abolished since the previous September, but by counting on her fingers Marie could work out this bloody October 1793 as the month of Brumaire in the Year II of the Republic.

In April the National Assembly had passed a decree ordering all members of the Bourbon family to be arrested in order to be used as hostages. Curtius's royal crony the Duc d'Orléans, who had adopted the name Philippe Egalité when hereditary titles were swept away in 1792, heard this to his surprise while dining in his mansion of the Palais Royal.

* The early portrait has survived. The death-mask has not.

'Good God,' he exclaimed, 'how is it possible I am not exempt? After all the proofs I gave of my patriotism, all the sacrifices I made.' He was guillotined on 7 November 1793.

Curtius had to dance carefully on the political tightrope. A news-sheet published by a violent revolutionary, Prudhomme, attacked him for not creating a tableau reproducing the execution of Louis XVI. 'Curtius whom we like to regard as a patriot showed us for such a long time Louis XVI at table with his family and all his pleasures. . . . Louis Capet on his scaffold would assure him a full house.' The attack ends with a sentence which would have a familiar ring in many countries today. 'The Republic will not harbour in its bosom any arts but those which encourage all citizens to consecrate happy events and good principles. If this had always been done, J. J. Rousseau would not have banned them implacably from every free and well-administered country.'*

Throughout the winter Curtius continued his legal battle to obtain that inheritance from his defunct uncle, an oddly mercenary obsession for one so deeply involved in the Revolution. The sadistic, pornographic Hébert often dined at his table, 'a fine-looking man with agreeable manners', according to Marie's memoirs, but in her 1803 catalogue he is 'the constant companion and friend of the Monster Marat'.

Double agents abounded. Over twenty deputies and several of their wives mounted the scaffold. In November Marie heard that Danton had returned from the country for the fight of his life. His friend Robespierre, grown envious, was out to get him. The deputies eyed each other nervously, each man wondering if he might save his own neck by voting his neighbour to the guillotine. While the ministers kept accusing each other of treason, life for the ordinary citizen became bewildering, terrifying and lugubrious. St Just, the handsome twenty-six-year-old lieutenant of Robespierre, revelled in the lethal powers granted by the Law of Suspects. Arguing that *leniency was treason*, he insisted that Danton's humane tendencies should be distrusted. To ensure 'safety' the Committee of Public Safety daily sent batches of victims to the guillotine. Robespierre genuinely believed it was safer to allow 'controlled Terror'.

In March 1794 Hébert and thirteen of his cut-throat followers were, to their surprise, arrested and promptly guillotined. Hébert, who had sent so many to the scaffold, went to his death screaming with fear. According to Marie she received a summons from the Assembly to take his death-

* *Revolutions de Paris*. No. 188, 26 February 1793.

mask at the Madeleine cemetery.* There is no evidence to prove such orders were ever issued by any official body. Perhaps Curtius wished her to add famous heads while he was away.

It is difficult to believe that Marie Grosholtz did not suffer pain when Madame Elizabeth was taken from her prison in the Temple to stand trial on the usual meaningless charges of conspiring against liberty. Marie did not attempt to see her former mistress drive through the streets to meet death. She only heard of her serenity and of the unusual hush that hung over the crowd as this lovable Princess mounted to the blood-stained guillotine. Madame Elizabeth stood a moment bare-headed, for her kerchief had blown off, and then she laid herself down with quiet dignity as had her brother and sister-in-law. She was the last of the batch of twenty-three victims to climb the scaffold, and for once no voice cried out, '*Vive la République*'. Marie shuddered. She kept thinking of this curious saintly Princess of France and of the ingenuous enthusiasm with which she had sought to serve humanity. Only one little girl and one small boy now remained of the Royal Family which had driven from Versailles five years previously.†

After the disposal of Hébert, Robespierre organized a 'Festival of the Supreme Being'. It would not be very clear if these junketings were in honour of the Supreme Being or of Robespierre – or to celebrate their amalgamation. Immortality of the Soul was solemnly proclaimed to be 'a social and Republican concept'. David artistically devised the ceremonies

---

* This cast survives at Madame Tussaud's. Her memoirs merely state 'a cast of his head was taken by Madame Tussaud at the Madeleine'.

† Marie Antoinette had good reason to weep at leaving her children on earth. Her daughter survived. The eight-year-old Dauphin, a delicate sensitive boy, was locked up in solitary confinement, his window was never opened, his clothes and bed linen never changed and for six months his excrement never removed. Developing a painful skin disease, he was untreated by any doctor. This Dauphin suffered from tuberculosis of the bones like his elder brother, and it is likely that the pathetic small body given an autopsy after death on 8 June 1795 was indeed that of the little King of France, and not, as many claimed later, that of a deaf-and-dumb substitute. Thirty-two different 'pretenders' would eventually claim rights, but none of them was recognized by the Princesse Royale who would surely have been glad to see her brother again. This girl stood up bravely to her own imprisonment, which lasted until December 1795 when the mood of blood-soaked Paris swung to tearful sentimentality for 'the orphan of the Temple'. Having become an embarrassment to the government, the sixteen-year-old Princess was driven to the frontier and exchanged for a prisoner of the Austrians. Ironically this happened to be the post-master deputy who had betrayed her father at Varennes.

and Robespierre, holding a bouquet of flowers, presided over a procession which stretched from the Tuileries to the Champs de Mars. Marie Grosholtz was there to watch the great bonfire intended to destroy the figures of Atheism, Discord and Selfishness.

Meanwhile the Committee of Public Safety turned its attention to Danton, whose noisy emotional outbursts rendered it easy to accuse him of almost anything. Growing uneasy, Danton tried to fall back on his old friendship with Robespierre – the man who had written him 'we are together till death'. But when Danton called at his rooms Robespierre proved coldly evasive. Always a dandy, the new dictator was preparing for a pleasant day of death-sentencing by elegantly powdering his hair. Danton looked at him lolling back in front of the mirror, a protective anti-make-up smock thrown over his smart green-striped coat. Using the familiar *tu*, Danton spoke of their close friendship, of how they had built up the Revolution together. But Robespierre chose to forget the good old days and replied using the formal *vous* – a chilling change of address which only the French language can convey.

During the next few days Danton's friends implored him to escape from France, but he relied on his own eloquence. 'Can a man take his country with him on the soles of his shoes?' he asked. And he returned to face the Revolutionary Tribune in Paris. Five days later, the great Danton, last of a batch of fifteen, had to mount the blood-slippery scaffold.

That was April. At the end of July Robespierre and his henchman St Just, ardent organizers of other people's deaths, were in their turn arrested and to their amazed disbelief sent to the scaffold.* It is particularly revealing that, never dreaming he could be indicted, Robespierre had left his apartment to address the Assembly clad in a particularly handsome sky-blue suit. When preening before the mirror little did he dream that, two mornings later, it would be the executioner who undid his cravat.

* This is described in her memoirs. 'When he found that he had no means of escaping execution, he endeavoured with a pistol to blow out his brains, but only shattered his under jaw, which was obliged to be tied up when he was taken to the scaffold. The executioner when about to do his office, tore the dressing roughly away, and Robespierre uttered a piercing shriek, as his lower jaw separated from the upper, whilst his blood flowed copiously. His head presented a most dreadful spectacle; and immediately after death, it was taken to the Madeleine, where Madame Tussaud took a cast of it, from which the likeness she now possesses was taken.' Her early portrait of Robespierre has not survived but this death-mask is in Madame Tussaud's, and on it the wound in his jaw made when Robespierre had tried to shoot himself is clearly visible.

Curtius was away in Germany, so it was Marie Grosholtz who waited at the Madeleine cemetery to take a death-mask of Robespierre.

After the dispatch of their leader and twenty-one of his cronies in one morning the French people ceased to applaud the guillotine as a means of general improvement. The Great Terror was over.

7

Aftermath

There seemed no end to the theatrical devices by which the deputies sought to amuse the querulous populace. In the spring of 1794 (between the executions of Danton and Robespierre) the National Assembly commissioned the great David to create a national costume. The painter designed 'dress for the French citizen at home'. While denouncing friends for not trying hard enough, or not marching to sufficient revolutionary festivals, Frenchmen were invited to wear a Roman tunic, breeches and a round bonnet topped with a plume. In winter a blue cape would float from the shoulders. But the decapitation of all the principals ended this governmental lark.

By the summer of 1794 most citizens, at home or out of home, were obsessed not with their costume but with worry over the falling value of money, the high cost of food and the prevalent difficulty of keeping heads affixed to shoulders.

Curtius was a cool individual, able to jump with agility on and off the band-wagons of changing times. He had never ceased to make capital out of the Revolution. There must have been moments of anxiety, depression and disgust, but throughout the years of turmoil this indefatigable modeller had continued to build up his fortune and to take advantage of each turn of the tide. In a grim way executions suited his book. Everyone who rose to fame, everyone who lost his head, provided his museum with an interesting new subject to exhibit. He moved carefully amidst his revolutionary friends, never making a false step, never going too far, never not going far enough, for the new laws made hesitancy an executionable sin. When the government called on citizens to contribute their gold and silver plate to the nation Curtius had scurried off the mark. A hamper containing all the plate he possessed was delivered to the Hôtel de Ville. When there was an opportunity of presenting the bust of a popular figure to the Jacobin Society of Friends of Liberty and Equality, Curtius would be quick to show his 'personal patriotism and civic virtue' by producing a portrait modelled by his own hand.* His exhibition flourished throughout the days of mass arrests. Despite the nasty fate which befell so many of his acquaintances, Curtius never became unstuck. It was not all that easy when 5000 went to the guillotine. Between June 1794 and July 1795 more than 1280 people were executed in Paris alone, but until the last minute the Curtius household remained safe from denunciation and imprisonment.

The one dangerous episode occurred shortly before the fall of Robespierre, when Curtius himself was away in the Rhineland on an official mission. (Probably his native German language made him useful to the Foreign Ministry.) The dreaded midnight knock sounded at the door of 20 Boulevard du Temple, and Marie, her mother and an aunt were arrested and taken to prison in a hackney coach. Half the horror of these arrests lay in their lack of reason. Marie suspected that they had been denounced by a *grimacier* and dancer from a nearby theatre. This fellow, Jacques Dutroy, supplemented his income by assisting Sanson, the executioner, as one of his 'lads'. Dutroy might possibly have grown envious of the Curtius household and seized the opportunity of the master's absence to denounce the women. He had only to cite some vague offence such as not wearing a sufficiently ostentatious tricolour cockade, or of sympathizing with a victim of the guillotine. Marie, her mother and aunt were taken to the Carmelite prison where they met an attractive young widow named Josephine Beauharnais whose husband had just been guillotined. She was awaiting her own fate bravely enough. Her husband, General Beauharnais, had been arrested on charges of military ineptitude during the battles around Mayence. Despite his wife's appeals he had been taken to the Conciergerie prison and guillotined on 22 July 1794.

In prison, Josephine Beauharnais was allowed to see her children, Hortense and Eugène, who visited her in charge of their governess, with a dog on whose collar messages from the outside world were concealed.

---

* Report on Session of the National Convention, 23 November 1793. *Moniteur Universel.*

Even in her own distress Marie felt a surge of admiration for Josephine's spirit in that filthy prison. Twenty women were locked in one room with dirty straw to sleep on and no sanitation. Marie would always remember little Hortense, who never gave way to tears, except once, when she saw her mother weep.

Marie has not recorded the dates of her imprisonment. It could not have exceeded a week for her name, Grosholtz, does not appear in any of the extant prison records. She and her mother and aunt were suddenly released, probably on a word from Curtius's friend, General Kléber. It is also possible that the influential David, who found Marie's death-masks useful, stepped in. The women were certainly free before Robespierre's execution, because Marie was moulding his severed head on the evening of 29 July.

In early August, the Assembly, frightened by crowds shouting 'Down with the Law of Suspects', freed nearly 500 prisoners, Josephine Beauharnais among them.

Curtius had not yet returned from the Rhineland, so Marie and her mother and aunt, not daring to return to his house, went to stay with a barrister friend, Monsieur Dejean. They were fairly shaken; it took time to recover from even a week in prison, where the food was foul and all had their hair cut short to be ready for the guillotine. One wonders how Curtius reacted on returning from his mission to find that his chief had been executed and his household was waiting in trepidation after their prison experience.

The three men who engineered the fall of Robespierre were acquaintances of Curtius. They were Barère, that Billand-Varenne who had so casually watched the slaughter of priests in the street during the September Massacres, and Collot d'Herbois, who had appeared to be a 'nice young actor' when first he met Marie. There seems to have been room for improvement in his performance, for in Lyons he was once hissed on the stage. A few years later, as Commissioner to that city, he took his revenge by making such hearty use of guillotine and grapeshot in a way that seldom falls to the unappreciated actor, that even the hot-blooded extremists of the south besought him to check his cruelties. To the Curtius household, however, d'Herbois had his uses, and he it was who arranged for the whole Curtius ménage to change their Swiss passports, issued during their residence in Berne, to French ones before Switzerland became an enemy country. Marie became very friendly with Madame d'Herbois, a Dutch woman whose father had cut her off without a penny for espousing that 'penniless actor'. The actor's situation changed and it was Collot d'Herbois who, as President of the Convention, prevented Robespierre and St Just from speaking in their own defence. His little bell constantly drowning their protests rang the way for them to the guillotine. Such characters are better kept as friends than enemies. Marie remembered Robespierre suggesting that he, Collot d'Herbois and Marat give their own clothes for the wax figures Curtius had made of them. Little did she dream of the day that Monsieur d'Herbois would request a death-mask of his dear colleague.

As France indulged in hysterical rejoicing at 'tyranny's end', Curtius retired to Ivry-sur-Seine for a rest. He was worn out; the journey to the Rhineland undertaken at the behest of a government headed by Robespierre, the return to a city which had beheaded Robespierre, the feeling of outrage on hearing of his household's arrest, and the city's aura of exhaustion, must have affected him. No one knew at the time if the Terror had ended for certain. Curtius obviously felt himself a sick man, but in no paper or letter does he intimate that he might have been poisoned during his mission in Germany as Marie always insisted.

There had been a tremendous amount of work over the last year. For the first time an exhibition of Curtius's wax portraits was to be shown outside France. Even now a collection of twenty life-size duplicate figures was on its way to India. This foreign exhibition was billed to include 'Kings and Princes who have been to Paris and were modelled by Curtius, the unfortunate Louis XVI and his family, as well as Voltaire, Rousseau and the principal members of the First Assembly'. It was well advertised in the *Calcutta Gazette* and *Madras Courier*. The whole exhibition travelled in the charge of an Italian named Dominick Laurency, obviously an experienced showman who knew how to get publicity. All the figures were guaranteed to be 'wearing their usual costumes'. He advertised 'The Cabinet of Curtius and the Optic of Zaler'; the latter seems to have been a form of optical illusion popular in Paris – 'the Optic Glass representing the rising of the Sun and the capital cities of Europe in their Natural State and Size . . . the illuminations in the houses are represented so exactly that persons who have been to any of these places will easily recognize the streets and houses they have inhabited'. The exhibition was completed by a model of the Bastille and the decapitated head of Foulon (once Minister of Finance and Curtius's neighbour). This particular piece had great popular appeal, for 'the blood seems to be streaming from it and running on the ground'.

While the Danish ship containing this exhibition was making its six-month voyage around Africa and across the Indian Ocean, France despatched Robespierre and company, and Paris danced with relief. Marie felt there was something frightening in the craze for street dancing. She had seen people dancing before – around the guillotine and behind the tumbrils. The city seemed to be reeling from its experiences.

When Curtius went to Ivry-sur-Seine Marie usually accompanied him, but she had to keep returning to Paris to attend to affairs on his behalf, and it looks as if her mother always accompanied her.

On 31 August 1794 Curtius summoned a lawyer and a witness in front of whom he dictated a last will. On this document only can the circumstances of that autumn be reconstructed. Although no symptoms are mentioned, the wording of the will makes it obvious that Curtius knew he was a very sick man. Dated 14 Fructidor, Year II (31 August 1794), the 'Will of Citizen Curtius' introduces his notary, Sieur Hubert Gibé, and the two witnesses, Citizen Antoine Boucheron of 14 place de Vendôme, Section du Temple, and Citizen Jean Dournel, Justice of the Peace of the Section du Temple, both of whom must have been neighbours summoned from Paris. These men attest that 'Curtius, painter and sculptor of Paris, resident at No. 20 Boulevard du Temple, being also this day at Ivry-sur-Seine in his country house, 3 rue de Seine' was found by them in his bedroom on the first floor of the same house, which looked out on the garden, 'ill in body but sound in mind, memory and judgement'.

The wording presents Curtius, 'who in the sight of death, made, dictated and named to the Notary in the presence of the undersigned Witnesses his Will as follows.'*

I declare I do not have, or know of, any female heir either in France or in a foreign country.

I give and bequeath to the poor of the Section du Temple in Paris, all my silver ware and all my jewellery. I desire that at my death the sale of these should be effected by the normal means, and the sum which results should be transmitted to the Welfare Committee of the same Section against the receipt of their treasurer. I charge them to distribute it according to their wisdom.

I appoint and institute as my residuary legatee the Citizeness Anne Marie

* The legal troubles concerning the inheritance of Mayence are not mentioned. The interesting paragraphs remain as above.

F

Grosholtz, spinster, of full age, my pupil in my art who has lived with me under my roof for more than twenty years.

I desire that she should have from my estate, immediately after my death, everything that the law allows me to give, in view of my not having an heir. I make her executrix of my Will.

This was dictated to the notary in the presence of the witnesses, and re-read to Curtius so that he could testify to his own clear understanding.

How strange that this man, who knew himself to be on the brink of death, should allow his beloved 'pupil' to return to Paris. Perhaps she had only just departed when, three weeks later, he had a relapse. Only the concierge and his wife were in the house. Philippe Curtius must have expected death; perhaps he preferred to be alone, to contemplate the paths he had followed from the respectable dullness of the lesser German nobility to the exciting artistic theatrical world of Paris and the dramas of the Revolution. He had cultivated friends in every camp, he had known the famous men of his time, and he had found one human being to love – Marie Grosholtz, whether his daughter or not – who was to inherit everything he possessed.

When Curtius realized that death was upon him, he sent for the concierge Guérin and his wife, who remained at his bedside during the final hours. His extraordinary life ended at four o'clock on the afternoon of 26 September 1794.

A galloping horse was the fastest method of communication, so Marie and her mother could not have learned the news until late that night, but the local Justice de la Paix had to be informed immediately so that his officers could put all property under seal.

Next morning Marie arrived with two neighbours from the Temple district to sustain her in this hour of crisis. These men were old friends of Curtius – Louis Gabriel Sallé, who owned the Théâtre Patriotique in the Boulevard du Temple, and Antoine Villon, a grocer. Marie wanted a post mortem, but the surgeon-doctor who had attended Curtius made no remark concerning the likelihood of poisoning, which she suspected, and the official *acte de décès* does not mention anything unnatural.

What could she have felt walking up the staircase to that first-floor bedroom where 'Uncle Philippe' now lay still and pale as one of his own untinted wax effigies. She was the one living thing that he had created. All the rest could break and melt and be forgotten. But she would carry on his name into the future. Not a line exists concerning her personal grief, but how could she not have wept at losing such a guardian?

What *have* come down to us are the fascinating inventories of Curtius's houses. These were taken in detail because of the complex legal situation. And it is interesting to note that however hard she may have been stricken Marie Grosholtz took charge of the situation with coolness and determination. Curtius had not only taught her to model, he had imparted his own business sense.

How strange it was for Marie to sit in the 'big room with five windows' and hear her voice taking the oath before the local officials. She had to declare herself present, that she was residuary legatee and that neither she nor Madame Guérin, the concierge's wife, had removed anything from

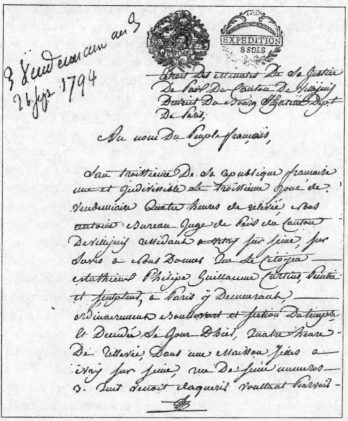

First page of the inventory of Curtius' house at Ivry-sur-Seine, made by the local authority the day after his death on 26 September 1794. *Archives of the Mairie of Ivry-sur-Seine*

the house. The detailed inventory then began. The listing of tables, curtains, mirrors, pictures and bibelots continued until nine that night. Curtius must have been a veritable jackdaw who loved buying things, for every corner was jam-packed. The busybody officials who had to rush around examining and placing seals must have been weary after five hours of it.

Meanwhile Sallé and Villon fetched the Registrar to the house and he painstakingly wrote a death certificate.* Curtius was buried at Ivry-sur-Seine. Then Marie returned to Paris and got down to dealing with affairs. There the local authorities had arranged for another inventory of the Exhibition rooms and the dwelling house. A copy of this inventory survives in the archives of the City of Paris, and it is evidence that every corner of 20 Boulevard du Temple as well as the Exhibition rooms were crammed. Chairs, tables, mirrors and an extraordinary number of folding camp-beds with their bedclothes were recorded; so were the contents of endless cupboards full of clothes, glass, china and domestic paraphernalia. There appeared to be no separate workshops or studios. The making of casts and modelling of wax took place in *all* the rooms. Boxes of moulding material were stored everywhere, and a large number of pictures left over from Curtius's picture-dealing days had to be listed. The poor of the neighbourhood did not grow fat on their inheritance, for only six silver spoons and knives could be found, and one snuff-box, which Marie claimed ought not to be included under the term jewellery and should go to her and not to the poor! The cellar held ten bottles of *vin ordinaire* and fifty of Bordeaux, with a few other items 'not meriting description'. The Cabinet de Cire must have been large, for thirty-six unglazed oil pictures and 114 under glass hung on the walls, all in gold frames. The mirrors, chairs and tables were all described along with the main items – thirty life-size portraits in wax, seven half-length figures (*à mis-corps*) fully clothed, and three wax figures reclining on beds. These were probably the young Madame du Barry,† the Princesse de Lamballe and that flirtatious Madame St Amaranthe, arouser of dangerous passions in gentlemen capable of sending ladies to the guillotine. The inventory also records many cases of busts and interesting objects kept for display under glass. There is a long list of lighting brackets and lamps, for Curtius

---

* The handwritten death certificate, with its errors crossed out and altered, is filed in the Mairie at Ivry-sur-Seine.

† Only that of Madame du Barry survives.

had been expert in illuminating his figures and Marie had learnt this lesson well.*

In fact Curtius left a substantial inheritance in a state of chaos. Having established her right with various tribunals, Marie found that she had got to deal with three houses – 20 Boulevard du Temple; another house bringing in rent; and the country house at Ivry-sur-Seine on which only one instalment had been paid. She waded through a confusion of small bills from doctors, locksmiths, masons, etc., paid out a portion of the 7600 livres taxes due and started to get all in order. Curtius had always taken on too much.

To the appropriate tribunal she applied to confirm her rights and obtain a judgment. Throughout the legal formalities following her uncle's death Marie showed an extraordinary calm. Doubtless Monsieur Gibé, the family lawyer, advised her, but there is no record of his presence when she was dealing with officials or supervising the making of inventories, which in those days had to be written out by hand in small meticulous copperplate. He must have perceived her hard-headed competence and left her to it. It was not easy for a woman to keep her wits at this time. The political scene with which the Exhibition had always been linked was in a state of confusion. New names arose and all groups kept jockeying for power. Now the 'Gilded Youth', a party drawn chiefly from artistic professions, made itself heard. Members affected long hair, sideburns, smart tightly buttoned tailcoats and boots with long pointed toes. Joining with the right wing of the Convention, they repudiated the Revolution and attacked the remaining members of the Jacobin Club. Busts and mementoes of Marat were smashed and thrown in the sewers and his remains removed from the Panthéon. Had they been able to find Mirabeau, doubtless his corpse would have been put back.

Marie had learned over the years to be cautious. She quickly removed the figures of revolutionaries from her Exhibition and replaced them by men of the opposite persuasion. The doormen, who in Curtius's day were dressed as National Guards or *Sans-Culottes* according to public feeling, were now tidied up to resemble the Gilded Youth.

By her thirty-third birthday in December 1794, Marie Grosholtz had everything in hand. She would continue to run the Exhibition and add figures of interest, but she often felt lonely – the lynchpin of her existence

---

*A typical extract from the closely written eight-page inventory is given in Appendix 1.

had gone. Her inheritance included three houses, complicated mortgages, the Cabinet de Cire with its wax portraits, valuable furniture, invested capital, and all the clutter of a prosperous complicated business which had taken Curtius nearly thirty years to build up. In the end it would be his skills and not his money which proved the precious heritage.

8

Marriage

The great Revolution was over but human nature did not change. When Chateaubriand questioned his concierge, she sighed: 'Ah, Monsieur le vicomte, those were the days! Every day there went past the windows little duchesses whose necks were white as snow and they were all cut. Now it's over. The people's pleasures have been taken from them!'

Such were the voices Marie heard in Paris. In November the Jacobin Club was closed down and Carrier, whose mass drownings in the Loire a year previously were now divulged, went to the guillotine in December. Whatever Marie's relationship was with the authorities, they permitted her to model the severed head and this was immediately shown in the Exhibition.*

As a bad harvest led to speculation in grain, thieving became endemic. But during all that terrible hungry winter of 1794–5 the Cabinet de Cire, with its valuable furniture and countless interesting objects, was never raided. By April 1795 the poorer classes, who could not afford black-market prices for bread, became desperate, and in May they attacked the Convention, now sitting in the Tuileries. It really was exasperating to go through a bloody Revolution and cut off 5000 heads only to find you were just as hungry as before!

Reaction brought a sort of mini-Terror. Collot d'Herbois and nearly all

---

* It survives in Madame Tussaud's today. Her memoirs note, 'Of five hundred members, four hundred and ninety-eight voted for the death of Carrier, who at last met his death with firmness and resolution, and his head was submitted to the talents of Madame Tussaud, who took from it a cast, still in her possession, which certainly represents him with rather fine features than otherwise.'

Curtius's revolutionary friends had mounted the scaffold; now came the turn of that most blood-thirsty of public prosecutors, Fouquier-Tinville. He had often dined in Curtius's house in the early dream days – five or six years before – when his sadism was less obviously apparent. He was a terrifying character – Fouquier-Tinville – and Marie had always hated his thin lips. Unlike Danton, he scorned affectionate relationships, unlike Robespierre he cared nothing for his appearance, and unlike Curtius at whose table he so often appeared, he was uninterested in food. On 7 May 1795, to general relief, the *accusateur publique* found that his turn had come for the guillotine. Marie, determined to keep her Exhibition up-to-date, proceeded to the cemetery and modelled the head of this former dinner guest. The catalogue noted that the mask had been made 'only a short time after the head had fallen'. Certainly the cast which can be seen at Madame Tussaud's today is a superb piece of work and a most revealing character study.*

Meanwhile Marie found herself in a financial predicament. It turned out that Curtius had died owing 55 000 livres, mostly on the country house at Ivry-sur-Seine which Marie particularly did not want to lose. To raise this sum Marie had to mortgage this partly paid for house and the house in rue des Fossés du Temple which was rented out. The mortgage document dated 17 May 1795 survives. In it a paragraph states that if Citizeness Grosholtz should marry, she must oblige her husband to accept responsibility for interest and repayment on the same terms as she had undertaken. Although such an obligation remained a legal necessity whenever a single woman took out a mortgage, if Citizeness Grosholtz had already set eyes on the young man who would change her name six months later the clause would be pertinent.

In June 1795, as a strong resurgence of Royalist feeling swept the country, came the announcement that the Dauphin – that unseen boy King called Louis XVII – had died in the Temple prison. Rumours that he had been smuggled away immediately abounded, but none would hold definite credence.

The Comte de Provence, he those face Marie had slapped at Versailles

---

* Her memoirs state: 'As he ascended the scaffold he did not appear to derive the same pleasure from viewing preparations for his own death, that he had on so many occasions evinced, when contemplating the requisite arrangements for the execution of others. . . . Madame Tussaud took a cast from his head a short time after it was severed.' This was the last guillotined head that Marie dealt with.

so many years before, now became Louis XVIII, and issued proclamations from Verona. The British permitted his younger brother, the Comte d'Artois, to sail with 700 armed *émigrés* for Brittany, but the landing at Quiberon proved disastrous. Blockaded in the peninsula, only three of the *émigrés* escaped death, and this premature Royalist invasion caused a resuscitation of revolutionary fervour. Many Jacobins who had been arrested during the reaction against the Terror were set free, and the strains of the *Marseillaise* were heard once again.

During this emotional see-sawing Marie struggled with her muddled financial affairs. While a new constitution was debated in the Tuileries, while the Gilded Youth attacked revolutionaries, and revolutionaries newly released from prison attacked the Gilded Youth, the value of the paper assignat fell from its original 100 to 1·4 livres in metal coinage, and it was not easy to keep the Cabinet de Cire solvent.

The only good news came from India where Dominick Laurency had exhibited profitably in Calcutta (in the Old Court House – tickets one gold mohur) and, having mastered the difficulties of preserving wax figures intact through heat and monsoon, had moved them on to Madras. Gentlemen of the East India Company and their families flocked to see what the personages they read about in the newspapers actually looked like. The *Madras Courier* of 12 August 1795 announces the exhibition's opening at Chaultry Plain 'in the large commodious airy house and garden of His Highness the Nabob'. Tickets cost two Star Pagodas three nights a week, and at other times, for an extra Star Pagoda, the wax figures could be seen privately.

But this enterprise did not contribute to the expenses of 20 Boulevard du Temple.

By October Paris was again under arms, and in the fierce street fighting around the rue St Honoré a young Corsican soldier distinguished himself. His name was Napoleon Bonaparte and he had already set appreciative eyes on Josephine Beauharnais whom Marie had met and admired in prison. During these weeks of political chaos Marie Grosholtz decided to marry a young man of twenty-six (eight years her junior) named François Tussaud. She never revealed how or when they met. He was a civil engineer, born of a family of coppersmiths and small wine-producers. The Tussauds had been settled in Macon since the seventeenth century. For reasons unknown François had left his widowed mother and come to Paris.

No. 2.

ETAT CIVIL.

PRÉFECTURE DU DÉPARTEMENT DE LA SEINE.

VILLE DE PARIS.

Sixième Arrondissement.

52

N° ~~340~~

EXTRAIT du Registre des Actes de
Mariage de l'an Quatrième.

Mariage
Tusseau
&
Grosholtz.

Du vingt-huit Vendémiaire de l'an quatrième de la république.
Acte de mariage de françois Tusseau, ingénieur âgé de vingt-six ans, né
à macon département de Saône & Loire, le vingt-huit avril mil sept cent soixante
neuf, demeurant à Paris rue Phelippeaux N° 27 section du gravillier, fils de
Claude Tusseau, et de marguerite Robin ses père & mère, lui décédé, elle
demeurante au susdit Macon. Et de anne marie Grosholtz âgée de trente
trois ans née à Strasbourg le sept Décembre mil sept cent soixante un, Dépt
du bas Rhin, demeurante à Paris boulevard & Section du temple N° 20, fille de
jean Grosholtz et de marie anne Walner, ses père & mère, lui Décédé, elle
demeurante à Paris ladite demeure.

Les actes préliminaires sont l'extrait du registre des actes de publication
de mariage du vingt-cinq Vendémiaire présent mois, affiché au terme de la loi,
et les actes de naissance desdits époux le tout en forme: Les dits
époux ont Déclaré prendre en mariage, l'un anne marie Grosholtz,
& l'autre françois Tusseau, en présence de gabriel joseph Girard, peint
âgé de cinquante cinq ans, demeurant à paris rue Phelippeaux, Section

---

Above and right: Extracts from the registration of Marie Grosholtz's marriage to
François Tussaud on 18 October 1795. *Madame Tussaud's Archives, London*

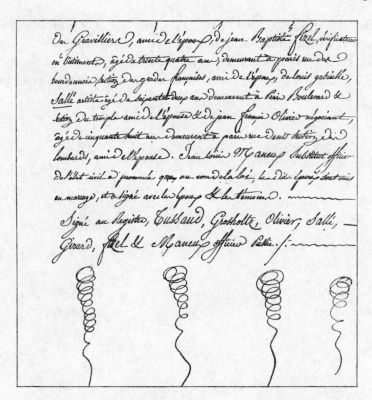

On 18 October 1795 Marie married this young man at the Préfecture du Département de la Seine, ville de Paris. It was a week in which Paris calmed down and renamed the place de la Révolution, where the guillotine had stood, the place de la Concorde.

The witnesses at Marie's marriage were, for François, a painter Girard, aged fifty-five, and an Inspector of Buildings. The witnesses for the bride were Louis Sallé, who had accompanied her to Ivry-sur-Seine and helped her at the time of Curtius's death, and Jean François Olivier, a merchant. Marie's mother is mentioned in the registration of the marriage as living at 20 Boulevard du Temple, but neither she nor any member of the Tussaud family signed as witnesses. Maybe Madame Grosholtz preferred not to use a pen and remained at home preparing the marriage feast.

It is perhaps surprising that Marie did not marry a man of the theatrical world around her. She had lived so long in the Boulevard du Temple, with its showmen, its tumblers, panoramas, rope dancers' booths, and little theatres thronged with people. François Tussaud retained his own profession, and though after marriage he participated in the Exhibitions, he could never have dreamed that the result of marrying this busy little woman would make his name the most famous of London bus-stops.

9

Wife and mother

A few days before her wedding, Marie undertook to pay a life annuity of 2000 livres to Citizeness Marguerite Reiss who inhabited the Curtius home. Business must have been variable, for this represented interest on a loan of 20 000 livres presumably made to help the Exhibition keep up its high standards. Added to the mortgage raised to clear debts and procure the house at Ivry-sur-Seine, it added weight to the burden with which the Tussauds began married life.

Nothing is known of Marie's domestic life except what a few letters can hint. Whether or not Curtius had been her natural father, she had loved and respected him and depended on him for every need – material and emotional. She may well have married young François Tussaud because he reminded her of the lost father-figure. But he may have disliked the role. He may even have been irritated at her business acumen.

Despite hostilities between England and France, considerable traffic continued between the two countries, and towards the end of 1795 a small exhibition called 'Curtius's Grand Cabinet of Curiosities' was sent over for show in London's Bond Street. Then it went on tour throughout England.

Madame Tussaud's first child, a daughter, was born in September 1796 and christened Marie Marguerite Pauline at the church of St-Germain-des-Prés. The baby lived only six months, and although there is not a letter or note concerning the sorrow natural to a mother who loses a first child, Marie's grief can be imagined when, in the following spring, this daughter died at Ivry-sur-Seine. Her mother had made a wax portrait of the little creature before she died. During the next three years Marie bore two sons, Joseph and François, who for a time would be brought up between the Boulevard du Temple and the country house. Their mother worked hard, ceaselessly approaching famous personages and asking if she could model them for her Exhibition. She knew Reubell, one of the important men of the Directory, and he helped her. The flamboyant dress worn by the five Directors lent glamour to the tableau she produced of France's new rulers. The cherry-coloured cloak, white silk pantaloons, boots with turn-down tops and Spanish-style plumed hat are described meticulously in her memoirs, for Madame Tussaud memorized clothes at a glance, just as she memorized the shape of a face and placing of features. The most exciting of her new portraits was that of Madame Beauharnais. She now again met the fascinating Josephine as mistress of Barras, the outstanding personality of the Directory, former vicomte and former Terrorist. The briefest acquaintanceship in prison can forge a strong bond, and Josephine posed gladly for the little woman who had briefly shared those days of fear.

On 10 March 1796 Josephine married the promising young General Bonaparte. Barras, tiring of her, had whispered to Josephine that Napoleon showed potentialities and was about to be given command of the French army in Italy. The honeymoon lasted two days, then Napoleon departed for the front and soon the news of his victories came seeping back to Paris. Josephine found herself, as Barras had promised, the cynosure of all eyes, but this did not prevent Madame Bonaparte from giving free rein to her amorous disposition.

The Directory ended the threat of civil war, but France's financial situation continued to deteriorate. As metal currency disappeared from circulation, a flood of assignats of decreasing value was printed until finally a new coinage had to be issued. The government wished to 'milk' the wealthy, but the wealthy had ceased to exist. Show-business suffered and Marie found her young husband was no replacement for the shrewd, experienced Curtius. But at least she now owned outright the house at Ivry-sur-Seine with its garden and poultry yard, and she had learned how to eke out supplies when the food became short.

The hardships of 1796 brought about a short-lived Jacobin rebellion. The conspirators were arrested and brought to trial, but they were small fry, hardly worth modelling. What Marie Tussaud needed to keep the public flocking through her door were dramatic new names.

In 1797, an electoral year, while Marie was recovering from the loss of her daughter and awaiting the arrival of another baby, existence grew easier. During the election nearly all the departments of France chose Royalist representatives. This swing to the right caused aristocratic *émigrés* to return, yet the armies of France remained revolutionary in spirit, and their successes alone could give power to the government. Of the generals no one was more spoken of than young Bonaparte and by the time the Peace of Campo Formio had been signed (leaving only England at war with France), Josephine realized – somewhat late – that she had married quite a remarkable man.

Marie Tussaud pluckily struggled on and kept her business up-to-date. When in December 1797 the Congress of Rastadt was held in Baden, a small 'Cabinet de Curtius', showing wax portraits of French revolutionary leaders, travelled to the town. Marie must have employed a well-trained staff to accompany these minor displays, or perhaps François Tussaud himself travelled with them. She could not leave Paris at this time for she awaited a second child, her first son Joseph, born there in 1798.

During the following year an amusing mixture of personalities came her way. Talleyrand, the fascinating old fox whose brain enabled him to work for the peace of Europe, while picking up fortunes for himself and dropping witticisms by the way, returned from exile to become Foreign Minister under Barras in the Directory. Marie made a portrait of this extraordinary man,* along with his lady cousin, the celebrated Abbesse de Perigord, whose political prophecies had come true. Then Charles Louis of Austria arrived in Paris and she modelled him. The Mameluke, Roustan, whom General Bonaparte brought back from Egypt, also visited the studio.

Josephine's spouse – for so he remained in Marie's eyes – had suddenly become the hero of France. After all the bloodshed and disillusion the nation longed for a hero – and here he was. Josephine, a graceful figure in her low-cut, bosom-revealing, classical dresses, became the most fashionable lady in Paris. So weary were people of strife and disorder that General Bonaparte's plan to replace the five-man Directory with three stable Consuls, who would unite all political elements, was hailed with joy. But Napoleon, being a realist, immediately saw the necessity of making a clean sweep of the government. Talleyrand recognized Bonaparte's genius and backed him. With brother Lucien and a small band of supporters Napoleon launched the *coup d'état* of 9 November 1799 which ended the rule of the Directory and dismissed the Councils which had governed under its aegis.

* Unfortunately this portrait does not survive.

The new government of France was invested in three Consuls, General Bonaparte, Sieyès and Ducos, both the latter having been members of the Directory. They proposed to govern France through two committees each consisting of twenty-five deputies. Bonaparte assumed the role of First Consul of France, fashions became hysterically Roman, furniture took an Egyptian bent and Josephine continually had her portrait painted with classical wreaths topping various piquant hair-dos.

Josephine had liked the wax portrait made by Marie four years previously, and she asked Napoleon if he would condescend to sit. Eventually word arrived from Josephine that she had prevailed on her reluctant husband. Madame Tussaud would please present herself at the Tuileries at six o'clock in the morning.

The excited Marie arrived at the palace on time – recalling with a shudder that other terrible dawn eight years before when she had searched through heaps of bodies in the Tuileries Gardens. Napoleon received her kindly; Josephine and Madame Grand-Maison, the wife of a deputy, remained present during the sitting. The babble of their conversation never ceased while Napoleon, not all that pleased at having been inveigled into this affair, spoke seldom and abruptly. When Madame Tussaud stepped up to press a plaster mask on his face she begged him not to be alarmed as the process, though disagreeable, would not hurt. 'Alarmed!' exclaimed Napoleon, 'I should not be alarmed if you were to surround my head with loaded pistols!' However, the First Consul did sit still while the liquid plaster was pressed on to his face and straw inserted in his nostrils enabling him to breathe. Presumably this process, while preventing talk, did not prevent thought. The great man may have come to some important conclusion during his half-hour in Madame Tussaud's hands. It is more likely that he was groaning at the boredom of it all, and wishing that his delectable Josephine would not coax him into such tiresome arrangements. When it was over and Marie had packed up her gear, Josephine whispered to her: 'Be very careful with his head. Please take special pains because he only consented after my special plea.' Of course Marie took pains and the portrait was shown for many years.

Napoleon must have been pleased with the result or he would not have suggested that his generals, Moreau and Masséna, also have their likenesses done. He also sent his aide-de-camp whose appearance he thought 'Christlike'.

Marie Tussaud also made a portrait of Cambacérès, the High Chancellor, who would work out the laws for France, which, as the Code Napoléon, have survived to this day.

Out of disorder Napoleon created order. But in the Boulevard du Temple show-business fell upon increasingly hard times. Portraits from life of Voltaire, Marie Antoinette, Robespierre and Napoleon ought to have attracted customers, but popular taste in entertainment was changing. In France wax portraits had lost their novelty. Marie knew everyone 'at the top' – no one could be more 'at the top' than the First Consul – yet door money dwindled. Parisians are easily bored, and however hard she tried, Marie's tableaux often failed to amuse. Despite the fact that Curtius had named Marie as his sole heir, despite the ownership of three houses and of a unique Exhibition, she had to carry a heavy mortgage and live in a state of perpetual financial worry. Curtius had taught her craftsmanship, but even he would have had to call on all his financial expertise to continue carrying on through such hard times. François Tussaud, an engineer, did not seem particularly interested in the Salon de Cire, which for twenty years had drawn crowds; he was not a promoter, and Marie, worn by anxieties over money, was awaiting another baby. This second son, François (later known as Francis), was born in 1800, when Marie was thirty-nine. He was to be her third and last child.

10

Departure from France

Marie had to date existed as the shadow of Philippe Curtius. Although not possessed of his relentless ambition – indeed, she had been a little afraid when he coolly went off to wait at the cemetery for a cartload of interesting severed heads – under his guidance she had become a very talented modeller. No one ever reproduced a human visage more competently than Marie, and she remained an indefatigable worker. The death of Curtius forced her to try to become a business woman as well as a super craftsman. She showed herself extraordinarily capable of grasping the legal complexities of her own monetary situation. In fact, in her strained state she appears almost too careful; her insistence that an ivory snuff-box should not be included in Curtius's bequest to the poor shows that, although distressed, no detail was too trivial for her attention.

Now she had given allegiance to a husband, and in her own way she would stick to him. François Tussaud was the only man apart from Curtius to have any emotional meaning in her life, but as wife and mother she needed a sense of security, and this was the one thing Tussaud could not give her. He had no business flair and was incapable of guiding or directing, and Marie found that every decision and all the work rested on her, making it impossible to relax. Her mother remained, as always, in the background. Madame Grosholtz was approaching sixty, and all she had ever done was to fuss around in the aroma of that Alsatian cooking which royalties and revolutionaries alike had found so tasty. Marie herself was reaching middle age. She had modelled Voltaire when she was seventeen and Napoleon when she was thirty-eight; the dramatic faces of a terrible revolution had been kept for posterity in her wax reproductions. Now that a new era was arriving and the Salon de Cire drew a diminishing public, she considered methods of improving the family fortunes elsewhere.

In 1801, Philipstal, that old friend and fellow showman, who had been arrested during the Terror and whose release Curtius had obtained through beseeching and bribing Robespierre, had taken his Phantasmagoria to London. Despite Pitt's refusal to accede to Napoleon's peace overtures unless the Bourbons were restored, it was occasionally possible for theatrical entertainments to travel between enemy capitals. In October of that year Philipstal, who may have found it easier because he was not French-born, booked the Lyceum Theatre in the Strand for his 'Grand Cabinet of Optical and Mechanical Curiosities'. The show was divided into three parts; first came automatons and mechanical devices, followed by optical-illusion 'different spectres, ghosts and spirits of deceased persons', and ending with a spectacular mechanical-optical firework. The advertisement adds, in the amusingly snobbish language of the time, that with reasonable notification 'the nobility and gentry' desiring to bring private parties, could command a special performance at any hour of the day.

Probably the spectacle of so much public guillotining had rendered Parisians *blasé* of mere 'mechanical curiosities'. London provided a fresh audience eager for entertainment. The novelty of Philipstal's magic lantern kept the Lyceum Theatre packed for months, and in February 1802 Philipstal announced proudly that he had obtained royal letters patent for his show. Optical illusions could be considered educational as well as amusing. The lower theatre of the Lyceum was occupied by 'Egyptiana', seductively extended by Philipstal into 'regions of spectography'.

The Peace of Amiens, the great aim of Talleyrand's life, was concluded in March 1802, and in June Philipstal reopened at the Lyceum, adding a 'Sorcerer's Anniversary' to his show. In August his Phantasmagoria was replaced by 'Auricular Communications of an Invisible Girl', run by a Mr Charles who would in time become a rival and, eventually, because of his championship of Marie Tussaud, an enemy of Philipstal's.

When Philipstal returned to Paris during a theatrical break, he talked a great deal about his London success. Then, taking Marie aside, he suggested that it would be easy for her to slip over with a collection of Monsieur Curtius's wax portraits which would add a new dimension to his show. He had never forgotten the fright of his imprisonment after inadvertently using that slide of Louis XVI, and he remained, apparently, grateful to the memory of the man who had saved his neck. Marie listened to this proposition with interest. How wonderful if she could arouse enthusiasm for Curtius's reproductions in a new country, and make another fortune to replace that one which seemed to be evaporating from the Boulevard du Temple. Philipstal remained encouraging and urged her into partnership with him. He insisted that, with his experience of the London theatre world, and her talent for arranging tableaux, the wax exhibition could not fail to draw. It seemed a natural adventure, a natural association between old acquaintances. Marie placed the running of her three houses and the direction of the Paris Exhibition in her husband's hands, and applied for the passport and documents necessary to leave France. The application was refused. She applied again, this time directly to a man she had known in the past: Fouché, the all-powerful Minister of Police. This strange, brilliant, terrifying character, the only man to survive right through the Revolution and the Napoleonic era, had early realized the power of the secret police, and he devised a network of spies which he alone could control. No ruler of France could do without him.

The interview must have made Marie tremble, for Fouché knew she must remember him in the old days holding forth against the moderates and calling for more bloodshed – views which were less popular in 1802. He had voted for the death of Louis XVI and became notorious for his cruelty when sent to Lyons to eradicate anti-revolutionary movements. During the Terror, when the deputies started to cut each other's heads off, Fouché moved stealthily, a sinister figure waiting and watching, moving out of danger just in time. With unerring instinct he avoided the guillotine and then, after being expelled from the Assembly on account of his frightening record, he calmly manoeuvred himself back into office. Extraordinarily able himself, he sensed Napoleon's potentialities, supported his *coup d'état*, and immediately made himself indispensable to the rising man. Fouché, who had dominated the murky shadows of the secret police during the Terror, was now foiling plot after plot against the First Counsul. Napoleon did not like Fouché, but he knew he could not do without him, and Fouché alone had access to his bedroom at any time of the day or night.

To enter Fouché's office was a chilling experience, but Marie's enthusiastic hope of making a success of her Exhibition in London must have been clear to this expert in dissimulation. He had often seen her flitting around Curtius's house and now he had but to assess the impact which her wax figures would make in a foreign land. They faced each other across the desk. The tiny little woman with bright eyes watched him like a bird. And Fouché, his own hooded eyes set deep in a pale mask, watched expressionlessly while she expounded the reasons why it might be good for France to export her portraits. Fouché seemed to hesitate. He said, 'We want to keep talent in France, and *you* have talent.' She replied, 'Most of the figures I will take were made by Monsieur Curtius – *he* had talent as well you know. They will be new to English people.' 'He was a good fellow,' admitted Fouché. It was difficult for him to decide what effect the effigies of revolutionaries who had died on the guillotine would have abroad.

Having put forth her plea Marie waited quietly, and after consideration he acceded to her request. Marie was, after all, in favour with the First Consul and his lady. Fouché was a happily married man, but he liked to please Josephine. After careful consideration he gave Marie Tussaud permission to leave France with thirty or more wax portraits. His cold dark eyes followed her out of the office. He could not quite assess her but felt she could do no harm.*

So it was that Marie got her way, and in October 1802 she was ready to leave Paris. It had not been easy to pack up fragile wax figures to be transported by road to a cross-Channel sailing ship and then carefully stowed in the hold. Marie had little time to spare for tearful farewells to mother and husband. She left a hundred instructions, bid them a brave *au revoir* and climbed into the coach with the four-year-old Joseph. Maybe she turned wistfully for a last glimpse of 20 Boulevard du Temple which, though she did not know it, she would never see again. Nor would she again see her mother or husband. As for that chirping, two-year-old baby – some eighteen years were to pass before she again held him in her arms.

Without thought of what this journey might eventually entail, and overwhelmed by the unkind choppy Channel and the number of things needing attention, Marie Tussaud was glad enough to see the white cliffs of England. After disembarking she had to struggle with a mass of formalities concerning herself as an alien and also for the vast packing cases. No lady had ever before arrived with such luggage. If the Customs officers officially insisted on opening any of her boxes, they saw wax faces and

* Talleyrand described Fouché as having 'a heart of diamond, a stomach of iron, and a tearless eye'.

stuffed leather bodies and wooden limbs. Marie can hardly have been asked to *name* any of the figures, certainly not death-masks, and so the guillotined heads reached England. Before proceeding further she had to obtain a certificate giving particulars concerning her country of origin and her profession. This all-important certificate must be shown to the chief magistrate of any town she visited, while the main copy had to be lodged in the offices of the principal Secretary of State to King George III. Even in that unbureaucratic age such precautions were necessary, with England and France technically at peace, but highly suspicious of each other.

On reaching London, Madame Tussaud found lodgings in Surrey Street near the Lyceum Theatre where her Exhibition was to be uncrated and arranged with skilful lighting effects. In early November Philipstal reopened his Phantasmagoria in the Upper Theatre, but his advertisements did not mention the 'wax models of Monsieur Curtius' which Madame Tussaud had set up in the Lower Theatre. Although wax portraiture was already well known in England, her figures evoked a unique portion of history. Philipstal could tickle the public curiosity with his optical illusions, while Marie could but portray the French Revolution and the old regime with consummate artistry. Happily, her show, magnificently displayed, proved immediately successful. She had set her heart on building a fortune as Curtius had in the past, but with Philipstal in control this was not to prove easy. Perhaps he was jealous at her success, for unexpectedly he refused to share her financial expenses and she found herself forced to pay for everything out of her own receipts. The maintenance work on an exhibition of over thirty figures was enormous. Although she had brought materials for modelling new faces, and she could herself repair wax breakage and torn clothes, dozens of items had to be purchased as she went along. The damage inevitable in transporting wax figures in those days of sailing ships and horse-drawn vehicles may be imagined. Madame Tussaud's travelling expenses were always heavy. How she missed the shrewd business advice which Curtius would have given her. Soon she realized she had signed a most unsatisfactory contract and that she was completely in Philipstal's power.

Little Joseph, a bright precocious child, had loved the travelling and he began to pick up English words immediately. During this successful yet gruelling November of 1802 his merry childish laughter kept her spirits up.

Of the wax portraits which Marie brought to England nearly 200 years ago, a remarkable number still exist. They include the group of the Royal Family of France, Voltaire, Benjamin Franklin, Marie's portrait of Marat stabbed in his bath, and the twenty-two-year-old Madame du Barry modelled by Curtius (now known as 'The Sleeping Beauty'). The guillotined heads of Marie Antoinette, Louis XVI, Robespierre, Hébert, Carrier and Fouquier-Tinville have all survived. The King and Queen must have been hidden away in some storeroom, for they were not mentioned or shown for sixty years. Marie recorded the French Revolution from its beginning to its end. She had known personally almost every leading character. Now that she had reached her forties with this unique knowledge of *how the participants looked*, it became a passion with her to keep her Exhibition intact. Certainly she wished to make money, but only because money meant success.

II

London, November 1802
to April 1803

If Marie Tussaud imagined that any man was going to look after her she now would learn a bitter lesson. Curtius had always protected and guided but her husband proved to be an inept businessman. He had a gambler's nature and was always interested in speculation, but the hard work necessary for show business bored him. Then Monsieur Philipstal, whom she had, till now, regarded as a true friend, soon made it plain that he cared little for her interests and simply intended to batten on her talents. When a woman, longing for security, finds herself let down by men in whom she places trust, she may weaken and go under, or she can get tough. Madame Tussaud got tough.

Maybe it was easier for her, who had undergone the harrowing experiences of the Revolution, to face hard reality. She had led such an extraordinary life, hearing so many brilliant men hold forth at her uncle's table and knowing them to end later under the guillotine, that perhaps determination to overcome financial disasters came naturally. But in London during the early spring of 1803 she must have approached cracking point.

Philipstal had made no bones about what he considered the superiority of his show – he brought Marie's wax figures over as a kind of subordinate exhibition to the Lyceum. He stressed the drawing power of *novelty* and this his optical illusions provided. Marie's beautifully produced, perfectly dressed, portraits could not in themselves be advertised as a novelty, for waxworks had been known in England for several hundred years. In fact, since the funeral effigies of the thirteenth century, wax portraits had appeared in various forms. A wax effigy of Henry III, who died in 1272, was probably the first full-sized figure made for this purpose, and that of the beautiful Duchess of Buckinghamshire, who died in 1743, the last.

Around 1642, one Abraham Simon, medallist to Queen Christina of Sweden, had come to England and won fame for his miniature portraits in wax. His clients included Charles II and Henry Cromwell, son of the Protector. Then in 1684 the highly skilled French artist Benoît visited London to produce wax busts of James II and members of his court. Benoît set a standard of workmanship which remained a criterion for later artists, including the celebrated Samuel Percy who modelled many of his miniatures in high relief. The subtle use of coloured wax, as well as white, entailed delicate technical craftsmanship.

During the latter part of the eighteenth century several women modellers obtained renown. One of these was an eccentric Mrs Patience Wright (who modelled Benjamin Franklin as had Marie). The well-born Mrs Wright found her models in high society and, like her smart-set contemporaries, she enjoyed pranks. Horace Walpole records that Lady Aylesbury when paying a visit to Mrs Wright's house, spoke to a housemaid on the stairs, received no response, and finally realized that it was a wax figure that confronted her. Mrs Wright lived until 1786 and the also fashionable Catherine Andras, sixteen years younger than Marie Tussaud, was already exhibiting at the Royal Academy and had in 1801 been appointed 'Modeller in Wax' to Queen Charlotte. Like Mrs Wright she held a place in society, and their renown may have goaded Marie's personal ambition. These ladies, however, had never descended to the entertainment world. Patience Wright and Catherine Andras enjoyed the privilege of being *artists in society*; popular exhibitions remained out of their ken.

As well as portraitists, there had been since the seventeenth century waxwork exhibitions of various kinds. A broadsheet of 1647 describes the 'wonders made of wax' at St Bartholomew's Fair, and the Lord Mayor of London's Waiting Book of 1685 notes permission given to one Jacob Schalek to show his waxworks in the City. A little later, in 1696, a Mrs Mills, advertised in the *Postman* as 'the greatest Artist in Europe', was showing full-sized waxworks in the Strand. Mrs Mills's exhibition included Charles II, William and Mary, and Oliver Cromwell 'in full stature'. In 1703 another woman modellist hit the news when the *Daily Courier* of 6 August announced, 'On Wednesday last Mrs Goldsmith,* the

---

* In 1797 *Mr* Goldsmith used the *Postman* to advertise his wax exhibition in Old Jewry.

woman famous for Waxworks, brought to Westminster Abbey the effigy of that celebrated beauty, the late Duchess of Richmond, which is said to be the richest figure ever set up in King Henry's Chapel.' During 1701, a Samuel Fry was travelling with a waxwork exhibition which he showed at the Angel Inn in Norwich and advertised in local papers. The avid curiosity of the general public, in those days before photography or television, to see what the famous looked like is understandable, but amidst so much competition only those able to offer dramatic, well-dressed figures could make really good money.

The most famous of Madame Tussaud's predecessors was the extraordinary Mrs Salmon, who modelled and exhibited from early in the eighteenth century. At her premises at the sign of the Golden Salmon in what is now called St Martin's-le-Grand, 140 wax figures 'as big as life' were on show, and her handbills drew attention to 'moving waxworks', so that some must have been animated by clockwork mechanism. Mrs Salmon advertised in the *Tatler* in 1710 and Addison commented on her show in the *Spectator* of April 1711. Eventually Mrs Salmon moved her exhibition to a house in Fleet Street near the Horn Tavern where, she announced, the gentry would find more room for their carriages which had blocked the narrow street of St Martin's-le-Grand. When Mrs Salmon died in 1760 at the age of ninety, her exhibition was purchased by a surgeon-solicitor called Clark whose wife took on the management under the trade name of Mrs Salmon. Towards the end of 1794 the Fleet Street house was purchased by a banking firm and the waxwork exhibition moved across the street to the room now known as Prince Henry's room over the archway leading into the Temple. To intrigue and astound, Mrs Clark arranged a figure at the exhibition door which kicked out at visitors.

The style and quality of this old-established show offered no serious competition to Madame Tussaud's fascinating, authentically gowned figures when she arrived at the Lyceum, though another group, Mrs Bullock's 'beautiful Cabinet of Wax Figures', may have offered some comparison. Certainly, if the Tussaud waxworks could not be offered as a *novelty*, they could be advertised as very high-class wax figures portraying unique personages, revolutionaries, kings and queens. Marie had to admit that waxworks had been seen before, but not portraits of this calibre, or with such extraordinary historical association. The chopped heads of revolutionaries were of great interest. No mention was made of the heads of Louis XVI and Marie Antoinette. Their daughter, the Princesse Royale, was alive and in her teens. It would have been poor taste to show her parents. No English public could have been pleased.

Trying not to feel too low when Philipstal refused to advertise her collection of figures, Marie made the best of things. She got through her first gloomy Christmas in lodgings and determined to make a success of her show. Determination became her strongest characteristic. Curtius had allowed nothing to daunt *him*. He had used his art to cash in on the French Revolution and she would cash in on the history of her times.

In the Lyceum Theatre Marie set up over thirty life-sized wax figures of well-known people in their perfectly copied clothes. They were well lit and entertainingly grouped. Her show remained in the Lower Theatre along with Philipstal's Egyptian collection, which included the Egyptian Mummy. Marie was a perfectionist: all day she worked at the Exhibition, slaving to see that every button had been sewn as it should, every collar just as the model would have worn it. Although he enjoyed taking half her earnings, Philipstal may have been a little jealous, for he still refused to mention her contribution in the press. The partnership had become very different from what she imagined, and had it not been for the sunny little boy who was always at her side, Madame Tussaud might have become very depressed. As it was, she remained on the alert for new subjects. The first interesting man who allowed her to model him was Sir Francis Burdett, the politician who had married Sophia Coutts, the banking heiress. Sir Francis was a lively member of Parliament who had visited France in the early years of the Revolution. He was also a reformer of prison abuses. He firmly opposed war with France and could talk sympathetically with the intelligent little Frenchwoman who modelled him. Through him Madame Tussaud met a few members of the aristocracy, and they could always speak French which made her feel less isolated. At forty-two she did not find it easy to pick up a new language, and the dangers that can befall an insolvent woman alone in an alien land haunted her all through that winter.

Then a curious opportunity to gain publicity presented itself, and Marie did not hesitate to make the most of it. A certain Colonel Despard, on failing to obtain compensation after being unjustly arrested, joined a senseless conspiracy to assassinate King George III and seize the Tower of London. After being caught red-handed and tried with six associates, he was condemned to death. On 21 February 1803 they were all hanged and then beheaded. On hearing that Despard's remains were to be given to friends for burial, Madame Tussaud saw an opportunity of adding to her Exhibition. One can imagine the surprise of Despard's cronies when this French woman modeller applied for permission to take a plaster mould of the severed head. But it did not seem strange to her. She had modelled the dead faces of Marat, Robespierre, Carrier, Hébert and Fouquier-Tinville, all of whom she had known intimately, not to mention the un-mentionable heads of the King and Queen. The grisly technical work merely meant good business. She knew her public – it liked seeing how villains looked after execution.

One is left to visualize that spring morning of 1803 when Marie left her lodgings in Surrey Street and did not as usual walk to the Lyceum Theatre. Did her little son ask, 'Where are you going, Maman?' And what did she answer her four-year-old? 'Maman has important work this morning. Be a good boy and we'll have a lovely supper together.'

Whatever story had to be told to Joseph, his mother's fingers knew how to go about the job. With unfailing care she took a mould of Despard's severed head and from this there emerged an excellent reproduction of the executed colonel. When this was put on view in a cleverly contrived scene, faintly lit in bluish tones to give an atmosphere of wicked conspiracy, the public flocked in to enjoy, gape and shiver. Gate money went up.

Marie had started a fashion whose appeal would prove lasting. Henceforth heads made from the death-masks of executed criminals became popular viewing for family parties. In the Exhibition catalogues the words 'modelled from the face after death' added to the attraction.

There was no lurid gloating in Marie's nature; only the business side of executions interested her. Exact portrayal of the visage of the criminal and the tragic brought in the money. People would *pay* for a shudder, so shudders she would give them. Curtius had shown that he had no scruples about sorting a particular visage out of a cartload of decapitated heads if it would embellish his Exhibition.

Marie's inner reactions can never be known. She may have been prompted by fear during the Revolution, but a certain callousness must have developed. She certainly chose to model Fouquier-Tinville and Despard when no possible pressure existed except the pressure of the box office. Now, however, she may have felt a renewed revulsion, for she had become a mother, she had known sorrow when her baby daughter died and to add to these softening influences a new facet of Marie's character was slowly emerging. She wished to present herself in England as a lady! It is slightly ironic that Curtius, who was born into the upper class, should have deliberately descended into the theatrical world and picked cut-throat revolutionaries as his friends, while Marie, born an unknown little girl of Strasbourg, should eventually desire to establish herself in society. Handling of decapitated heads could hardly be deemed a ladylike accomplishment in the drawing rooms of 1803, and those with social ambitions might do well to talk of the days spent at Versailles rather than of the Madeleine cemetery. So, while ready to adorn her Exhibition with suitable executed criminals, Madame Tussaud let it be known that she had modelled many royal personages from life. It might even be pleasanter to be an artist acceptable to society than the modeller-manager of a touring exhibition.

Her first royal commission in England arrived from the Duchess of York, wife of the second son of George III. Madame Tussaud was charmed to obtain this sitter, and HRH allowed her name to appear on handbills and posters when her portrait was exhibited. Separated from her husband (who was at this time heading towards trouble with the infamous Mary Ann Clark), the Duchess endured a lonely life at her country house, Oatlands, lavishing affection on pet dogs. She had no children, and it was with a certain wistfulness that she requested Marie to make a sleeping child of wax. Marie did this and kept a copy for her own Exhibition. Presumably she used her adored little Joseph as a model.

In April 1803 the Lyceum booking ended. Philipstal was keen to transport the whole show to Scotland, for judicious enquiries had revealed possibilities in that country. Marie agreed to take her own Exhibition under his aegis to Edinburgh. Having survived the winter in London, she felt renewed confidence in her own abilities. Any fear she had known of Philipstal now turned to indignation at his selfish demands. But just as she was getting really angry with him and threatening to pull out, a letter would arrive from Paris which changed the flow of her anger. François Tussaud wrote solely of financial worries and failure. Why couldn't he make the Paris Exhibition pay? How exasperating men were. Why did she have to do everything herself? Maddening as it was to have such a husband in Paris and such a partner in London, she knew in her bones that the struggle would be worth while. An Exhibition such as hers only needed new audiences. The problem lay in the vast expense of packing and transport. She dreaded having to face setting up the figures again, of unpacking and ironing their clothes and finding things missing, of mending chipped noses and broken fingers, and replacing lost buttons and laces. It seemed almost too much for one woman alone, but her fighting spirit had been roused. One evening she heard herself explaining to Joseph that they were off to a new country. He couldn't have been more pleased – change, excitements, chaos delight a child – the longer and more uncomfortable the journey the better he would enjoy it.

But there was one aspect which Madame Tussaud dreaded – Scotland would take her even further away from her baby son. Joseph was now five; he had nearly forgotten his little brother, but for Marie the vision of François remained a torment and at the same time a spur to success.

12

Scotland, April 1803
to February 1804

Although by now on extremely bad terms with her partner, Marie agreed
to travel ahead to Edinburgh. One thing made her extremely glad to leave
the Lyceum Theatre – Mr Winsor, the inventor of gas lighting, was giving
demonstrations of his spectacular new method of piping gas from room
to room in a part of the theatre. The sudden glare of gaslit chandeliers
filled Marie with trepidation. Always, and with reason, afraid that a fire
might destroy her precious figures, she could hardly wait to get the
effigies safely packed and away.

Maybe her sharp tongue was souring Philipstal. He had probably ceased
to appreciate references to his own near escape from the guillotine, and as
it clearly dawned on Marie that the contract she had signed gave un-
reasonable power to her partner, she may have hinted rather often that
it was hardly *gentil* to repay Curtius's confrontation with Robespierre
by taking advantage of his pupil.

It is possible that only Marie's wax figures were making real money.
Philipstal does not sound very flush at this time, and an individual referred to in letters as 'the Baron' was helping him financially.

During her last days in London, in the midst of the arduous process of
dismantling, labelling and packing, Marie had a flaming row with her
partner. She threatened to abandon the whole enterprise and return to
Paris. This did not suit his book, and while still refusing to let her see the
accounts Philipstal hastily paid her fare to Edinburgh by sea and gave her
to understand that the transport of her exhibition was also paid for. She
had to be content with £10 handed her in cash to cover extras during the
voyage and glib promises. Yet she was determined to battle on. In a furious
frame of mind she attended to the wrapping and crating of the life-size

figures. The wax heads and hands were affixed to bodies of stuffed leather with carved wooden arms and legs. The removable clothes of each personage had to be labelled and parcelled correctly. This alone was sufficient to give brain fever to the person responsible. It was a weary woman who returned to the lodging house to pack her personal belongings while Joseph scampered around in transports of joy at another move. Marie always called him by a pet name – 'Nini'.

The only surviving letters written by Marie Tussaud belong to this travelling period. Her big, clear, open handwriting, sliding slantways across the paper, gives an extraordinarily modern impression. As testified by herself and her family she 'hated to guide a pen' and some of the letters appear in quite a different hand. When she could hire or inveigle some other person to take dictation, the writing appears in perfect copperplate and the spelling becomes less erratic – for Marie, who was so accurate in reproducing what she saw and in memorizing details of manner and of dress, could not spell *at all*! It remains curious, not that she should show by phonetic spelling that she spoke French with a strong German accent, for it is natural to write words as pronounced, but it is odd that one so meticulous in her craft should spell the same word in different ways in a single letter. Writing obviously bored Marie – whereas human faces held her attention. She completely ignored the need of using 's' in the plural and 'e' in the feminine.

On 25 April 1803 a letter in Marie's own handwriting went forth from London addressed to Monsieur Tussaud:

Boulevard du Temple No. 20. Cabinet de Curtius, Paris.

Mon ami, mon cher amie et mes cheres amies [already she is muddling her genders but presumably this missive was for husband, mother, auntie and baby son], I received your letter with great pleasure. Nini and I cried with joy and pain at being unable to hug you all. But today is Tuesday and we leave next Tuesday. The Cabinet de Cire has been closed since Saturday and all is packed up. M. de Philipstal treats me as you do. He has left me all alone. He is angry. . . .

A description of financial entanglements ensues and it is explained that Philipstal has to remain in London negotiating with 'the Baron'. Marie continues her letter rather sadly:

I must go alone to seek a fortune. I will send you my address immediately on reaching Edinburgh. I beg of you beloved to reply to me at once as your letters are my only consolation. I will end by embracing you a thousand times. All my love to mon cher Francison [the baby François] to Ma cher mer and Ma tant.

After these amusingly ill-spelt declarations of affection she adds that Nini is well, hugs everyone with all his heart and sends a thousand *bese* which must mean *baisers*. Then, switching to the familiar tense she signs for her husband alone, 'Pour la vie. Ta femme – Tussaud.'

So it was that on a late April day in 1803 a neat little foreign woman with a lively child climbed into what she called *un fiacre* and drove to London docks. Whatever trepidation Marie may have felt was well concealed. No one could know what it meant to sail away northward to a strange land where even the few English words she had learned would be rendered incomprehensible by the Scottish accent.

Despite the risks entailed to her Exhibition in travelling, Marie knew that she had made a sensible decision, for, if the Treaty of Amiens broke down and hostilities recommenced, the situation of a stranded enemy alien could become extremely disagreeable. Feelings would not be so high north of the Border – or so she hoped. Philipstal, probably not of French nationality, seemed to have been less nervous of getting caught up in the war situation.

None of François Tussaud's letters to his wife survive. We only know that he was not making a success of the Paris exhibition left under his control, either because he was incapable or because public taste had changed. From now on Marie's husband seems to have become ever more desperate for money, and there is never a word about his own earning capacity as an engineer. He may well have had more charm than ability, or he may have disliked financial responsibility. The little fortune which Curtius had laboriously scraped up was disappearing as fortunes often do in troubled times. Marie still owned two houses in Paris and the one at Ivry-sur-Seine, but No. 20 Boulevard du Temple, which also housed the Cabinet de Cire, was still mortgaged to Marguerite Salomé Reiss. When François wrote that he was anxious to raise money on what property remained in her name Marie responded generously.

Before leaving London she visited her lawyer, Mr Wright of Duke Street, off Manchester Square, and endowed her husband with all that she possessed in Paris. By signing a power of attorney giving François Tussaud full control of all her French properties, she enabled him to raise fresh mortgages.* She herself faced life without a penny save what she could earn, but she remained confident. She had nothing to fall back on save her wax figures and her knowledge, but that was enough.

* This document survives in the archives of Madame Tussaud's in London.

H

Marie *must* have loved and trusted her husband even if his business incapacity was beginning to make her heart sink. Having signed away the French properties, she sat down to assess her personal predicament. At all costs she must keep up appearances and then her talent would see her through. She never considered turning to lovers for help. Men meant nothing but trouble; she saw through them quickly and believed nothing they said, even when they believed their own boasts. All that she achieved would be done without aid. Men talked, ranted, promised and let you down. By now she knew them – or thought she did. Her husband was yet to tender final disillusion.

Always aware of the effect that dress could make, Marie Tussaud attired herself carefully but conventionally. She did not seek to allure or astound, although the fashions of Paris were at this time set on shocking. In London the ladies never went as far as those Parisiennes who, in a kind of post-Revolutionary frenzy, dispensed with underclothes and wore only skin-coloured tights to give the appearance of nakedness under transparent classical draperies. Frenchwomen were studied for style, and the tiny Madame Tussaud in her bonnets and high-waisted dresses caused interest in a modified virtuous form.

No sooner had Marie agreed to go to Scotland than she discovered she had to attend to the Exhibition's shipping without help from Philipstal. While that gentleman flitted around, presumably discussing business matters with potential backers, the tremendous responsibility of packing up delicate wax creations and supervising their transport from the Lyceum Theatre to the docks fell entirely on her shoulders. All that Marie had heard of conditions in Scotland gave cause for optimism. Although the term 'industrial revolution' had not yet been invented, the actual happening had begun. Suddenly wool, linen and cotton industries flourished in the north. Roads were improving, the population expanding, and people had more money to spend than ever before. As the likelihood of renewed hostilities with France grew more imminent, this industrial boom must continue. Marie knew that although the voyage would take her yet farther from husband, mother and baby, to make it was wise. If Philipstal thought only of himself and her husband could but write of debts, she must become successful entirely on her own. Only one man, called Tenaveil, would accompany her on the journey. He seems to have acted as a kind of secretary to Philipstal.

Little Joseph helped to cheer her up – he was a lively cherub. When things went badly she took comfort from his high spirits. Tenaveil, she soon discovered, had, like herself, been placed in an odious financial situation by his master.

Because of gales, the voyage up the east coast of England in a sailing ship proved a horrible experience. They departed from London docks on 27 April and did not reach Edinburgh until 10 May. On arrival, exhausted by days of retching and her own imaginings of the damage being done to her figures in the hold as the ship pitched, Marie discovered that Philipstal had not, as she had understood, paid for the transport of the waxworks. Now she found herself faced by bills, including one for £18 for moving the enormous crates. A lesser woman might have collapsed, but she set out into the town and discovered one good friend. This was Mr Charles, the English ventriloquist whom she had known in Paris and at the Lyceum. He was now working in Edinburgh and he came to Marie's rescue with a loan. When the figures were unloaded and unwrapped she found that, just as she had feared, many breakages had taken place. After going ashore she could not throw off the effects of seasickness, but in spite of a cracking head she set to work on the repairs. Philipstal was not expected for a fortnight, but Madame Tussaud, having fought her way out of the monetary fix in which he had landed her, resolved to repair, dress, and set up the wax figures and open to the public within a week. She was fortunate in immediately finding a large, suitably furnished room and a landlady who spoke French. Still reeling, she sat down on 11 May to recapitulate her adventures for her family. Her letter begins in the same vein as the others:

Mon cher ami, mon cher Françison, cher mer et cher tant. I hope this letter will find you also in good health. We are very well here . . . in good, good health and in good company. But we suffered 36 breakages and because of the bad weather everyone was seasick – even those who did not expect to be. The sea was terribly rough. We had three storms in three days and no one could go on deck. The boat rolled in a terrifying manner and the Captain, who has made this voyage a hundred times said he had never seen anything like it. But Monsieur Nini was not afraid. He made friends with the Captain and everyone else. In fact the Captain wished he had a child like him. He said Nini was a marvellous sailor and he would like to train him for the sea. He said he would do honour to France. Everyone adored Nini & called him 'Little Bonaparte'. . . .

She went on to describe her row with Philipstal:

I threatened to return to Paris and when he saw I meant business he gave me

£10. One has to be wary of that Philipstal. The expenses on arrival appalled M. Tenaveil who hadn't got a sou. If I had not found Mr Charles we should have been obliged to lose all. Mr Charles lent me £30, and £18 had to go to Tenaveil to pay for the sea voyage of the figures. I then found and rented a very nice Salon well furnished & decorated for £2 a month. I am lodging in the same house with very nice people. The landlady speaks very good French which is lucky for me. And Mr Charles is going to remain throughout the opening of the show. I hope the Salon will be ready in a week and that M. Philipstal will reach Edinburgh within a fortnight when his business with the Baron finishes. Through the good offices of the Baron I now have an interpreter, he is a German, a very worthy man who speaks fluent English and French as well. . . .

This is Marie's second day ashore and everything is looking up; she has found a good English friend in Mr Charles and a helpful interpreter and she has fallen in love with Edinburgh.

We are in a beautiful little city from which one can see snow-covered mountains. I still have a bad head as though I was on board that boat but I have discovered some compatriots at the Castle and one Lady-in-Waiting has spent all her life in France. She is friendly and we spend a lot of time together. Really I feel as if back in Paris & this consoles me greatly. Monsieur Nini is dressed like a Prince & can spend all day at the Castle playing with a little French boy.

Now my beloved remember me to my mother & aunt, and to my Francis be a good father, as his mother is so far away & cannot see him. Nini & I hug you with all our hearts a thousand times. I am for life your wife. Tussaud.

Here is my address. I beg you to reply as soon as possible. Mrs Laurie, Bernard Rooms, New Town, Edinburgh.

From these missives it looks as if Marie's mother and aunt, either through lack of education or because of failing sight, could not read. Despite the envelopes addressed to Monsieur Tussaud, the letters are written for the family, yet she constantly has to call her husband's attention to the elder members. The exuberance with which she describes a flicker of gracious treatment at the castle and the pleasure of finding French-speaking people, give an idea of Marie's loneliness. She was a middle-aged woman struggling entirely on her own.

During the period in which she had to wait for Philipstal to arrive with his Phantasmagoria, Marie grew bolder and more confident. Now that she realized she could stage her show without help or backing she was completely self-sufficient. She always took care to travel with adequate materials for repairs: she could melt wax for broken faces, mend wooden limbs and sew torn costumes, and she had great theatrical sense. Years of experience had given her an eye for dramatic lighting, and she possessed a real flair for cleverly improvising props and background. The alluring handbills she now sent out were truthful – nothing quite like these wax figures ever *had* been seen before. She never thought of using her own name in advertisements. Her teacher Curtius had been famous throughout Europe and so she tried to promote the exhibition by way of posters which described 'accurate models from life in Composition from the Great Curtius of Paris'. By working from dawn till dusk she managed to get the display well arranged, and on 18 May the opening proved a huge success. Marie made full use of her own dramatic taste and experience; she showed each individual figure to advantage; she could arrange limbs so that they revealed a person's character, she knew how to drape material and how to use lights. It was indeed a splendid assembly that met the eyes of visitors who paid what was then the large fee of two shillings to enter the Salon. There stood the exact replicas of the late Royal Family of France and the Princesse de Lamballe, of Voltaire, Rousseau, Frederick the Great, Mirabeau, Benjamin Franklin, revolting Marat rolling his eyes in death, Madame St Amaranthe and Madame du Barry both young and lovely, Charlotte Corday, Robespierre, Hébert, Carrier, Fouquier-Tinville, and a cruel portrait which Marie had done at Versailles entitled 'The Old Coquette'. Most fascinating of all to the public was England's new enemy – General Napoleon Bonaparte and his spouse Josephine.*

Suddenly Marie knew the euphoria of success. Mr Charles continued to help while hinting that he would like to become her partner. She refused to entertain this idea, but she did discuss with him the possibilities of disengaging herself from Philipstal. When, however, on Mr Charles's advice she paid a visit to a sound Scots lawyer, she learned the truth. That contract she had signed in Paris placing everything in Philipstal's favour was virtually impossible to break. She could but strive to earn a sufficient sum to buy him out. On 26 May she wrote to her husband.

I am still waiting to hear from you. This is the hundredth letter which I have written to you without reply. Why have you not written? I pray you to remember that I am your wife and that you are the father of my children. If only I had little Francis with me and my dear mother and aunt – however, I hope this

* A copy of Madame Tussaud's Biographical Catalogue for this Edinburgh show of 1803 has recently been acquired by the Victoria and Albert Museum. It is the earliest and longest of her surviving catalogues. Its points of interest can be read in Appendix 2.

finds you all well. I opened the Salon on the 18th May at 3 o'clock in the afternoon. The first day brought in £3. 14s.: the second day £5: the third £8. 9s.: the fourth £9. 12s.: the fifth £7. 12s.: the sixth £5. 5s.: the seventh £7. 17s. and the eighth £13. 6s.

It is very satisfactory and I hope to make real money in this city. Everyone is amazed at my figures. Nothing like them have ever been seen. Everyone loves Nini and regards him as an Englishman! The town is full of him. . . .

Philipstal is worrying at my success in Edinburgh and wondering how to get more money out of me. He has the reputation of a 'ranter' & cannot understand why everybody is on my side. I am liked here as much as in my own country & not treated as a foreigner – We are always gay, Nini and I – we have hardly time to take a meal! He is a very hard worker and keeps his little head down. Sometimes we are too tired for supper but we have promised ourselves a trip to the country on Sunday to get some wild honey. It is so nice to get a day in the country & the people are so kind. Oh Philipstal is jealous to hear it! He wants us to mix with no one. In fact I know him as my enemy wishing me harm. But I hope in six months to have done with him. His business is in a bad way & he has only my *Cabinet* on which to really rely. . . . I embrace you with all my heart – I am for life, Ta femme, Tussaud.

Send news as soon as possible. If the Channel is closed – write by way of Hamburg.

A few days later she wrote another jumbled letter addressed to Madame Allemand, who may have been that aunt, probably a German-speaking sister of Madame Grosholtz, residing at 20 Boulevard du Temple. By now the daily receipts were passing £13:

The show gives a great deal of pleasure and is open from 11 in the morning until 4 o'clock in the afternoon and from 6 o'clock until 8 o'clock and is always full. Nini is very proud of his portrait. . . . All the women want to have a child like him. Tell Monsieur Tussaud he is very sweet and everyone asks if he resembles his father.

I think I shall stay in Edinburgh for 3 months and if all goes well pay off Monsieur Philipstal. . . . I have good friends & if he thinks I am afraid of him he is mistaken. According to our dreadful arrangement I alone have had to pay all expenses and buy materials out of my half of the receipts . . . I do hope to be finished with him. I am regarded as a great lady here & have everyone on my side. . . . They look on Philipstal with his Phantasmagoria as a charlatan.

In this country the law in on my side. . . . Nini is growing prettier every day. We charge 2/– for admission to the Salon.

A very long letter to her husband dated 9 June, in someone else's copperplate hand, runs over the same legal ground but it resounds with affection for she has received a missive:

My Beloved, I received your dear letter of the 18th ultimo. . . . As to myself and our son Nini we are very well thank God. . . . Today is the 18th day our wax-works have been on show and we have taken £190. We hope it will continue. In July we are going to have the Fair and Horseshow here. Everyone will come to Edinburgh from the country and we hope to have a bumper fortnight.

Now about Mr Philipstal. I have been advised to wait until enough money comes in to square my account . . . if he demands an exorbitant rate of interest I shall bring an action to dissolve the partnership & be free of his insupportable domination. . . . I have had the good fortune to become acquainted with the Governor of Edinburgh Castle – a nobleman of high estate. His wife is a French woman* who made friends with Nini who told her all about our difficulties and she has promised me her protection and that of her friends. . . . As you complain about my writing I am using the hand of the interpreter who explains our models. You know him – he is the Swiss with whom you once went to the Opera in London†. . . . When we leave Edinburgh we intend to spend some time in Glasgow. . . . Mr Charles is doing good work here & again suggests joining me but once bitten by Philipstal I do not want any more joint ventures. . . . I have had an unhappy experience and am better off on my own.

Beloved, you have told me nothing of what is happening at home – if you take a turn at the cooking, or if you have altered the Salon? I am not ready to return yet & can't help being surprised that you suggest it before my business is cleared up, and when all the ports are closed – anyway there is no travel between France and Britain.

I hope to keep my word to you – I will not return without a well-filled purse. It is very fortunate that I brought all our equipment along because most of the heads have been broken & I have had to remake them.

I do urge you to take my place at home – work hard & change the exhibition as you like while I am not there to argue with you. I just beg you to look after my dear mother, aunt, Françison and your sister – she should have come with me she would have been useful. My compliments to all our friends and also to Nini's 'wife'! He hopes she remains faithful and will not take a lover while he is away – otherwise he will be sorry for her when he returns for he has bought a pistol and a sword. . . .

---

* Madame Tussaud must have meant the French wife of a castle official, for the Governor was unmarried.

† While it is not known when François Tussaud made this earlier visit to London, it probably took place in 1795 or 1796, when Curtius's Cabinet of Curiosities was taken to England and shown in a number of towns.

This is the only attempt to crack a joke in the correspondence; and, indeed, this letter which ends on an imploring note asks for lette rsthrough Hamburg. Letters were Marie's only joy and show how anxious she was not to allow war to sever the family ties. Also it is amusing to note how after all those years spent among Curtius's blood-stained revolutionary friends, Marie now desires to be well thought of by the upper class, as she had been when in Madame Elizabeth's household. The Comte d'Artois (youngest brother of Louis XVI and later Charles X of France) had made his headquarters in exile in Holyrood Palace, and aristocratic French *émigrés* crowded around him. Conveniently forgetting certain episodes in her past Marie – who had been patted on the head by Marat and Robespierre – rejoiced that now she herself, with her perfect manners, could be 'taken for a great lady'.

While she worked throughout the long hours of her show, Nini remained at the castle playing with a little French boy. She could not but be happy at her own success. The place she hired was always full and no one quibbled at the entrance fee of two shillings, but it is revealing to see how much a little kindness meant, how grateful she was to discover any person who could talk French. Nini, of course, provided her main consolation. Like many another proud Mama she cannot keep off the subject of her small son – but despite the description of him playing at the castle dressed *en prince*, Joseph does not seem to have become insufferable. He may, as a child can, have realized that for Maman he had become the man of the family – the one human being she could rely on.

With everything going so well, it must have been difficult for Marie not to chuckle when, some three weeks later, Philipstal arrived to open his Phantasmagoria, and it proved a complete flop. He had added a collection of automata to the usual show and advertised these as 'original, astounding and unparalleled experiments in the Science of Optics'. According to broadsheets lauding himself as 'the sole inventor', these experiments would *do away with the belief in ghosts.* But many people *like* to believe in ghosts, and on the first night his apparatus broke down – 'it failed of producing the effects intended'. Philipstal then had to make public apology in the press. Few people hankered to view these gadgets, whereas everyone wanted to see the wax portraits. The contrasting popularity of the two shows became apparent, and Marie flaunted her own success. Edinburgh was a sophisticated, stimulating town; she loved the views, the air, the architecture and street life, and the abundance of public functions. There

Extracts from a letter dated 25 April 1803, written from London by Madame Tussaud to her husband, François, in Paris. After a successful five months at the Lyceum Theatre, Madame Tussaud has packed her Exhibition and is about to leave with it for Edinburgh. *Madame Tussaud's Archives*

By Permission of the Right Worshipful the Mayor.

LATELY ARRIVED FROM EDINBURGH,

THE GRAND EUROPEAN
Cabinet of Figures,

MODELLED FROM LIFE;—AND NOW

Exhibiting at No. 4, MARKET-PLACE, opposite the REIN-DEER INN:

Where the Curious may be gratified with a View of all the SEVENTY Characters at once.

Madame Tussaud, Artist,

RESPECTFULLY informs the Gentry and Public of HULL and its Vicinity, that her unrivalled Collection has just arrived here.

The full-length PORTRAIT-MODELS of their Most Gracious MAJESTIES

Geo. III. & Queen Charlotte,

THEIR ROYAL HIGHNESSES

THE PRINCE AND PRINCESS CHARLOTTE OF WALES,

Duke of York—Prince Charles Stuart;

LIEUTENANT-GENERAL SIR JOHN MOORE,

Admiral Lord Nelson,

GENERAL WASHINGTON.

Right Hon. Ch. Js. Fox—Right Hon. Wm. PITT,

SIR FRANCIS BURDETT,

Right Hon. H. GRATTAN—Right Hon. J. P. CURRAN,

The Philanthropic Mr. ROSEBERRY, of Dublin,

Mons. TALLEYRAND—L'ABBE SIEYES,

COUNT DE LORGA,

The famous BARON TRENCK—The EMPRESS of FRANCE,

MADAME CATALANI, the celebrated Singer,

A SLEEPING CHILD—The ARTIST and her DAUGHTER.

AN EXACT LIKENESS OF THE BEAUTIFUL BUT UNFORTUNATE

Mary Queen of Scots.

JOHN KNOX, and JOHN WESLEY.

THE CELEBRATED

MRS. CLARKE.

A Coach and a Cannon,

Formed in Gold, Ivory, and Tortoise Shell,—to the Astonishment of the Spectator, is, with great Facility,

DRAWN by a FLEA!

The other Subjects composing this UNIQUE EXHIBITION, chiefly consisting of Portrait Characters, in full Dress, as large as Life, correctly executed, may be classed as follows:

I. The late Royal Family of France, viz.

King, Queen, Princess Royal, and Dauphin; with M. de Clerie, Valet de Roi.

Celebrated Characters of the past and present Times, viz.

Henry IV. of France—Duc de Sully—Frederick the Great—M. de Voltaire—Pope Pius—J. J. Rousseau—Dr. Franklin—Buonaparte—Madame Buonaparte—Archduke Charles—General Moreau—General Kleber—Ex-Consul Cambaceres—Elfi Bey, and his Son; with a favourite Georgian Slave, and two most beautiful Circassians.

II. Remarkable Characters:—Subjects, viz.

Madamoiselle Bruiser de Perigord, who foretold the French Revolution.

Princess de Lamballe, who was murdered by the Revolutionary Mob in Paris.

Madame du Barri, the Mistress of Louis XV. who was guillotined in Paris.

Madame St. Amaranthe, guillotined for refusing to be the Mistress of Robespierre.

Charlotte Corde, who suffered by the guillotine for the Assassination of Marat.

Marat in the Agonies of Death, immediately after receiving the fatal Wound.

Heads of Robespierre, Foquilier, de Thionville, Herbert, and Carriere, as they appeared after the guillotine.

A Soldier of the French National Guards, in full Uniform.

An old Coquette, who teased her Husband's Life out.

One of Buonaparte's Mameluke Guards.—Madame St. Clair, the celebrated French Actress.

III. Curious and Interesting Relics, viz.

The SHIRT of HENRY IV. of France, in which he was assassinated by RIVAILLAC; and an accurate Portrait of Rivaillac himself; with various original Documents relating to that Transaction.

A small Model of the original French Guillotine, with all its Apparatus; and two Picturesque Models of the Bastile in Paris;

(In which Count de Lorga was confined Twenty Years:)

One representing that Fortress in an entire State, the other as destroying by the Revolutionists.

A real EGYPTIAN MUMMY, 3299 years old, in perfect Preservation.

Colonel Despard.

☞ OPEN EVERY DAY, from ELEVEN in the MORNING till TEN at NIGHT.

∗ Admittance, One Shilling.—Children under Ten Years of Age, Half Price.

N. B. A Free Ticket, (not Transferable) Price 5s. will admit a Person any Time during the Exhibition.

No. 4, Market-Place, Hull, February 28th, 1812.   ROBERT PECK, PRINTER, & PACKET-OFFICE, HULL.

Left: Poster for Madame Tussaud's Exhibition at the Reindeer Inn, Hull, February 1812. *Madame Tussaud's Archives*

Above: Page from an account book of 1812 when Madame Tussaud took her Exhibition from Leeds to Manchester. *Madame Tussaud's Archives*

Above right: Part of a poster advertising Madame Tussaud's Exhibition in fashionable St James's, where she showed in September 1816 on one of her visits to London. Note the Royal patronage. *Madame Tussaud's Archives*

Right: In February 1829 Madame Tussaud was in Liverpool, and added the body-snatchers Burke and Hare to her Exhibition. Burke was executed in Edinburgh on 27 January. Hare, who turned King's Evidence and was released, was advertised on 6 March. *Liverpool City Libraries*

THE DUKE AND   DUCHESS OF YORK,

THE COUNT   D'ARTOIS.

MADAME TUSSAUD,

Lately arrived from the Continent,

Artist to Her late ROYAL HIGHNESS MADAME ELIZABETH, SISTER to LOUIS XVIII.

Most respectfully informs the Nobility, Gentry, and the Public, that her

UNRIVALLED COLLECTION

Of Whole-Length

FIGURES,

AS LARGE AS LIFE,

CONSISTING OF

83 *Public Characters,*

Which have lately been exhibited in Paris, Dublin, Edinburgh, &c.

IS NOW OPEN FOR INSPECTION, AT THE

MAGNIFICENT MERCATURA,

No. 29, St. James's Street.

CHARACTERS AS FOLLOW:

THE FULL-LENGTH PORTRAIT MODELS

OF

THEIR MOST GRACIOUS MAJESTIES GEORGE III. AND QUEEN CHARLOTTE,

---

NEW ADDITION.

THE INFAMOUS, THE DIABOLICAL HARE,

The Associate of the monster Burke.

EXHIBITION AND PROMENADE, PANTHEON,

CHURCH-STREET.

MADAME TUSSAUD, *ARTIST,* respectfully announces that, influenced by the great satisfaction which the introduction of the figure of Burke has produced to her Friends and the Public, and in consequence of numerous inquiries for a figure of the wretch HARE, she sent her Son to Edinburgh, in order to procure a good Likeness of him, together with a description of his person, and she is happy to say, that, after considerable difficulty, he succeeded in getting one, which Madame Tussaud pledges herself may be depended upon as being a good resemblance; and she trusts it will convince her Friends of her great wish to render the Exhibition as interesting as possible, in order to make it worthy of the patronage of the inhabitants of Liverpool. The Likeness of Hare was taken a short time previously to his leaving Edinburgh; and the countenance is fully indicative of his character. The original Bust (in plaster) of BURKE, is now added to the Exhibition.

Admittance One Shilling.

The BAND will play every Evening, from Seven to Ten.

Open from Eleven to four, and from Six to Ten.

Bristol Riots, 1831. On 30 October Madame Tussaud's Exhibition was endangered by rioting mobs who set fire to the north side of Queen's Square. William Muller made a water-colour drawing, from sketches made on the spot, showing her figures being carried to safety from the Assembly Rooms where she was showing. *Madame Tussaud's Archives*

had been good theatre in Edinburgh for fifty years, with a renowned supply of native talent. She was also impressed by the water pipes newly laid in all the main streets. She hardly noticed that the famous traditional cry of the 'water caddies' was vanishing, for the chorus of street cries remained loud enough, especially at night when the women came up from the coast with creels of shellfish. Cockles and mussels and oysters were sold at street corners as were curdy cheeses, buttermilk, gingerbread and sweetmeats. Joseph listened to the cries and mimicked them, and begged for coconut from the man who cried 'Cocky Nit, Cocky Nit, a ha'penny the bit, bit, bit'. The streets were so alive, so full of different calling voices and the crowds had a kind of freshness. This was the lively, enthusiastic city which Marie Tussaud really preferred to all others. The fact that Philipstal had arrived late and established his Phantasmagoria in the Corri Rooms entirely separate to the building she had rented helped her to work out a mode of attack. This unsatisfactory partner who allowed her only half her own receipts was on the way out.

On 28 July, after the Edinburgh Horse Show, when visitors fell off, admission had to be reduced to one shilling. Marie wrote her husband a long outburst:

I have delayed so long in writing to be able to tell you now of the final settlement of the account with Philipstal. . . . Here are the accounts:

Receipts from the opening day 18 May to 23 July   £420. 10s.

Deduct the transport of effects from London,
payment of wages of 2 men, rent, tickets,
advertisements etc.   118. 18s.

Net Profit   £301. 12s.

I have parted with Philipstal's share £150. 16s. sterling. . . . We had plenty of rows in arriving at a settlement. I have been forced to accept his accounts as he placed them before me. . . . He treats me like a slave. I have made all possible efforts to break the association. I have shown our agreement to different lawyers who say there is not the least chance of it being broken legally. The agreement is entirely in his favour and at his discretion. The only proper solution is to separate and he will have none of it. . . . Now he wants to go off without telling me where – I have got to go to Glasgow but he holds my nose to the grindstone. . . . He seeks only to flout and ruin me so he can take all.

Tomorrow I am going to make yet another visit to a lawyer in case there might be any means of getting out of this mess. . . .

In spite of the crisis don't be anxious and don't be upset – I have every hope of surmounting my difficulties with the aid of the Almighty. . . . Send your letters here still. Mrs Laurie will forward them. Send a greeting to Mr and Mrs Laurie, they are very kindly people and I am grateful for their interest and their many little kindnesses to me. I am glad to learn that all are well at home – as I am, although bowed down with anxiety and fear. Nini is learning English so quickly and has started to read. He does lessons every day – We want to see you again. A million kisses to darling Francino. . . .

The interpreter sends you his best wishes. He is no longer with me – a few days absence through illness was sufficient pretext for Philipstal to replace him.

This final insult from the detested Monsieur Philipstal does not, however, seem to have had permanent results. Whether paid or merely mesmerized by Madame Tussaud and her wax Exhibition, the interpreter remained a fixture.

Marie was sad enough to leave Edinburgh for Glasgow. She would miss the comfortable lodgings in Thistle Street and the kindly landlady, and Sunday outings into the beautiful hills with Joseph. It would be more difficult to alleviate her homesickness now that she began to realize the impossibility of returning to Paris. Europe was growing frightened of Napoleon, ports were closing and all communications between France and England would soon be severed.

At the beginning of October she moved to Glasgow, found lodgings with a highly respectable pastry cook – respectability meant a great deal to Marie Tussaud, and this new landlord, Mr Colin of Wilson Street, came into the highest category, for he was not only a top pastry cook but on the way to being made a Guild Brother and Burgess of Glasgow. The Exhibition, well placed in the New Assembly Hall in Ingram Street, had a great success.

On 10 October Marie sent a letter by the hand of a personal friend travelling in some way or other to France. It is addressed to Madame L'Allemand at 20 Boulevard du Temple. Perhaps it seemed safer this way. The letter itself begins: 'Cher ami, cher mer, cher Françison', and covers the whole family as usual. It goes on:

I am seizing the offer of M. Careborlion who has promised to see that you receive this letter. It is over three months since I have heard from you – is it possible you have forgotten me? Nini is so popular and his portrait stands outside the Salon. Everyone is astonished and he is the child they all want to have. He speaks English like a native and his answers come so easily that I can use him as my interpreter.

It is three months since I saw Philipstal – the scoundrel. . . . I made a mistake not to finish with the monster in Edinburgh. . . . By bad luck I have lost his written answer – now he does not want to be found in the same town . . . I have the approach to everybody – which is impossible for him. As soon as I pay him off I hope to give him the go by. . . . We made £600 in four months in Edinburgh . . . and I have good friends. I have been in Glasgow since October 1st and all goes well – the first receipts amount to £40 which more than pays our expenses & I hope to do still better – there are plenty of other towns.

I hope my friend that you take on the duty of head of the family? Look after my mother and my aunt – Don't worry about us here. . . . Nini embraces all his friends. . . .

This torn letter is written in Marie's own strong hand. The spelling makes very hard reading but at the end in large exquisite copperplate someone else has written: 'My address is: Mrs Tussaud, at Mr Colin. Pastry Cook, Wilson Street, Glasgow.'

Marie now kept to the idea of two separate Salons. In the first room she tried to astound the public with brilliant historical figures and in the second room she showed the death heads of Robespierre, Hébert, Carrier and Fouquier Tinville, as well as her own full-size model of Marat expiring in his bath (journalistically this could be called a scoop which lasted). She also showed a scale model of the guillotine, models of the Bastille before and after its destruction, the shirt worn by Henri IV when assassinated and to add a final spinal shiver – the Egyptian Mummy which had somehow become her property.

In the *Glasgow Herald* advertisements of this autumn, Madame Tussaud offers to take portraits in 'the fullest imitation of life' adding 'The artist can also model from the dead body as well as from animated nature.' In December, as visitors fell away, she planned to move to Greenock. The best method of keeping receipts high was to constantly seek a new public. A letter written around Christmas says:

Our show was successful until this week which has fallen off. I plan to close three days after the New Year and go to Greenock eight leagues from here – but after that I do not know and will have to tell you later. . . . Suffice it to say I have received £250. M. Philipstal is at the moment in Dublin with M. le Baron and their servants. I heard today of his arrival. I am alone with my dear Nini and the interpreter and I can breathe much more freely. . . . According to Philipstal's plan I must follow him to Dublin . . . but I am still undecided. I will not go there, at least not this winter and during the bad weather, until I am sure that there is no danger for the Exhibition and myself and when peace is restored in that country. . . . Don't worry about me and my darling Nini. We are well & comfortable and often eat with the family. . . . But oh to be again in the bosom of our family. Nini so wants to see his little brother & to talk to him in English. He is very busy at his lessons and is making such progress.

A little later she wrote to her husband: 'I leave at six o'clock tomorrow for Greenock and have so much to do. As soon as the Cabinet is opened I will write to you. In the meantime goodbye, goodbye. To end this Nini & I send kisses from our hearts. Goodbye, Goodbye, Goodbye.'

A fragment of another letter assures Monsieur Tussaud that she would not think of travelling to Ireland during winter gales. Yet in February 1804, either because the Scottish tours she planned fell through, or because she was so anxious to catch up with Philipstal and buy him out, Marie Tussaud faced the stresses inevitable when packing up her fragile figures with their expensive costumes, and set sail for Dublin.

13

Ireland, March 1804 to June 1808

It can be horribly rough in the Irish Sea, but this voyage in February 1804 proved lucky. As the ship reached Dublin Bay after a calm crossing, Joseph stood on deck staring at this new land, the alluring outline of the Wicklow Mountains stretched on one hand and the ancient Hill of Howth on the other. His mother must have felt a certain trepidation, for after her experiences in the French Revolution she feared violence, and Ireland was in a most unhappy state. Pitt and George III had four years previously wrecked the country's economy by forcing through the Act of Union, and the Habeas Corpus Act had been suspended for two years. Martial law prevailed and Dublin, which after Dresden ranked architecturally as the most beautiful city in Europe, had entered its long, tragic decline. The great houses were not yet slums however, for although the politicians tried to govern as absentee members, the Irish gentry could not all afford to travel to the English capital for their pleasures. Balls took place nightly and theatres flourished. In fact, the Dublin to which Philipstal had ordered Marie was still a city of elegant houses and squares. It stretched for a mile each side of the Liffey quays where a forest of masts marked the river. There was terrible poverty and terrible drunkenness, but the cobbled streets hummed with laughter and sense of life. Dublin society had always placed value on wit and erudition. When Marie Tussaud was introduced to the ladies she found them highly educated and nearly all spoke fluent French. Concerts and opera were of the highest standards. Dublin had heard the first performance of Handel's *Messiah*, and its playgoers had seen Garrick act Hamlet before London did.

Marie realized the possibilities. Whatever the discontent, Ireland could not be a dull land. The people would be interested in what she had to show. With an exhibition to arrange and the chance of finally disentangling herself from Philipstal, she had hardly time nor inclination to listen to the torrent of political talk which resounded on every side, and after a close view of the French Revolution she was finished with politics, but it was hardly possible to exist for a week in the Dublin of Grattan and Daniel O'Connell without realizing that these two great men, one a Protestant and one a Catholic, were engaged to fight to the death to regain proper government for Ireland.

Marie did not care for ideas or theories. All she wished to do was record the faces of men who wove history. Let them become famous and she could take just one look, imprint their expressions in her memory, pour the hot wax into neat perfect moulds and finish off the exact likeness. It was not for her to be involved in political arguments – all she could do was to *see* and reproduce. She would not talk, she could not talk. But while assessing her own position in this new world, she enjoyed strolling through the wide, well-proportioned squares, watching the sumptuous carriages driving by with postillions, and the fashionable residents taking their daily walks in a large field called St Stephen's Green on the city outskirts.

Delighted by the outward show and impressed by the education of all she met, Madame Tussaud did not perceive the disintegration of what appeared to be a brilliant social life. It was, after all, only four years after the Act of Union and most country gentlemen still kept their town-houses in Dublin. Only gradually would they sell out and move to London.

The Act of Union! How incessantly they talked about it. Marie could only understand that the Dublin Parliament had been closed down and that magnificent building where its bribed members had voted for its extinction had been taken over by the Bank of Ireland. '*Ah, je comprends,*' said Madame Tussaud, but she didn't. The effect of removing the government and all intellectual, social and political forces to London would wreck Ireland slowly.

She had no time to lose. The Exhibition with its heavy expenses must be kept incessantly before the public. Marie opened in the Shakespeare Gallery near Grafton Street and found success. Then she tackled Philipstal, and after thrashing matters out, induced him to accept her Scottish earnings to buy him out. At last the partnership ended. Philipstal and his friend Monsieur le Baron are not heard of again.

This spring of 1804 was to prove the watershed of Marie's life. She now knew her own value in the entertainment world and had obtained freedom by hard-earned monetary payment. But something else happened. We do not know what severed the link between her and her husband, but '*ta femme pour la vie Tussaud*' was in no uncertain terms to explain to Monsieur Tussaud that henceforth they each went their own way. The change in relationship is puzzling, but obviously Marie now realized her own potentialities. Her industry and her talent would pay off, but how could she suffer indefinite separation from her second son?

Within a week or so of the Dublin opening Marie was organizing a tour – the first tour in which she would be completely on her own, the taker and keeper of all her own earnings. She learned that owing to the hunger and unrest prevalent, up to 14000 British troops had to be kept in Ireland. They were spread out over the countryside, not in tents, which would be dangerous, but in some twenty garrison towns. And the soldiers as well as the country Irish were longing for entertainment. In between insurrections both military and civilians grew bored. Every theatrical touring company of merit encountered an enthusiastic reception. What a success her superbly mounted show might have if she could organize its transport from one captive audience to another.

In late March she received a letter that had taken five months to travel, and she replied to it addressing her husband and family as usual in that curious fashion, partly plural, partly feminine singular:

Mes chers amie. I have just received your letter of Sunday 27 October on 17 March. It made me very happy to learn that you are all in good health. We are very well also and if only I had my darling Françison with me I could ask for nothing more. My son here no longer speaks a word of French. I can tell you that I finished completely with M. Philipstal last February. God be thanked. Now I work for myself and my children and everything is going well. When I am in Dublin the takings can reach £100 sterling a month. People come in crowds everyday from six o'clock until 10 o'clock. My Cabinet is already well-known with its portraits of famous and infamous men. I am very proud of it and I feel full of courage. My Cabinet is very much in demand and I have had a letter asking me to visit other towns, so I leave for Cork which is about 100 miles to the South. I hope by working hard that I can give my children a good start in life and that they may then turn out so that their father and mother can be proud of them. This is the real wealth we can give them. There will then be no cause to reproach me for doing them harm. I have no regrets. The day I finished with M. Philipstal my enterprise became more important to me than returning to you. Adieu, Adieu – we can each go our own way. Address your letters to the same place in Dublin and they will be forwarded. My compliments to all friends. We embrace you from the depth of our hearts a thousand times –

I am for life

Ta femme Tussaud.

I hope that you are looking after my mother and my aunt so that I never have reason to reproach you.

Just what is to be made of this letter? What has occurred to make possible that statement about her enterprise becoming more important than seeing the family again? It was now a year and a half since she had seen her baby – in fact he was emerging from babyhood. She admits to a longing for 'Françison', but there is not a word about the family group joining up with her travelling Exhibition when the advent of peace made it possible. The cool 'Adieu. We can each go our own way' is followed by the regular formal affectionate ending, and the injunction to look after her mother and aunt seems to imply some expectancy of meeting up again. Yet *Adieu* is final in France.

If Marie seems to have finished with her husband, she had not finished with her family. She regards mother, aunt and younger son as being in her husband's care and the exact implication of those thousands of embraces are difficult to discern. Who was to embrace whom and why?

It does seem likely that the financial speculations of François Tussaud had irritated Marie. After all she had made over to him everything she owned in France – mortgages included – and if that October letter which had finally reached her in Dublin contained bad news it may have proved a last straw. She had just got rid of Philipstal. Now she wanted to be free of her husband as well. But here there were complications. She could hardly paddle off in her own canoe leaving an unreliable man in charge of the family in Paris. To hold the situation together she must concentrate on earning.

By June she was back in Dublin, advertising the Exhibition in Exchequer Street near to Grafton Street. *Faulkner's Dublin Journal* and the *Dublin Evening Post* would carry the following announcement:

SHAKESPEARE GALLERY, EXCHEQUER STREET

To be seen, this and every Day, the most beautiful

Collection of

FIGURES, EXECUTED FROM LIFE,

Consisting of

ACCURATE MODELS IN WAX,

Of the invention of the celebrated Curtius, than which nothing can be a closer resemblance of Nature – the Figures being elegantly dressed in their proper Costume, are scarcely to be distinguished from Life: and have been exhibited at the Lyceum, London, and at Edinburgh, with the greatest applause.

The Exhibition is open from Eleven o'Clock till Four, and from Five till dusk.

Admission 2s. 2d. – A perpetual Ticket (not transferable) 7s. 7d.

Ladies and Gentlemen may have their Portraits taken in the most perfect imitation of Life; Models are also produced from PERSONS DECEASED, with the most correct appearance of Animation.

Evidently curfew problems were avoided by keeping the opening hours from eleven in the morning until dusk, with an hour's closure at tea-time. A full-length portrait of the great Irish statesman, Henry Grattan, who was incessantly working for Repeal of the Act of Union, was added with the subject's consent on 14 June. The notification that clients could order their own wax portraits and that models could be made of 'persons deceased' shows the taste of days before photography. Madame Tussaud did not yet presume to attach her own name to the Exhibition, deeming that of the renowned Curtius the greatest draw imaginable.

After three weeks, Marie took her exhibition to Waterford by sea, which was always the best mode of travel. On 20 June she wrote to 20 Boulevard du Temple a letter which began with that puzzling, inaccurate *Mes chers amie*, and in it she rejoices at receiving a letter from her husband dated 7 June (it must have been brought by hand from France). She and Joseph are still elated at having got 'rid of the Monster M. de Philipstal', and one can imagine how enthusiastically the six-year-old joined in the 'hate' against this gentleman who now vanishes from history. Marie feels twice the woman now that she is free.

I am sure to do well and succeed now that I only have to work for myself and my children. The Salon *will* make money. Also people will help me because I am alone and have to pay all expenses myself. There are about 50 towns I could go to but they are far apart and transport is dear. I plan to spend the winter near a big town which can provide plenty of visitors, and then go on to some big city in the North which has invited me. . . .

You ask if I speak English? I speak enough to carry on my business. And I *have* to speak English as my son no longer understands a word of French, and we live entirely with English people. I never call Joseph my son because everyone regards him as a little English boy. He does not even remember how to say

I

'Bonjour'. When he returns to Paris I hope he will pick up his French quickly. Oh I wish I had my beloved Françison with me so that he could have the same chances as his brother. I would be so happy if he could travel to me by land or sea.

We endured a very bad storm on our way down to Waterford and everyone was seasick. It was a terribly rough voyage but by merciful providence here we are safe and sound. Your son is a very good sailor. He is happy at sea and fancies the idea of becoming a sailor. Goodbye and write a little whenever possible to the same address in Dublin, No. 16. My compliments to all my friends – we embrace you with all our hearts a thousand times. And I am for life *ta femme Tussaud.*

By 27 June she was back in Dublin after a fearful voyage up the Irish coast. One has to presume the three vessels which were sunk went down on leaving Waterford and that crews and passengers were rescued. Young Joseph who was, luckily for himself, immune to seasickness, may have shed his ambition to be a sailor.

Mes chers amie: It gives me great pleasure to learn you are enjoying perfect health since we endured a terrible voyage. A storm struck us and three vessels which left port with us were sunk beside us in five minutes. You can well imagine my loss. I have to make good everything broken. . . . I hope to remain here quietly and am making portraits of famous Dubliners for my Salon which is drawing big crowds. The slack summer season is starting but everyone is so pleased and they say I will make a lot of money in the winter. The receipts grow continuously and average £6 to £7 a day. Our expenses remain small – 25 guineas for the room for six months. I plan to stay here until March and then go to Cork, Limerick and Belfast which are good cities in which to exhibit. From Belfast I can return to Scotland until God sends us peace.

My dear ones be patient because I suffer so far from you. I press you against my heart and darling Françison will no longer know his mother – or his brother become a proud English gentleman – for he really is English now and everybody believes him so. He speaks English perfectly and at the moment is taking piano lessons from one of my friends who loves him. Nini is a child of great promise and of an intelligence without equal – he is liked by all. And now my friends I hope you are taking proper care of my poor Françison. Don't be afraid for us, all is well. *I* have no fear Monsieur Tussaud, but take care of my mother, my aunt and dear Françison. When I return let there be no reproaches. . . . Goodbye dear friends – I embrace you thousands and thousands of times. My address is No. 16 Clarendon Street, Dublin – ta femme – Tussaud.

This is the last surviving letter written by Marie Tussaud to her husband.

One has to presume that having made over to him all her material possessions she tired of constant requests and complaints, the love she had borne for him withered, and although eager to entrust him with the Paris household she recoiled at the thought of seeing him again. *Ta femme pour la vie Tussaud* had said *Adieu*. The disenchantment with this attractive, younger man may have been gradual, or some incident may have proved a final straw. The human story remains unclear. It was difficult to envisage any return to Paris at the time, so it seems reasonable to leave an old mother cooking for a cast-off husband, but how could Marie Tussaud who was such a devoted and doting mother to her first-born son give up the baby?

War with France was now intensifying. The ports were closed as England came under blockade, and it is amazing that any letters from an enemy alien actually reached Boulevard du Temple. As no letters from François Tussaud survive, we can but guess how he took the injunction that henceforth he and she would 'go separate ways'. Presumably he accepted her dictum and settled down with his mother-in-law and younger son. From now on Marie Tussaud forgets her personal life and concentrates on the problems of taking the Exhibition on tour.

She remained in Dublin throughout the winter, busily accepting commissioned portraits and making new models of people for the Exhibition. Marie must have been able to work in the most uncomfortable circumstances. The inventory of 20 Boulevard du Temple taken after Curtius's death reveals the presence of modelling materials in almost every room. Marie needed only sufficient space for plaster and wax and tools; craftsmanship and concentration out of the ordinary were the real ingredients of her success – and that dauntless determination which set her to mend breakages after every unfortunate journey. The roads in Ireland were fairly good, but the carts and carriages of the period must have been hard on delicate crated objects, so whenever possible she transported the exhibition by boat.

In the spring of 1805, when travelling conditions improved, she set out on a tour across Ireland. Cork, Limerick and Galway were busy cities, each sheltering two regiments, and the populations of smaller towns received her with acclaim. Very few Irish towns possessed a local press and Marie had to rely for publicity on her own posters and handbills (none of which have survived). In May, however, when she arrived in Kilkenny, *Finn's Leinster Journal* provided her with the chance to advertise, and we learn that the 'Grand European Cabinet of Figures' was open every day in the Grand Jury Room of the City Court House by permission of the Mayor, from 11 a.m. until dusk. Admission cost one shilling and one penny and included the innovation of a 'Flea Parade'. Tiny models of 'carriages curiously formed in Gold, Ivory and Tortoiseshell each drawn by a flea *to the complete astonishment of the Spectator*'. Astonishment was indeed complete and crowds flocked to the Court House. Those who were not actually starving enjoyed life in Ireland – the Kilkenny races were accompanied by balls and concerts and the fashionable folk of Dublin travelled down by mail coach. As if to lure visitors and perhaps attract commissions, Marie asserted in her advertisement that 'her departure from hence will be for ever'. In a country as small as Ireland she could hardly have meant this seriously.

All that summer and autumn the 'Grand Cabinet of European Figures' was on tour, and what a blissful experience this must have been for Joseph. No country is more magical for a small boy than Ireland. The kindly people, the uninhibited talk, the jolly soldiers and poetical country-folk filled him with delight. And now that packing and moving the Exhibition had become routine, his mother must have obtained a certain enjoyment from the contrasting beauties of the scene. She never left the show during its opening hours, but she can't have spent *all* her time doing accounts.

On 25 November she opened in Cork at Mr Snagg's Hotel. Curfew restrictions had been lifted and the Exhibition remained open until 10 each evening.

John Carr, writing his *Stranger in Ireland* in the year of Madame Tussaud's visit, describes Cork with its 'superb barracks, handsome houses, and refined, elegant society'. One would give much for the little Frenchwoman's own opinion of the audiences that paid the two shillings and two pence entrance fee that she found possible to demand of the élite. Marie's advertisements continued in the *Cork Evening Post* until Christmas Day. Then she probably returned to Dublin for the rest of the winter.

During the next three years we know only that she continued to tour Ireland, presumably following the regular route of theatrical companies, travelling from Cork to Limerick, Galway and back overland to Mullingar. It is maddening not to have her own account. One only knows that she herself sat in the box office taking the cash, counting every penny each night and working to keep her wax figures in fine array during the early hours. Joseph must have had some kind of schooling, for he would later emerge very well educated. It probably did him no harm to remain the apple of his mother's eye and join in the effort of making a livelihood in a most original way. Certainly it must have been puzzling for a little French boy to learn in 1805 that the Battle of Trafalgar was a cause for rejoicing. Had not Maman been in prison with Napoleon's wife? Had she not modelled the great man's head? But by now Joseph hardly thought of himself as French – he spoke only English (though surely with an Irish accent and the changing rhythms of Dublin pith, Cork roar and Galway melody). Surely all this sharpened his ear.

The next printed record of Marie's travels appears in the north of Ireland. In May 1808, the *Belfast News and Letters* carried advertisements to say that the Exhibition would open at No. 92 High Street, Belfast. And for the first time Madame Tussaud dares to present the show under her own name. Continuous success had increased her confidence. The famous Curtius had been dead for fourteen years and his pupil was now forty-seven years old. She had herself built up this travelling Exhibition and now she dared to place herself as head of the concern. The Belfast newspaper advertisement ran referred to:

MADAME TUSSAUD
ARTIST OF THE GRAND EUROPEAN
CABINET OF FIGURES
MODELLED FROM LIFE

It was also the first public use of the term 'waxworks'. So after four years touring in Ireland, Marie left Belfast to return to Scotland. On 29 July the Exhibition was established in the Masons Hall, Greenock, and local advertisements announced that Madame was on her way to London.

She would never go back to Ireland, but the years of travel through a country which, whatever its miseries, was always intensely alive and receptive had turned Marie Tussaud into a woman who was very sure of herself. She seems to have abandoned all idea of returning to her husband; she no longer needed him; he must have injured her in some way which no letters explain. The hurt may have been financial or perhaps she learnt of infidelities. The situation remains curious, for little François is still living in the house she made over to Monsieur Tussaud who is still keeping her mother and small son and maybe that old aunt as well. Then in the September of 1808 her husband took an action which must have caused her great sadness. Possibly it was only then that she resolved *never never* to see him again.

14

Twenty-six years touring England (1808-34)

It is not known if Madame Tussaud reached London in September 1808, but wherever she was, the news from Paris must have hardened her resolve never to set foot there again. Certainly she knew she would no longer find a patron in Josephine Bonaparte. In the previous year Fouché, who had been the Empress's friend, had, reversing his opinions about divorce, declared in his harsh realistic way: 'It is much to be hoped that the Empress will die. It would remove many difficulties. Sooner or later he must take a wife who can bear children. For as long as there is no direct heir, the danger remains that his death will be the signal for an upheaval.'

But it was not the fact that Napoleon had dispensed with Josephine or that England and France kept going to war that embittered Marie; it was the news that her husband was handing over, lock, stock and barrel, 20 Boulevard du Temple, complete with its Exhibition of wax figures, to Madame Salomé Reiss in exchange for the annulment of her annuity of 2000 livres interest on the mortgage arranged in April 1795. It seems likely that François had been unable to pay this interest since Marie's departure, and in the end he may have been thankful to be shot of the whole business. Under the power of attorney which Marie had granted him, François ceded to Madame Reiss, as well as the house which had been Marie's home since girlhood, 'all the objects comprising the Salon of figures known as the *Cabinet de Curtius*. These objects include all the wax figures, all the costumes, all the moulds, all the mirrors, lustres, and glass. . . . Monsieur Tussaud herewith renounces any rights in this regard'. In return for 20 Boulevard du Temple and its unique contents, Salomé Reiss renounced all claim to her original loan of 20 000 livres in assignats and the interest thereon.

François Tussaud could not have been very hard up for he had just purchased the lease of the Théâtre des Troubadours, a building erected on a plot of ground already owned by him. It was only too likely that anyone not fascinated by the art of wax-modelling would get bored with the very demanding work entailed by it in running such a show. Henceforth Monsieur Tussaud concentrated on speculation in property and, as Marie had decreed, he and she went their own ways.

If at this stage Marie had desired to return to Paris, it would have meant starting from scratch. She would have had to rent or buy a salon, and equip it with new chandeliers, furniture and mirrors. Even if there had been no domestic rift, it was more sensible from the business point of view to continue touring. By now she knew just how to pack and transport the figures, how to mend wax faces as she went along, how to attract attention by advertising, and, above all, how to do her sums!

François Tussaud moved 'the family' to Curtius's other house in the rue des Fossés du Temple, and there they were to live until death overtook Madame Grosholtz and 'Françison' had grown into a young man. However painful the loss of her former home may have been, Marie faced the prospect of an indefinite round of travel with equanimity. She was now irrevocably committed to ceaseless packing up, setting up, taking down and repacking. The splendour of Curtius's Salon de Cire had vanished for ever. English towns would not expect costly background scenes. If she kept on the move no public would tire of her, and there were many expanding cities which must welcome a show so beautifully set up and carefully contrived. The artistry she had acquired would be put to full use.

With Joseph as company she tried to face the future bravely. In middle age Marie emerges as a woman ahead of her time, a career woman determined to be self-supporting and to maintain the prestige of her exhibition through merit alone. Monsieur Philipstal had taught her to avoid entanglements, and François Tussaud in ways unrevealed had taught her to prefer an independent life. Madame Tussaud could assess a situation. She had, since her arrival in England six years previously, realized the importance of building up her own image as a French Royalist, and so her nationality caused no complications when Napoleon invaded Spain and Portugal and general Sir Arthur Wellesley engaged him in the Peninsula War. She could put *both* great military leaders in her show!

Marie now worked out an established routine for touring. She must never allow the Exhibition to grow stale in any district. During the next twenty-six years she visited seventy-five towns, as well as many small places possessing no local press, where all advance publicity had to be achieved by use of posters and handbills. She gauged accurately the Exhibition's drawing power. It must be kept spectacular, educational and topical. History would be presented in the guise of kings and queens, daily events by ceaseless additions of famous personages or notorious criminals, and the core of the show must always remain the French Revolution which she had witnessed from so close. She perceived that the separate room for horrid sights would always bring cash, but along with murderers, royalty, and famous politicians, Marie did not underestimate the appeal of ordinary individuals briefly become the subject of contemporary talk. One of these she approached was the millionaire manufacturer of patent medicine, Dr S. Solomon of Liverpool, whose 'Balm of Gilead' was considered indispensable as a cure-all, especially for persons who travelled to hot eastern climes. Visiting the doctor at his splendid Liverpool mansion, Gilead Hall, built from the proceeds of his medicines, Marie followed the usual procedure of spreading a life-mask over her subject's oiled countenance, but for once Madame Tussaud was not concentrating – she forgot to insert the breathing straws in his nostrils and the doctor had started to asphyxiate when Marie realized with horror her omission and tore off the mask. He allowed her to continue, however, for Dr Solomon *wanted* to join the ranks of the famous.

Marie was lucky in the sense that her travelling years coincided with the achievements of the great road-builders, Telford and McAdam. When she first started out with her delicate figures the going must have been horribly rough, but Telford's system of road surfacing and McAdam's 'macadamizing' increasingly improved the highways. She had to transport her figures by wagon, while she and her son travelled by coach, the fastest of which flew along at ten miles an hour. What a fascinating upbringing Joseph had; for a little boy – what a lot he saw of life!

Madame Tussaud always stayed in lodgings and, as surviving ledgers reveal, she and Joseph travelled from one town to another by HIRED COACH. It must have been imperative for her to arrive in advance of the closed 'caravans' that carried the figures, costumes, settings, moulds and wax-modelling materials.* The ledgers note that these caravans had to be

---

* Even teeth could be realistically modelled in white wax, but there is a report that in the earlier years of her travels (and probably when she worked in Curtius's Exhibition in Paris) Madame Tussaud purchased real teeth when a subject's features made it

occasionally regilded, and certainly they carried her name in elegant lettering, so each arrival must have meant an exciting procession.* There are occasional personal entries for food, day-to-day living expenses and many for the purchase of candles – brilliant illumination of the Exhibition was imperative and remained Marie's *forte*.

In 1810 she collects her son's French watch left for repair with James Ritchie and Son, clockmakers, Edinburgh, and later she leaves one bought in Dublin. In 1812 she moves from lodgings in Briggate, Leeds, to Manchester, and hire of her coach amounts to £1. 4s. The weekly accounts for 1812 survive and include 'Easter expenses on the road', listing essentials in her clear hand and confusing spelling of such items as Meat, Tea, Cafe, Laundrie Women, Lamp Oil, Candles, Porter and Snuff. A sip of porter and a pinch of snuff must have been very welcome at the end of a long day. Wages to staff are a main expense and workers must have travelled with her. The only extravagance cited is a Hat, costing £1. 10.

All during these years Joseph travelled with her and helped with the Exhibition, while somehow getting an education and continuing to study the piano. In 1814 when in Bath an additional attraction was added. This consisted of a 'machine' with which silhouette portraits could be taken by J. Tussaud for prices ranging from two shillings to five shillings. Madame Tussaud may have been in an indulgent mood, for her sixteen-year-old son appears in posters and advertisements as 'Joseph Tussaud, proprietor', but this title is never used again, although he continued to produce silhouettes for over thirteen years.

When the Emperor Alexander I of Russia came to London, where he readily showed himself to the crowds, Marie Tussaud added his portrait to her travelling group. A Coventry local history describes Madame Tussaud in 1823 when she lodged in Hay Lane as 'an affable woman who told many queer tales of the French Revolution'. She stayed in Coventry

---

desirable. Human teeth were not difficult to obtain. It is known that looters on a battlefield would remove teeth from the slain and sell them to 'the trade'. After 1815 such teeth were called 'Waterloo teeth', though the Duke of Wellington's own dentures were of walrus ivory.

* Until Madame Tussaud could afford her own special vehicles she must have used a firm like *Pickford & Co. Caravan Office* who advertised, 'Land and Water Conveyance. Caravans on springs and guarded (for conveyance of goods only), leave Nottingham for London, Manchester and Liverpool every morning at five o'clock.' The word caravan then meant a horse-drawn pantechnicon, not a sleeping-wagon.

for about three months, not only occupying St Mary's Hall for a wax-works show, but also turning the Mayoress's Parlour into a 'Chamber of Horrors'.

In the early nineteenth century, elegant Assembly Rooms were built in most towns and these provided Madame Tussaud's first choice of venue. The long pillared rooms enabled her to present that brilliantly lit *coup d'œil* on entry which is frequently praised in local newspapers. The number of full-length, richly dressed figures varied between seventy and ninety and she hated to be cramped for space. In 1819, according to the *Norfolk Chronicle*, her Exhibition was 'as well arranged as the size of the room will admit but certainly would have appeared to greater advantage in a larger space'. In Norwich that year she has to delay her opening as the shortage of daylight makes the arrangement and dressing of ninety figures difficult. In the larger towns such as Doncaster, Peterborough and Dover where no Assembly Rooms were available she used a theatre.

After the Battle of Waterloo Marie had the extraordinary experience of modelling a second portrait of Napoleon. According to her catalogues this was 'taken when he was on board the *Bellerophon* off Torbay'. *Bellerophon*, which was transporting the fallen Emperor to St Helena, was surrounded by scores of small craft loaded with sightseers eager to catch a glimpse of the villain who had for so long endangered their country. With her indefatigable push Marie must have obtained permission to go on board. If he did not choose to pose in this moment of defeat, a glimpse of the broken Napoleon would have enabled her photographic mind to register the changes in that face she had moulded in plaster so long before.

Marie had natural journalistic talent. She scented what was of public interest and she was quick to act. In May 1820 she added two figures which were in different ways what would now be called 'hot news'. The Exhibition was given an extra few days in Leeds so that gaping crowds could view a likeness of 'the Cato Street conspirator', Thistlewood, who had planned to assassinate the entire Cabinet while the ministers were at dinner. The plot was discovered, and Thistlewood and four of his fellows were hanged at Newgate on 1 May. Three months later, opening her Exhibition at the Large Room at the Exchange in Manchester, Madame rushed in a portrait of Signor Bergami, the alleged lover of George IV's estranged wife Queen Caroline. The Queen's brilliant defence lawyer, Brougham, would make his name in this case and himself eventually entered Madame Tussaud's show in wax. Marie had done a likeness of

Caroline in 1808 when she was Princess of Wales, and the catalogue, amusingly moralizing, states: 'The separation of the "Royal Pair" – an event greatly to be deplored – is too delicate a subject to be entered into.'

In 1810 Madame Tussaud was back in Edinburgh with her Exhibition established at the Panorama, Leith Walk, opposite the Botanic Gardens. Her detailed and enthusiastic poster is the earliest that survives, and it lists a mixture of old and new portraits. There is one of Mary Queen of Scots and Prince Charles Stewart newly added especially for this Scottish tour. Full-length portrait models of George III and Queen Charlotte are listed in surviving catalogues as 'taken from life in 1809'.* Nelson and Sir John Moore mingle with English and Irish politicians, and Napoleon stands there with some of his generals, two ex-consuls and not only Josephine, but his second Empress, the recently modelled Marie Louise.

Madame Tussaud's handbills and advertisements are always an indication of which personages are catching the public attention at the time, and the largest type on the 1810 poster is given to Mrs Mary Ann Clarke, mistress of the Duke of York, whom Marie had modelled seven years previously when the lady was living in style in Cumberland Place. Now Mrs Clarke was even more prominently in the news, for the Duke of York had been charged in the House of Commons with wrongly selling commissions under the influence of his mistress. Mary Ann had defended herself saucily, and her good looks and fortitude during long examinations at the Bar of the House had won her many new admirers. Public interest in the crackpot conspirator Despard had not waned and we see that he remained in the show for six years after his execution. The Egyptian Mummy had survived sea crossings and being trotted around Ireland, and the fleas were still drawing their little gold, ivory and tortoiseshell carriages.

In 1816 Marie Tussaud met in Southampton the brother of that Pierre de Paris who had stabbed to death deputy Lepelletier, who had voted for the King's death, on the evening of the execution. This brother lived in the town teaching French. How far away that grey day seemed.

In 1816 Marie was again exhibiting in London at the 'Magnificent Mercatura', an arcade or bazaar on the east side of fashionable St James's Street. It must have been satisfactory to return to the capital where she had started out, nerve-racked and anxious, fourteen years before. Then off she went on fresh travels, knowing that no other itinerant show had ever achieved such success. In the first three decades of the nineteenth century

* The mould of Queen Charlotte, which is a particularly striking portrait, survives.

many English and Scottish people never saw a newspaper. News travelled without the aid of print, and important events were discussed and the participants' names became famous even in remote areas, but no one knew what the people they were talking about *looked like*. Even when a local press existed, few news-sheets outside London carried illustrations, and where these were used, artists had to depend on impressions gained from drawings for their pen and ink representations. The impact made wherever Madame Tussaud's Exhibition arrived became tremendous. The public flocked to see what the great and wicked really looked like, and brought their children because it was educational. Marie could skilfully group and illuminate her figures in telling poses within a few hours. She was close to the eager, gossiping, seething crowds of her time, aware of their pulse and desire for excitement. When there was no local press, handbills and posters were supplemented by catalogues. A surviving catalogue, dated 1819 and printed in Cambridge, is very Royalist in tone, claiming the patronage of Louis XVIII of France (he who had tried to kiss her on the stairs at Versailles and got smacked for his pains). She showed portraits of the Comte d'Artois, HRH the Duke of York and the Duchess of York (Mrs Clarke was shown separately), and the Duchess of Wellington, that lorn Irish girl whom the new Duke had felt duty-bound to marry. Perhaps the portrait we would most like to see is that listed, 'The Artist. Taken by herself', but the moulds of all Marie's early portraits have disappeared.

The catalogue is a compendium, like its successors, of information about the characters portrayed in the Exhibition and the events with which they were concerned – this is History without Tears. A short introduction begins:

Madame Tussaud, in offering this little Work to the Public, has endeavoured to blend utility and amusement. The following pages contain a general outline of the history of each character represented in the Exhibition; which will not only greatly increase the pleasure to be derived from a mere view of the Figures, but will also convey to the minds of young Persons much biographical knowledge – a branch of education universally allowed to be of the highest importance.

A catalogue carried back to an isolated hamlet could be read aloud to those who could not decipher it themselves. Topical as well as historical information would thus be conveyed, for it was not only townsfolk who visited the Exhibition. People came in from miles around, and from time to time Madame Tussaud's advertisements announce that, owing to inclement weather, she will remain a few days longer for the benefit of those whose visits have been prevented by rain, hail or floods.

As she became well known in dozens of English towns, Madame Tussaud began supporting charities. There are considerable records of her efforts. Often they concern special benefit openings, such as that for the Infirmary at Leeds mentioned on 27 May 1820 by the *Leeds Mercury*; sometimes they reflect the hardship of the time, such as that on 8 August 1822 in Shrewsbury when the proceeds of her opening day in the Town Hall were given to 'the distressed peasantry in Ireland'. On 4 December 1821 the receipts of a first evening in the Exchange Rooms, Manchester, were given to the House of Recovery. Beneath the report of this the following details are listed: 'Admitted 4, Discharged cured 5 – Dead 7 – Remain in House – 10.' On 23 December 1826 an unusual charity is designated. Madame Tussaud was showing in the Assembly Rooms of York where a pre-Christmas Ball took place in a room adjoining that in which the Exhibition was arranged. When the dancers retired from the ballroom to take tea, Madame Tussaud's son Joseph cut away the canvas screen separating the two rooms, thus allowing guests to troop in among the figures. The takings that evening amounted to £15. 10s. and this sum was donated without any deduction to 'the Distressed Manufacturers of York'.

No exceptional event was allowed to pass without some kind of representation. The accession to the throne of George IV gave Marie opportunity for her first great spectacular production. In October 1820 the *Exchange Herald* of Manchester announces a magnificent allegorical Coronation group with a 'new figure of George IV modelled from a recent bust and universally allowed to be one of the best likenesses ever taken'. The setting for this ambitious project reproduced the crimson and gilt throne room at Carlton House, and the construction of the splendid throne 'got up' by Messrs Petrie and Walker of St Ann's Street had taken a considerable time. Viewing of this magnificent royal group was accompanied by what Madame Tussaud called a 'Musical Promenade'. Cleverly she saw how to enhance the pleasure of her audiences with background music. A 'truly elegant spectacle' should be accompanied by piano player and fiddlers playing suitable melodies. Joseph, at twenty-two years old, had become a knowledgeable musician, so he could control the small orchestras which now added to spectators' enjoyment. Madame Tussaud might well be called the originator of the Promenade Concert.

Encouraged by Manchester's enthusiasm over her elaborate Coronation group, in the following year Marie unveiled her first actual tableau. She chose the Christmas season in Liverpool to present 'The Coronation of Napoleon', based on the dramatic picture by David. There were eight figures to be authentically attired in this tableau. Napoleon in his coronation robes is depicted in the act of crowning himself; Josephine kneels at the foot of the altar; the Pope, attended by Napoleon's uncle Cardinal Fesch, gives a blessing; and two mamelukes in their native costumes with pages complete the picture.

The catalogue for an 1822 visit to Manchester announces a 'special room' for the more harrowing exhibits which did not really mix with royal splendour and that *coup d'œil* which Marie deemed so important.* 'Highly interesting figures and objects, in consequence of the peculiarity of their appearance, are placed in an Adjoining Room and form a separate exhibition well worth the inspection of artists and amateurs.' The additional charge for 'peculiarity' was sixpence. And for this small extra sum could be seen: 'Marat taken immediately after his assassination by Charlotte Corday', the ancient Comte de Lorge stumbling from the Bastille, that well-travelled Egyptian Mummy, Henri IV's bloody shirt, the model of the guillotine, and moulds of the newly guillotined heads of Robespierre, Carrier, Fouquier-Tinville and Hébert. There was no mention of Madame once having dined with these gentlemen at Curtius's table.

According to family tradition, it was at this time that Madame Tussaud's second son François came to England to join her. He had not established himself in a career in Paris, having disliked his first apprenticeship to a grocer, and having failed to settle down in his second which was with a billiards-table maker, in whose workshop he learned to carve wood. His grandmother, who had brought him up, would have been seventy-nine, and it is possible that her death may have occurred and influenced his decision to leave France. According to the story he was horrified to learn, on his arrival in England, that his mother had just perished in a shipwreck and he had already turned back to France when the report proved to be untrue. He then travelled to Liverpool and found her there. This story is confirmed by an extraordinary happening in 1822 when Madame Tussaud was indeed in Liverpool and had on 23 June announced her last week in the city owing to 'a particular engagement in Dublin'. George IV

* It was a university don who first objected to the close proximity of the heroic and the criminal.

was making a state visit to the Irish capital and Madame Tussaud, who knew her Dublin well, most certainly realized that it would be an opportune moment to return and show her Coronation group.

But she never got there. Why? There is not a line in her own records, and one might attribute the story concerning François and the shipwreck to fantasy, but for the printed recollections concerning two Lancashire families, Fynes-Clinton and Mathew, published privately in 1924 under the title *Annals from our Ancestors*. In these *Annals* there exists an astonishing story concerning Marie Tussaud which exactly fits into that Liverpool summer. The author of these family recollections writes:

Before finishing with the ffaringtons I had better relate the adventure of Madame Tussaud which must have occurred before 1830. One stormy evening, Mrs ffarington (my gt aunt) and her two daughters Susan and Mary Hannah with some guests staying in the house [Worden, near Preston] were sitting after their dinner in the room called the morning-room, a comfortable apartment opening off the hall on the left as you enter, in the front of the house. They heard footsteps on the gravel outside and heard the bell ring, and the servants go across the hall to the door. A colloquy seemed to be taking place amidst a babel of voices which no one could understand. Mrs ffarington's curiosity was aroused and she went to the door herself, where she found the butler was being addressed in voluble French by a party of people outside. She brought them in and found them to be a little company of foreigners who had suffered shipwreck on their way to Dublin. The leader of the party was Madame Tussaud, a middle-aged lady who had fled from Paris during the Reign of Terror, after having been a favourite of the Royal Family and suspect in consequence and forced by the Communists to exercise her art of wax-modelling on the decapitated heads of many of their victims. She brought some of her models with her to London and started an exhibition there; afterwards touring with them about the country.

The shipwreck cast her and the survivors of her party on the Lancashire coast, and all her possessions went to the bottom, except one small box which the unfortunate companions carried between them when they all started to walk to Preston which they were told was the nearest town. Darkness fell upon them, and they struggled along in the rain and wind, soaked to the skin and caked with Lancashire mud. They mistook their road and instead of arriving at Preston, they found themselves at the lodge gates of Worden. How they got past the lodge I don't know, but they arrived at the house as described and were taken in and housed; supper was got ready and dry clothing, and they turned out to be such charming and interesting people that their stay was prolonged for several days.

The small box contained miniature models of various historical figures, and Madame Tussaud announced her intention of setting to work at once with fresh life-sized models of those that had been lost.

Mrs ffarington took her upstairs to a room where a number of old chests were kept, full of costumes which had belonged to former members of the family, and presented her with a good many of these to clothe her new figures, and to help her to re-start her exhibition. In addition to this Mrs John Mathews [Mrs ffarington's step-sister] at North Shields who also became interested in Madame Tussaud, gave her a quantity of valuable old Venetian point lace, of which I possess two or three pieces left over.

This extraordinary tale rings true, all the more so as the author writes artlessly for private perusal. It also gives an idea of the way in which Marie presented herself as a refugee from the French Revolution.

Her courage after shipwreck is typical. Marie would think only of getting back to Liverpool and reconstructing all that she had lost. She would not want sympathy or publicity. One kept quiet about disasters. It was bad business to allow the public to suspect that a subsequent opening might not be up to standard. And, of course, Marie would not have transported her actual moulds to Ireland, only some wax figures suitable for that 'particular engagement'. Much would have been left in Liverpool.

A search through newspaper files reveals that on 8 August 1822 a ship named *Earl Moira* bound for Dublin was wrecked just outside Liverpool. A heavy storm drove the vessel on to Burbo Bank, and subsequently on to the Wharf Bank, where it stuck and was battered by big waves. The decks were torn apart and the mast collapsed. We are informed that the captain, who was drunk, was washed overboard, and some passengers 'on their way to Dublin to meet His Majesty' were drowned. Lifeboats and other craft put out and a number of exhausted people were rescued. As no record had been made of passengers' names, the number drowned remained uncertain. It was surmised that about one hundred people had been aboard and nearly half of them perished. Marie Tussaud and her staff must have managed to climb on to one of the rescue boats which landed them along the coast. The *Liverpool Mercury* and the *Preston Chronicle* printed news of the disaster, but made no mention of Madame Tussaud. She kept very quiet about it all, and within a short time there she was back in Liverpool reopening the show in its full glamour. Marie Tussaud was the bravest of women, but nothing ever induced her to set foot on a ship again!

K

When he was in his twenties, Joseph married a Birmingham girl named Elizabeth Babbington. The Exhibition visited Birmingham in 1822–3, so it is quite possible the young couple met then. Their only son, Francis Babbington, was born in 1829 and named after his uncle and grandfather. There were also two daughters, Mary and Louisa. Later on François Tussaud, now known as Francis, married an English girl named Rebecca Smallpage, and they produced eight children, so in her old age Marie Tussaud did not suffer from lack of company.

In 1831 Madame Tussaud got caught up in the Bristol Riots and might well have lost all her wax figures in the disturbance. It was the third time her Exhibition had visited Bristol and all through August, September and October she had done good business in the Assembly Rooms in Prince Street. As winter approached she contemplated the usual move to Bath, and then the Second Reform Bill failed to pass the House of Lords. Violence broke out. The inhabitants of Bristol rose in wrath to protest against the Lords. On Sunday, 30 October, a mob started to loot and burn, criminals were freed from prison and there was a serious attack on the houses in Queen's Square, near to the Assembly Rooms, before the military could arrive. Felix Farley's *Bristol Journal* describes Madame Tussaud's situation:

After the destruction of the north, and during the conflagration of the west section of the Square, the inhabitants of Princes Street were in a state of great alarm. Parties of ruffians proceeded to several of the houses to warn the inmates of their intention to burn their premises and in some of them they actually commenced operations. During this awful state of suspense, among others Madame Tussaud and her family experienced the most painful anxiety. It was stated, among other places, that the Assembly Rooms were marked out for destruction, containing at the time their invaluable collection of figures. These, at an immense risk of injury, were partly removed, as hastily as circumstances would permit. The house in which Madame T. lodged, on the opposite side of the street, was among the number that became ignited from the firing of the west side of the Square; and we regret to hear that the lady's constitution has received a severe shock.

Madame Tussaud's cast-iron constitution probably suffered more from fear of losing her precious waxworks than of being herself injured. She did not flee, but remained manfully near the scene while a Negro servant helped to keep the rioters away from the figures being carried out. Danger to life and limb was not so bad that a passing youth, named William

Muller, could not take notes and produce a water-colour sketch of the scene.* Among the losses that Madame Tussaud would have sustained had the rioters succeeded in setting fire to the Assembly Rooms would have been Henri IV's blood-stained shirt and other treasures, the whole 'brilliant assemblage' as well as the unlovely objects in that 'separate room' which would later be called the Chamber of Horrors.

And so the years rolled by, with the Exhibition ever expanded and embellished. Historical curiosities, sculpture and paintings were constantly added, and larger orchestras increased viewers' elation. With two strong, talented sons to help her, Marie Tussaud did not find the constant tours as onerous as when she began. The tradition of keeping up with current affairs continued. Exciting new models drew the crowds. There were, for example, portraits of one Stewart and his wife, hanged for poisoning and robbing a sea captain, 'from casts taken from their faces three hours after execution' and, of course, the famous body-snatchers, Burke the murderer and the 'infamous diabolical Hare'. Later would come Mr Holloway, 'who murdered his wife in a manner too horrible to describe', and, to go with Henri IV's bloody shirt, which never lost its attraction, a full-length figure of his assassin Ravaillac was made.

The late spring of 1833 found the Exhibition in the Town Halls of Oxford and then of Reading. In Reading Madame Tussaud seized the opportunity of procuring a likeness of the current most interesting inmate of the gaol. Probably she did not perform this job herself, but sent one of her sons, who were both by now adept at their craft. A wax portrait was made of the prisoner of the moment – one Dennis Collins, a feeble-minded sailor with a pension grievance who had hurled a stone at William IV during the Ascot Races. The King was not hurt, but the incident was blown up into an assassination attempt, and the unfortunate loon was sentenced to transportation. He died during the voyage. Crowds came to the Exhibition eager to see what Collins looked like, as well as to gape at the latest sumptuous Coronation group, in which allegorical figures representing England, Scotland and Wales attended William and his Queen. The group was set beneath 'a magnificent canopy surmounted by a large Fancy Coronet'.

As Madame Tussaud grew older, her tableaux and her patrons grew

---

* Ironically this sketch was burned in the great fire of 1925, but before then it had been photographed and so a reproduction is possible.

grander. She deserved the open acclaim. No woman could have worked harder.

In 1833 Princess Augusta-Sophia, sister of George IV and William IV, brought her nephew Prince George of Cambridge to see the waxworks at the Brighton Town Hall and graciously wrote: 'We have been afforded much amusement and gratification.' Such royal compliments did not have to be discreetly read to friends. Madame Tussaud knew exactly how to use such praise. She published her gratitude at receiving this royal favour in advertisements, and when for some reason the County Hall of Lewes was refused her by the magistrates, she remained in Brighton for some weeks with the enhanced prestige which royal patronage could in those days bestow.

Madame Tussaud sometimes offered special prices to poorer sections of the community. Such was the snobbishness of those times, however, that she had to make sure that no embarrassment would be caused by 'mingling of the classes'. For instance in Portsmouth around 1830, when showing in the elegant venue of the Assembly Room in Green Row, the Management announced:

. . . considering that a large class of persons are unavoidably excluded from viewing the collection, in consequence of the pressure of time, they have made arrangements to admit

THE WORKING CLASS

During the time the Exhibition remains

FOR HALF PRICE

From a quarter before nine till ten in the evening. By this arrangement sufficient time will be given for the classes to view the collection without interfering with each other, and they hope that none but those so situated will take advantage of it. . . .

Even at half price, sixpence must have meant a strain on a working-class budget, and many would have gone to bed wearily before a quarter to nine at night.

During the autumn of 1833, Madame Tussaud moved slowly through Kent, setting up the Exhibition at Canterbury, Dover, Maidstone and Rochester, until it reached the outskirts of London. She planned to draw audiences from the suburbs throughout that winter.

In early November she opened at the Assembly Rooms at the 'Green

Man' in Blackheath. The area south of London had grown increasingly fashionable since Caroline, Princess of Wales, estranged wife of the future George IV, had chosen to live there. Caroline was long fled, but the 'Green Man', a picturesque long-established inn, in which the Assembly Rooms were incorporated, was constantly packed with holiday-makers from London, as well as by local residents. The number of excursions declined in the winter months, however, and Madame Tussaud and her sons decided to close on 17 December and move right into the city centre where bad weather would not hamper visitors. A Christmas advertisement announced that, while grateful for the welcome given by Blackheath, the Exhibition must move on to the Old London Bazaar, Gray's Inn Road, near King's Cross in the City of London. The recommendation of those who had friends in the metropolis was respectfully solicited.

For thirty years Madame Tussaud had been on the move. She did not, of course, realize that her days of wandering were over. The Exhibition would, however, never again leave London.

15

Madame Tussaud settles in London

Early in 1834 Madame Tussaud opened her Exhibition in what was called the Old London Bazaar in Gray's Inn Road. The enormous building, which surrounded three sides of a square, had until five years previously been the London Horse and Carriage Repository. It was then turned into a bazaar – that is, a collection of small enterprises, one of which was Robert Owen's short-lived National Equitable Labour Exchange which bartered goods without the use of cash. The first floor of this three-sided building consisted of a number of large rooms with tall windows. The largest of all, an Assembly Room, allowed sufficient space for a really splendid display of figures. The advertisements in the metropolis stressed the fact that this room alone offered sufficient space for such a show.

A press cutting extols 'one of the most remarkable exhibitions that has been seen in London for a considerable period'. The writer, who seems to have been bored by other attempts at wax portraiture, praises the Tussauds for their successful efforts to overcome the 'vapid velvet faces and gazing but unspeculating eyes' usually portrayed in this medium. He remarks on the care and expertise with which the large room had been prepared.

The two major Coronation groups were shown oppositely. Napoleon's tableau was at one end of the room and King William's 1830 tableau at the other. In between these splendidly attired brilliantly lit *pièces de résistance*, all the other figures were arranged and, in their midst, stood Madame Tussaud herself! Wearing one of her own bonnets and a favourite silk cloak, the wax portrait was so exact that acquaintances hesitated whether to cross the floor to address the proprietress. Marie had always possessed a charming vivacity of expression, and this had been caught to perfection. She appeared to be welcoming her visitors.

As always, the Exhibition was cleverly lit, and this London reporter continues: 'When the whole is aided by the effect of lamplight, it becomes highly interesting; the mellow, artificial illumination throwing a deeper tone over the flesh colour in the figures, and rendering the glare of the glass eyes less remarkable.'

Apart from the Assembly Room in which Marie as always sought to astound the public on entry, there was another room, alluded to by the reporter as 'that ghastly apartment', into which the ladies were advised not to enter. Such advice, of course, is extremely tempting, and the death-masks of murderers and decapitated revolutionaries had enormous appeal. Guillotined royalty and aristocrats were not yet for open display. It was not until some years after her death that they were shown publicly.

During the five profitable months in which the Exhibition remained in Gray's Inn Road, the Tussaud sons supervised and themselves played in the orchestra which accompanied the promenades. They were a talented pair, artistic and musical, and they learnt from their mother to relish history.

On 22 March 1834 they attended a sale of 'Waterloo spoils' and for the sum of £12. 13s. 7d., they purchased Napoleon's carved eagles which were carried with his standard into battle. This memento started off their quest for Napoleonic souvenirs which resulted in due course in a superb collection. For twenty years or so after Waterloo mementoes of Bonaparte aroused little public interest; then a new generation became intrigued.

In the early summer of 1834 the Exhibition moved for a time to the Lowther Arcade in King William Street at the west end of the Strand. This place lay only a short distance from the Lyceum Theatre of nostalgic memory, where an unhappy little Frenchwoman had toiled thirty-two years before. The arcade featured various forms of entertainment as well as shops for fancy goods. The show remained open from eleven until six and then again in the evening from seven until ten. Madame Tussaud's advertisements in the *Morning Post* reminded patrons that her Exhibition was 'admirably calculated to induce youth to make themselves acquainted with History and Biography', and that a band played during the evening promenade.

In August the Exhibition moved again – to Camberwell, where the Old Grove House, an inn lying in one of the numerous pleasure gardens which surrounded London, made a delightful summer background. The

Old Grove House had its own adjoining coachyard, so that Londoners could easily escape the city heat and come to enjoy a meal or use it as an hotel. A spacious room with three tall windows provided sufficient space for the figures, and here the Tussaud family (for it was a family once again, with grandchildren arriving frequently) spent a pleasant three months.

At the end of October the Exhibition moved on seven miles to Assembly Rooms attached to the Mermaid Tavern at Hackney. The Mermaid was also easily accessible to Londoners, standing on the west side of the High Street, and a covered way connected the tavern to the Assembly Rooms, so that all who entered for food or drink must have had their attention caught by ideas of self-improvement and entertainment; above all the young were always eager for acquaintance with 'history and biography' in such an amusing form. From the back of the inn, extensive grounds ran to a bowling green and archery lawn. A shaded 'dark walk' skirted the kitchen garden to a brook running through the grounds. The show was, of course, open all through daylight hours and then 'at half past seven the music began and from eight o'clock all would be brilliantly illuminated'.

Although the winter dispelled the pleasures of strolling down shady walks to the brook, Madame Tussaud found visitors still arriving and she extended her stay in Hackney from two weeks to two months. In the wording of her own advertisements, here the Exhibition was 'favoured with the most brilliant reception since its arrival in Hackney, the Assembly Rooms being filled every evening with the most respectable company'.

Apart from the special sessions for the *labouring* classes, Madame Tussaud took care to entice the well-to-do and, above all, the well behaved – the last thing she wanted were roistering drunks.

During these months at Hackney, the Tussauds were preparing for a triumphal return to Gray's Inn Road. Obviously the great capital city was the proper place for an Exhibition of such quality. London could unendingly produce respectable clientele. Francis became particularly enthusiastic, and he busied himself with exciting transportable decorations for the great room of the bazaar, seventy feet by forty-five feet, 'Magnificent and Unequalled Portable Decoration, superior to any ever exhibited representing a Golden Corinthian Saloon'. This glittering project was well advertised, and Francis took care to give credit to craftsmen who helped him. Mr Bielefeld of New Road was responsible for the elaborate *papier-mâché* ornamentation; joinery work was carried out by Mr Hunt of 22

Left: Joseph Tussaud, Madame Tussaud's elder son. He was born in Paris in 1788, and she brought him with her when she came to England with her Exhibition in 1802. He died in 1865, his only son having pre-deceased him. *Right:* Francis Tussaud, second son of Madame Tussaud, was born in Paris in 1800. She left him there with his father and maternal grandmother when she came to England with the Exhibition in 1802. He joined his mother and brother when he was about twenty-one, and worked in the Exhibition until his death in 1873. Joseph Randall, the eldest of his three sons, then took over control. *Madame Tussaud's Archives*

Below: Family group of silhouettes by Joseph Tussaud. His mother is on the left, a self portrait on the right, and his wife Elizabeth Babbington sits at the harp. *Madame Tussaud's Archives*

Above: Contemporary engraving showing part of Madame Tussaud's Exhibition at The Bazaar, Baker Street/Portman Square. It includes the tableau of George IV and his Coronation Robes, which was set up in 1841. *London Interiors*, Mead, 1843.

Above right: Cartoon by George Cruikshank from *The Comic Almanack* for 1847. Madame Tussaud's Exhibition at The Bazaar, Baker Street/Portman Square.

'I dreamt that I slept at Madame Tussaud's
With cut-throats and Kings by my side;
And that all the wax figures in those abodes
At midnight became revivified.
I dreamt that Napoleon Bonaparte
Was waltzing with Madame Tee . . .'

Madame Tussaud's Archives

Right: Madame Tussaud's new purpose-built Exhibition in the Marylebone Road was opened on 14 July 1884, anniversary of the Fall of the Bastille. 1) First hall with painted ceiling panels by Sir James Thornhill, with the Hall of Kings beyond. 2) Entrance Hall with 'Baron Grant's' marble staircase supported by caryatids. 3) William Cobbett, modelled *circa* 1837. 4) The exterior with grand entrance. 5) The Napoleon Salon, lined with oil paintings and containing the Shrine of Napoleon and many relics. *The Illustrated Sporting and Dramatic News*, 2 August 1884

SEASON OF 1846.

M^{ADAME} TUSSAUD & SONS

Have the high gratification to state that THE GROUP of the

ROYAL FAMILY AT HOME !

CONSISTING OF

Her Gracious Majesty, Prince Albert, and their Four Lovely Children, the Prince of Wales, the Princess Royal, the Princess Alice, and Prince Alfred,
HAVE GIVEN COMPLETE SATISFACTION TO THOUSANDS. The novelties for the present season consist of a

Magnificent Display of Court Dresses,

OF SURPASSING RICHNESS,

Comprising TWENTY-FIVE LADIES' AND GENTLEMEN'S COSTUMES, intended to convey to the **MIDDLE CLASSES** an idea of **REGAL SPLENDOUR**, a most pleasing novelty, and calculated to convey to young persons
much necessary instruction. Amongst them will be noticed the FULL DRESS of His Majesty

LOUIS PHILIPPE, AS LIEUT. GEN. OF FRANCE

As King of the French, worn by himself on all public occasions, with the Grand Star, Cordon, &c., of the Legion of Honour.
The truly beautiful

GREEK WARRIOR COSTUME,

Of surpassing workmanship, conveying an idea of a GREEK OFFICER in full Costume, of matchless beauty, and a curiosity
for the ladies, as a specimen of NEEDLEWORK. The Ladies' Dresses comprise such as are Worn at Court by the Highest
Classes. The Collection now contains upwards of ONE HUNDRED AND TWENTY PUBLIC CHARACTERS. Also,
THE MAGNIFICENT

CORONATION ROBES of GEORGE IV.

Worn and designed by himself, and which cost upwards of £18,000.

THE RELICS OF NAPOLEON,

OF SURPASSING INTEREST. The GOLDEN CHAMBER containing the Camp-bed on which he Died, the Coronation
Robes, the Cloak of Marengo, and the highly celebrated MILITARY CARRIAGE, taken at Waterloo. The magnificent
Rooms fitted up for the purpose, at a great expense. The recent Novelties are

THE NATIONAL GROUP OF EIGHTEEN FIGURES,

IN HONOUR OF THE DUKE OF WELLINGTON,

The Group of the House of Brunswick,

CONSISTING OF FOURTEEN CHARACTERS;

Showing the whole of the British Orders of Chivalry, never before attempted ; consisting of the Robes of the
Garter, Bath, St. Patrick, Thistle, and Guelph, with their Orders, &c. ; the whole
producing an effect hitherto unattempted.

"THIS IS ONE OF THE BEST EXHIBITIONS IN THE METROPOLIS."—*Times.*

Bazaar, Baker-street, Portman-square.

Admission, **1s.** Children under Eight Years, **6d.** Napoleon Rooms and Chamber of Horrors, **6d.**
OPEN FROM ELEVEN IN THE MORNING TILL DUSK, AND FROM SEVEN TO TEN.
G. COLE, Printer, Carteret Street, Westminster.

Handbill of 1846. The words relating to the display of Court Dresses aroused the wrath of *Punch*, expressed in an article which gave 'The Chamber of Horrors' its name for perpetuity. *Madame Tussaud's Archives*

Berwick Street, and the 'glorious gilding' was carried out by Mr Syffert of 55 Great Queen Street, giving maximum effect with his contrasting gold burnish and matt. In all there was 2000 feet of gilding and the entire structure, 'any description of which must fall short of reality', had cost over £1000, a very considerable sum for those days.

In this splendid setting were arranged the Coronation groups and tableaux and various new figures including the popular Duke of Sussex. In spite of the cost of the new décor, Madame Tussaud insisted on keeping admittance at one shilling, with children at sixpence. The macabre Second Room, called inadvisable for ladies to visit, yet advertised as 'highly interesting', cost another sixpence. And the biographical catalogues so revealing of public taste of the time also cost sixpence.

The 29 December 1834 was the day on which Madame Tussaud and her sons opened the most elaborate presentation they had ever attempted. This was even more splendid than the gilded mirrored rooms of 20 Boulevard du Temple. The press reported a striking *coup d'œil*, while 'pleasing modern music' was played morning and evening.

For three months the Tussaud show enjoyed tremendous success, but then the Assembly Rooms were needed, and another move had to be arranged. The sons settled on a location in London's smart West End, and, although they did not envisage the Exhibition remaining there for over fifty years, they thought that at least it would be a more permanent setting for objects which were becoming of increasing value and world-wide interest. At the junction of Baker Street and Portman Square there then stood a large building of curious history. The premises, formerly known as King Street Barracks, had since 1778 been the living quarters and stables of the Royal Life Guards Regiment. In fact, a regiment of the Life Guards marched out of the King Street entrance to embark for Belgium and fight at the Battle of Waterloo.

In 1820, when it ceased to be a barracks, the building was let out in segments, and became known as The Bazaar, Baker Street – Portman Square. This bazaar lay in a very smart area. The eighteenth-century mansions of Portman Square were inhabited by aristocratic families, and Oxford Street lay near by and would, on every morning of the London Season, become alive with grand people jogging their horses to exercise in Rotten Row.

Madame Tussaud took over the large room on the upper floor which had originally served as 'Mess Room of the Guards'. In this special room, and in various small sections jutting out from it, she could arrange her tableaux and figures as she saw fit. The attached private house that faced on to Baker Street provided accommodation for 'the Tussaud family'.

In fact, the place proved ideal. An open area at the back where horses had once been sold was now used for the display and sale of carriages, harness and household goods. The products of the Panklibanon Iron Works, whose saleroom adjoined the Exhibition premises, brought a constant flow of visitors to this corner of Baker Street. The company's advertisements boasted of

general furnishing, ironmongery, tin, copper and iron cooking utensils, table cutlery, best Sheffield plate, German silverware, *papier-mâché* tea-trays, tea and coffee urns, stoves, grates, kitchen ranges, fenders and fire irons, baths of all kinds, shower, vapour and plunge etc. Garden engines are always kept on hand by the proprietors of this establishment and patent radiant stoves.

Exhausted shoppers who had made their purchases would necessarily look with curiosity towards the Exhibition up on the first floor.

Madame Tussaud quickly assessed the benefits of the locality. The Bazaar was conveniently placed for transport. Horse buses were working the Oxford Street route nearby and beginning to rumble down Marylebone Road at the other end of Baker Street. These horse buses accepted advertisements, and Marie was one of the first to make use of them. She had learned the importance of publicity and in 1836 she had no less than 500 handbills and 400 posters printed.

Francis must have been delighted that a lease of several months was in view, for the 'up sticks and move on' life was particularly hard on his glittering decorations, and Joseph certainly heaved a sigh of relief at the thought of remaining in one place for a time.

So in March 1835 the move took place. The 'portable decorations' went first – all that gilding and the stunning chandeliers had to be set up in the great room. An extra 'caravan' had to be hired to transport the Golden Corinthian Saloon from Gray's Inn Road to Baker Street.* Workmen fitted the gilded carvings into place and hung the chandeliers, while Madame and her sons hurried around with costumes, new wax faces and repair tools for the old faces whose noses had been chipped in transit.

---

* The Exhibition reopened soon after the move, but the extensive replanning took three months to complete.

16

The last fifteen years (1835-50)

On 1 June 1835 *The Times* reported:

MADAME TUSSAUD'S EXHIBITION: A completely new arrangement of the figures which comprise this splendid Exhibition has taken place, and the effect is much improved. . . . The effigies of many of the great have not, like the originals, absolutely turned their coats, but they have been accommodated with suits which are much more in keeping with their characters than when they were first exhibited to the public . . . the whole appearance on entering, especially in the evening, when the whole is brilliantly illuminated, is peculiarly imposing and splendid.

The *Court Journal* also commented on the lighting:

When the spacious room is brilliantly lighted up, and the strains of music enchant the ear, this is a scene for a pleasant and instructive hour. The music was provided by Messrs Tussauds and Fishers, and the promenade lasted from 7.30 until 10 in the evening.

In the following July 1836 the *Morning Herald* announced that HRH the Duke of Sussex had honoured Madame Tussaud with a visit and approved of her artistry to such an extent that he was now permitting her to remodel his portrait for her collection.

Among the visitors who often looked in was the Duke of Wellington, who dubbed the Exhibition 'the most entertaining place in London'. He had given sittings for a portrait which was to join a new group entitled 'Great Men of the Late War'. His caustic humour must have been aroused by the sight of himself gazing at General Bonaparte – however, it was not to laugh that he returned and returned again and again to Napoleon's deathbed scene. The sight of his enemy lying there in wax seemed to hypnotize the old soldier – Waterloo, after all, had been the 'nearest-run thing you ever saw in your life'.

Meanwhile, in France, Louis XVIII (that Comte de Provence who took liberties with girl art tutors) had reigned and died, and been succeeded by his brother, witty ridiculous Charles X who abdicated. Since 1830 there had been no King of France but a *King of the French*, as Louis Philippe, son of the Duc d'Orléans, called himself, and in this July the worst of many assassination attempts was made on this King. Louis Philippe was driving through Paris reviewing the National Guard with several of his sons when a Corsican named Fieschi discharged what was called 'an infernal machine'. His invention consisted of twenty-five rifles mounted on a frame which could be discharged by one man. Having obtained 500 francs from a moronic grocer of revolutionary tendencies, he rented the third floor of a house, 50 Boulevard du Temple, overlooking the royal route. When Fieschi let off the trail of powder leading to the twenty-five rifles, the guns went off mowing down the crowd. Eighteen lay dead and twenty-two wounded. But the royal party escaped injury. Fieschi and his two associates were captured running into the rue des Fossés du Temple – how well Marie knew that district. They were guillotined. Soon the Separate Room was showing a wax impression of Fieschi's head beside a model of his ingenious death-dealing machine. Madame Tussaud's Exhibition really *was* an education!

Sixteen months passed in Baker Street and the old lady still seemed unsure of correct tactics. One of her posters urges people to see her figures *soon* because the large premises had been rented for a limited period only. Her sons with their growing families must have been frantic to settle down, but she could not quite make up her mind if this was the best thing for her Exhibition – the waxworks always came first.

In the autumn of 1836 the outstanding success of a certain wax figure consolidated the project of remaining permanently in London. There had been a celebrated young opera singer named Maria Malibran whose melodious voice and dramatic genius won her acclaim throughout the world. After nine years of triumph Madame Malibran was singing in a September festival in Manchester when she was suddenly taken ill and died. The public could hardly believe they had lost their favourite, and even those who had never heard her grieved that she had to leave this world at twenty-eight. There were many portraits to work from and

Marie reproduced the *prima donna* in wax – as only she knew how. She issued 500 posters advertising this one portrait. Those who had never heard Malibran, as well as those who had, flocked to see the beautiful, almost radiant, wax face. 'Now we know exactly what she looked like,' was the cry. A surviving ledger shows that attendances doubled after Madame Malibran's figure entered the Exhibition.

This revelation of the effect a single new figure of a personality could have in the capital decided Madame Tussaud to remain in London. The crowds could come to her instead of the Exhibition travelling to seek the crowds. A long lease for the first floor of The Bazaar, Baker Street, was negotiated. The Tussaud family rejoiced, although none of them dreamed that for over fifty years Madame Tussaud's Exhibition would not leave this corner of Baker Street, or that here it would become a national institution.

She was seventy-six now – a little old lady in fact – and her sons, Joseph, who had been her delight when she started touring, and Francis, that distant, longed-for baby, had turned into bearded middle-aged gentlemen wearing frock-coats and stovepipe hats. They took houses for their own increasing families, and sought a certain amount of independence, but they remained dedicated sons and understood their mother's gifts. Not only had she taught them modelling techniques, but she drummed her theories into their heads. The show must be kept both entertaining and instructive; past and present should be combined, so should the great and the humble, and, above all, they must always produce an atmosphere of glamour. When presenting human history in visual form, it was essential that the figures be accurate in every detail. These admonitions were accepted by her sons, and they maintained the Exhibition's standards as she decreed.

With good reason *Chambers Journal* commented that 'within its doors we can walk, as it were, along the plank of time'. Before the year 1836 expired Madame Tussaud modelled 'from life' the young Princess Victoria and her mother, the Duchess of Kent. At this stage Marie Tussaud did not need to use life masks; like a sculptor she could reproduce in wax by personal observation. Later she added to her collection Lord Melbourne, Joseph Hume the Radical reformer, the elderly Princesses Augusta and Sophie, Prince George of Cambridge, the Duke of Cumberland and Lords Brougham, Harrowby and Auckland.

When the young Queen was crowned on 27 June 1837 the Tussauds already had models of the principal men of England waiting, and within a few months the Exhibition was offering a superb Coronation scene. In the centre sat Victoria, enthroned, wearing her crown and robes and holding orb and sceptre. The Archbishop of Canterbury, supported by the Archbishop of York and Lord Bishop of London, 'implored a blessing.' All personages were carefully 'dressed in strict accordance with the regulations', and a contemporary catalogue illustrates the scene on its cover. Coronations were, of course, jam on the cake which Madame Tussaud had to offer. Everyone longed to know what Westminster Abbey looked like inside and even those present at the ceremony could see very little. The large salon at Baker Street had a coffered roof and elaborate plaster mouldings into which Francis's golden decorations were fitted. The gas chandeliers hung down each side of the hall illuminating all the figures. Visitors, gasping at the *coup d'œil* on entering, found eight long upholstered benches placed so that they could sink down to rest before making a detailed inspection.

George Cruikshank, the artist and cartoonist, was among the thousands who enjoyed the show and, for a series entitled 'London Fashion Plates', he painted ten large aquatints, one of which was called, 'View in Honour of the Coronation. Bazaar. Baker Street. Madame Tussaud's'.

So famous had Madame Tussaud become as an authority on the French Revolution that occasionally admirers wrote asking her opinion on the various 'pretenders' who claimed to be the Dauphin. In August 1839 a lady wrote asking if she would like to accept a book on the Duc de Normandie who was considered a possibility. Marie always hated writing letters and she told Francis to reply, explaining that owing to an indisposition his mother found herself reduced to 'so nervous a state as to be unable to guide her pen'. This was nonsense. She had always disliked guiding her pen, but, as the correspondent particularly requested an answer in her own hand, she signed the letter – the signature is almost as firm as that which ended her letter to François Tussaud thirty-five years before. She did not want the proffered book – it had already been sent to her, 'and we have every reason to think from the Dauphin himself. We are of the opinion he may still be in existence.'

Thirty-two persons had claimed to be Louis XVII and one of these had evoked the interest of Madame Tussaud. As she had seen the Dauphin as a very small boy she had the right to an opinion. Marks and scars were remembered by many who had been at the court of Versailles, but

Madame Royale, the Dauphin's sister, who shared his imprisonment until he was eight years old, never accepted a 'pretender'.

The particular marks that Madame Tussaud could have recalled were a scar on the left instep made by a shoe-buckle prong in an accident with his sister, an unusual vaccination scar on the right arm due to the surgeon's clumsiness, and a distinctive mole on the breast.

More than thirty years after the announcement of the Dauphin's death a Frenchman named Augustus Mèves, brought up as the natural son of a Monsieur Mèves, was told by his mother that he was the son of Louis XVI and Marie Antoinette. Having inherited a substantial sum of money on the death of Monsieur Mèves, Augustus made no official claim. He was (like Marie Antoinette) extremely musical and had given his first public violin recital at the age of seventeen in Edinburgh. No attempt was apparently made to show him to his possible uncle, the Comte d'Artois, who was holding court there, but in the early 1830s Augustus contacted Madame Royale, now the Duchesse d'Angoulême. Although she did not receive him, some accounts state that she placed money to his credit. In 1838, after falling into financial difficulties due to unwise investment, Augustus resumed his musical profession. During this time he played the violin in Madame Tussaud's orchestra and showed her his marks. She was impressed and thought perhaps he might be Louis XVII, but he never could explain his lapse of memory, possibly traumatic, concerning incidents that had befallen him up to the age of eight. Nor did Madame Mèves, his official mother, say why he had not been brought to his sister when young.

Having established herself as a celebrity, Madame Tussaud now agreed, reluctantly, it is said, that a book of her memoirs should be published. A family friend, Francis Hervé, himself of a French *émigré* family, undertook to edit the anecdotes she related, and set them in their historical context to form, he said, 'an abridged history of the French Revolution'. He was not a good historian, and his background facts often go astray, but it is from these *Memoirs*, published in 1838, as well as from contemporary documents and writings, that much information can be gleaned about Curtius's Cabinet de Cire, and Marie's experiences at Versailles and during the Revolution. On her personal and private life and on her marriage she says nothing, though describing in great detail, and with her own assessments, the very wide range of personalities with whom she came in contact.

Madame Tussaud was in her late seventies, and as her editor Hervé says, her dates and chronology sometime became muddled, and her facts not entirely correct, but her recollections of incidents and persons remained remarkably clear and vivid. She had, of course, been a trained observer from childhood. A unique picture does emerge of life in the house of a highly intelligent, artistic showman in the Paris of the late eighteenth century, and the impressions made on the mind of an astute and observant girl by the varied characters of those who visited it.

There is another curious aspect of Madame Tussaud revealed by this book. She was apparently very talkative. No matter who was mentioned she could produce some comment. But amidst innumerable anecdotes she remained extraordinarily discreet. The French Revolution had taught her the danger of airing opinions. Long before she became Madame Tussaud, little Marie Grosholtz had learned that it was safer to hold forth concerning collars and costumes and laces than people. 'Amiable manners' she might cite, or the becomingness of Marie Antoinette's velvet riding habit, but of the dangers and pressures which she had known under the Terror she never spoke. The thin cruel mouth of Fouquier-Tinville and the *amours* and corruptibility of Robespierre are among her few personal revelations. Marie Tussaud had cultivated a habit of carefulness, for carefulness had once kept her alive.

Several members of Francis Hervé's family were silhouettists, and in 1840 one of them made a portrait of Madame Tussaud. With her large bonnet and full bunchy skirts, it shows her stout yet somehow very alert. Joseph may have learned to work his silhouette machine from the Hervés. He took it up again around this time and made a picture of the whole Tussaud family with Rebecca, his wife, seated at the harp and *Grandmère* plumply presiding.

In 1841 there was an innovation at The Bazaar. The large open place where horses and carriages had previously been sold became the scene of the first Royal Smithfield Club Cattle Show. The mooing and bellowing caused anxiety to some business firms in the building, but on the whole the show benefited all in its proximity. Hundreds of country visitors who would not otherwise have come to London flocked to Baker Street, and there must have been many who were overjoyed to leave the cattle pens and climb the stairs to the first floor where they could bask in a different atmosphere.

The Cattle Show proved outstandingly successful and was repeated annually at the premises of The Bazaar for twenty years. Large poultry shows also took place and the tarpaulin overhead coverings were replaced by a lofty roof of wood and slates to improve ventilation. Flaring gaslights illuminated 'vistas of animals' and the aisles were widened so that ladies in their crinolines could move through the show 'with perfect safety'. According to one contemporary account the *coup d'œil* rivalled that of the Exhibition above.

Madame Tussaud, ignoring any disadvantages of noise and smell, welcomed the thronging visitors. 'Who does not remember dear old Madame Tussaud?' wrote one, 'her sharp twinkling eyes, eager look and the truly French style in which she would *faire l'aimable.*'

The custodians of Westminster Abbey asked the expert Madame Tussaud to undertake the restoration of the Abbey's ancient wax effigies, but she answered tartly: '*Voyez, messieurs*, I have a shop of my own to look after!'

In February 1840 the excitement of Queen Victoria's marriage gave Marie the opportunity to enthral romantic crowds. She produced a charming group showing the Prince Consort in Field Marshal's uniform placing the ring on his bride's finger. The little Queen's dress was of real Honiton lace 'by Miss Bidney'.

Soon after this, the insane youth Edward Oxford, who tried to assassinate the royal pair as they drove along Constitution Hill, joined other felons in the Separate Room. When Dickens's *The Old Curiosity Shop* appeared, it became obvious that he had based the description of Mrs Jarley's Waxworks on Madame Tussaud's.

In October of 1840 Madame and her sons made an important purchase, one that would for many years add lustre to the Exhibition. They acquired the Coronation robes of George IV which he had himself designed at the enormous cost of £18000. After the King died leaving many debts, the robes were sold, for his brother William IV preferred less magnificent apparel for the ceremony. At the original auction of George IV's costume on 11 June 1831, *The Times* reported, 'there was very slight competition for any of the articles, and we did not observe that they were knocked down to persons of distinction'. Madame Tussaud did not heed this, but when the robes were put on the market again nine years later by an unspecified vendor, the Tussaud family were in a position to purchase these grand mantles. It took six months to design and build an appropriate setting. In April 1841 the ledger records: 'Set up George IIII' [*sic*]. These

L

laconic words cover the most ambitious project that Madame Tussaud had ever been able to present. The Coronation groups of Napoleon and Queen Victoria were simple compared to this tableau 'acknowledged to be the most splendid sight ever seen by the British public'. She had not forgotten how Curtius drew all Paris to his 'Royal Family at Dinner' all those years ago. Not even felons held the appeal of royalty. Joseph and Francis must have had unusual judgment, for at a time when George IV's flamboyance was out of fashion they designed and supervised his tableau as 'an attempt to do honour to his late Majesty's taste'.

The main portrait of George IV was based on Sir Thomas Lawrence's picture of the King attired for his coronation. The robe he wore in the tableau was the one he had designed for the procession to Westminster Abbey; this was of purple velvet, seven yards long and three yards wide. Draped on each side of the King were the gold-embroidered imperial mantle which he had worn when returning from the Abbey to Westminster Hall and the parliamentary robe of red velvet which he wore at the opening of Parliament. It was claimed that these three ermine-lined robes contained 567 feet of velvet embroidery. Also in the tableau was an exact copy of the ornate throne which George IV had used when, as Regent, he had received the allied sovereigns after Napoleon's defeat. Careful replicas of the crown, orb and sceptre were included. The public got their money's worth in this tableau, which became 'the focus of the gorgeous spectacle offered by the entire Exhibition', said Mead in *London Interiors*.

A reporter from *Chambers Journal*, reeling at the magnificence of gilding and *papier-mâché* ornamentation, gives a general description: 'The walls are hung with crimson silk velvet, and the floor laid with crimson, the whole got up into most tasteful and superb style.'

Criticism would be aroused in the future – not of the actual presentation but of George IV himself. In 1854, in his periodical *Household Words*, Dickens fulminates in an article called 'History in Wax', 'It is in a tone of deep regret that our historian, speaking of these robes, observes, "Their like will never be seen again." I for one do most fervently hope and believe not.' Six years later Dickens could still feel indignation at the sight of these rich robes: '. . . here the writer would meekly ask whether there is not something compromising to the dignity of royalty in the sale of such wares, and their exhibition in this place.' Thackeray expressed an equal sense of outrage in *The Four Georges* in 1861. 'Madame Tussaud has got King George's Coronation Robes; is there any man now alive who would kiss the hem of such trumpery?'*

However, Madame Tussaud never allowed spectacle to destroy the atmosphere of participation. That was the magic: make the people feel they are mingling with the great, do not allow spectacle to destroy intimacy. A contemporary almanac, *Colburn's Kalender of Amusements*, remarks that 'the first people of the day (past and present) appear as if attracted by the hospitality of Madame'. And *Punch* called her 'one of the national ornaments of the feminine species'. Marie Grosholtz had become an institution.

But now that she could afford them, she made no attempt to acquire houses, jewels, fine clothes, *objets d'art*. She met the high-born but evinced no desire to enter Society, to entertain or be entertained. Her sons had to realize that she had not made a confidant of either of them, nor had she a single close friend. At this stage no one dared to question her about her youth or the emotional shock she must have suffered. She never said what she really thought about Marie Antoinette or the revolutionaries – she described what they *wore*! How deeply had she felt the deaths of Curtius and that baby daughter? What had driven her on when things looked dire? To Joseph and Francis she was always affectionate, but of herself – she told nothing.

Unexpectedly, in 1841, François Tussaud came back into the picture. Marie had for years avoided contact with her husband. Now he evidently had heard of and wished to share in her success. Feeling his way somewhat gingerly, he asked a French lady living in London to call on Madame Tussaud. The letter written after her visit by this widow Castille has somehow survived and gives a clear picture:

---

* In the 1860s the robes had to be removed from open display because the foggy air of Victorian London was causing them to deteriorate. Although kept under glass henceforth, the Parliamentary robe disintegrated. The other two survived the fire of 1925 because they were rolled away in a loft at the end of the building, and they were in sufficiently good condition to be shown in the Empire Exhibition in Glasgow in 1938. Their ermine linings had rotted but the velvet and embroidery, even of the fragile red robe, remained intact. When a bomb damaged Madame Tussaud's in 1940 the robes were again safely rolled away. They lay forgotten until 1965 when work began on archives and relics. A search brought them to light, and the splendid purple robe was displayed on the wax figure of George IV in the Brighton Pavilion Exhibition of 1968.

Monsieur Tussaud, On receiving your letter I hurried to find Madame your wife and I succeeded in seeing her today and I submitted to her the letter you wished her to read. The reading aloud of this letter seemed to make a deep impression on the lady. I truly think that this letter will have an effect beneficial to your interests. She asked me to leave the letter with her so that she could read it quietly and doubtless to enable her to make a decision of some sort and let you know later.

All the same I must tell you, Monsieur, that she appears to hold something serious against you, as at first she did not seem at all glad to hear news of you, and she told me that she had given all that she possessed to her sons. These sons have married English ladies – For the rest, Monsieur, I must tell you that she has lived in London for many years and you could write to her simply as Madame Tussaud, owner of the Salon of Figures. You could be certain your letter would reach her for *Madame votre épouse* is very well known in London.

It is impossible for me to describe the beauty and richness of her Salon. In my life I have never seen anything more magnificent. The entrance costs one shilling [chilin] each person which equals more than one French franc. Herewith Monsieur all the information that I can give.

> Receive my salutations and believe me I remain ready to be useful to you as far as lies in my power,
> *M.C. veuve Castille*
> I salute you.

So François had a request and Marie was anything but pleased to hear from him. The letter of the widow Castille makes no bones about the matter. She is willing to try to restore the link between husband and wife but describes the situation with asperity. Why does François use an intermediary who more or less tells him that any letter addressed to Madame Tussaud in London would reach her? Whatever François suggested, he met short shrift. On 27 August 1841 his sons sent a joint reply to his overtures:

Monsieur: Madame Tussaud and ourselves do not wish to correspond with you. We think that you have been supported at ease long enough. At our age we can tell you however that we wish you all that providence can bring you and hope the eternal God can pardon your scandalous conduct.

> F. Tussaud.
> Joseph Tussaud.

The Exhibition is our property.

From this note it appears that old François who had been given power of attorney over all Marie's property in France, who had sold the houses at Ivry-sur-Seine and 20 Boulevard du Temple, and was still living in the house Curtius had built in the rue des Fossés du Temple, had now evinced a desire to share in the fame and fortune of his wife.

Having sent their uncompromising reply, Joseph and Francis forgot about the matter and turned to help their mother with the next major project.

They had often looked at the eagles they had purchased at the sale of Waterloo spoils, and gradually the concept of special Napoleon Rooms emerged. Madame Tussaud had witnessed Versailles and the Revolution; she would make Napoleonic scenes and mementos the apotheosis of her career. Marie had always been fascinated by Napoleon. She had met him as First Consul and again in defeat; his face she had created in wax exactly as it was, and now nearly thirty years after Waterloo he was beginning to arouse interest as a personality. Entries in the Tussaud ledgers between 1841 and 1842 record a steady collecting of Napoleonic relics, many of which came from the estate of Prince Lucien Bonaparte. Items purchased included Napoleon's bedstead, the cloak he wore at Marengo, his riding whip, personal clothing and the 'mantles of Napoleon and Josephine'. The most important acquisition was the great travelling carriage which Napoleon had used at Waterloo. After its capture on the field it was given to the Prince Regent who subsequently sold it to a Mr Bullock for £2000. This gentleman exhibited the carriage in 1816 in the Egyptian Hall where it drew crowds of visitors. Then it toured the British Isles and must have been viewed by thousands. It changed hands several times, eventually going as part payment of a bad debt to Robert Jeffrey, a coach-builder in Gray's Inn Road. There it lay forgotten for a long time. The Tussauds may have seen it dust-covered and cobwebbed when they first came to Gray's Inn Road, but the actual purchase price of £52 was not entered in the ledgers until the week ending 23 January 1842. Although she paid so little, Madame Tussaud had to spent a certain amount of money in getting it back to its original pristine state. Then it became the centrepiece of the Napoleonic Rooms, and at the start people were even allowed to climb into it. Then, as barbarous visitors kept cutting off bits of the upholstery as souvenirs, the carriage had to be railed off.

As the Exhibition, with its various historical tableaux and forty-three single figures, filled every corner of the original premises, rearrangement was essential, and the New Rooms were devised. These were ready in March 1843 and a special catalogue, additional to the regular catalogues, stated that the two Napoleonic Rooms were

effected at a cost to the proprietors of £5,000; magnificently fitted up after the designs of Isabey and Fountain the Emperor's artists, forming a series of *National Reminiscences* of great interest, declared at the Public Office in the Court of Chancery, Southampton Buildings before the following Masters – J. M. Farrer, Esq., A. M. Lynch, Esq., and Sir G. Wilson, Knight.

The ceilings were particularly splendid and great care was taken with the picture frames which were made expressly to show 'the peculiar fashion of Napoleon's time'. In the first, or Golden Room, there was a kind of shrine to Napoleon with the great man standing there, taken 'from the best authority, David' and wearing his own clothes from St Helena (bought from Prince Lucien). Among the mementoes here was the cradle of his son, the King of Rome, with a wax model of the baby in it, taken from Gérard's picture. The second room contained the Waterloo carriage and the famous Table of Marshals which the unnamed owner offered for sale at 4000 guineas. An extra sixpence was charged for admission to these Napoleonic Rooms and this fee included the Separate Room.

As the collection of murderers and felons increased, the public always felt it got its money's worth. So carefully documented and attested was the authenticity of the Napoleonic relics which Madame Tussaud put on display that no one ever raised a query. 'This altogether matchless exhibition', as she called it in an *Illustrated London News* advertisement, had now attained the quality of a small museum. Her New Rooms proved a sensation and remained packed all through the immensely long opening hours from 11 a.m. until dusk and again in the evening from 7 until 10 p.m.

The old lady must have known final fulfilment. She was eighty-one when she modelled her last self-portrait, and this is the one we see today. It shows her much thinner, a tiny person in a big black bonnet, eyes glinting through steel-rimmed spectacles, seeing and enjoying her own creations.

Meanwhile, during the months in which the new Napoleonic Rooms were attracting crowds, Monsieur François Tussaud was still looking for money. He took up the almost forgotten issue of Curtius's inheritance in Mayence. Curtius had never settled the matter satisfactorily; he had – all those years ago – claimed that owing to the disappearance of his brother Charles he had sole right to the entire fortune left by their Uncle Raben. So much water had run under the bridges since the Revolution and Curtius's death that Marie had dropped the matter. But François Tussaud knew that if as Curtius's heir she could make a claim, he as her husband, with power of attorney, could by French law enjoy the money. So now, in 1843, nearly fifty years after Curtius's death, Monsieur Tussaud started to make investigations. He discovered the capital had remained intact, lodged in the Caisse Centrale du Grand Duc in Mayence. It amounted to approximately 3500 French francs and was earning interest. The difficulty lay in producing documentation to further any claims. The authorities demanded details of all sums which Curtius had taken from the estate in his lifetime and the dates on which payments had been made. François enlisted the help of one Steinbreck, but this man was soon appealing for the aid of a notary. The whole business seemed impossible to clear up. Eventually François tried to sell his rights to the inheritance. No one nibbled. So in 1844 he turned again to his family in London, and this time he met with more success. The letters which his sons wrote to old François are conciliatory. The first we have, dated 27 May from Joseph in London, remains cool: 'Monsieur et Père', it begins:

In reply to your letter telling us that you are aged and infirm and incapable of looking after your own affairs we think it is our duty as sons to come over and give assistance. We will come to see you in a few days time to see in what manner we can be useful.

Your servants
J. and F. *Tussaud*

P.S. Send a reply to say if you will be in Paris.

The meeting took place and it must have been a strange one. Francis had grown up with his father, but Joseph had not seen him since leaving France at the age of four. Their mother agreed to this *rapprochement* but remained determined not to become involved herself, and according to family tradition she forbade her elder son, who was now in his late forties, actually to confront his father, and to let Francis do the talking. Maybe she felt she could not trust the charm of that man who had consistently let her down in the past. Joseph complied with his mother's wish but, torn by curiosity, he accompanied Francis to the house in the rue des Fossés du Temple, and managed, without being seen, to peep at his father over a screen. There in an armchair sat a dear old gentleman of benevolent appearance. But whatever appeals Monsieur Tussaud made, they proved vain, for on 16 September his sons were angrily writing a joint letter:

Mon cher père, Since you have enjoyed a life-interest in our mother's property and she has received no profit for so many years, she cannot possibly grant what you ask of her, because, as we have already explained, this would harm *our* prospects. So enjoy your interest as you wish to the end of your days . . . We hope you remain in good health.

J. and F. Tussaud.
P.S. Have the goodness to tell Monsieur Laurier, if he visits you, that we have no wish whatsoever to enter into any speculation concerning a theatre.

This postscript probably gives the clue to Madame Tussaud's wariness when dealing with her husband. He had charmed her in the past, she had given him all she possessed, and over the years every speculation he touched appeared to lose money. Alarmed by old François's desire to obtain a share in her Exhibition, Madame had consulted a London lawyer and on 3 July 1844 signed Articles of Partnership with her two sons. This action secured Joseph and Francis in joint ownership of the business should their mother die before old François. As François was the younger by eight years, this seemed very possible, and they could well imagine the chaos he could create – in fact the whole business might be put in jeopardy. They must have been frank on this subject, and on 5 October they again wrote a firm joint letter:

Mon cher père. After having carefully thought the matter over our mother has decided she cannot grant your requests and has taken the advice of her London lawyer to do nothing whatever.

On 30 December 1844 a long incensed letter reached François from his sons. They accused him of having left their mother for years struggling alone. There is much underlining of words, 'she surmounted all the difficulties by perseverance without asking for one sous from your *pocket* . . . you have had the *sole* enjoyment of her properties for so many years . . . you cannot pretend she has not rendered you *some service*.' Writing as one, they add: 'I do warn you that every time our mother receives a letter from you it makes her ill, and especially when you write that you are coming to see her. To talk of your role as husband is really ridiculous.'

During the next weeks, however, they did ask a long-suffering friend to visit their father in Paris and try to get his projects on paper.

Madame Tussaud's iron health kept steady except when she was sorely tried. Her husband's letters were enough to prostrate any woman, but she kept going with the diversion of work. The years had not lessened her skill, and it was far more entertaining to produce a new group showing Queen Victoria and Prince Albert conferring honours on the Duke of Wellington than to worry herself sick over François.

A Glaciarium with scenic ice attractions departed on expiry of its lease from the ground floor of The Bazaar, but the enlarged, increasingly hygienic Cattle Show continued to bring visitors to Baker Street, and Madame Tussaud could guarantee advertisers that at least 8000 copies of her catalogue would be sold each year. She was amused and flattered by her first mention on the stage. In *The Drama At Home*, played at the Theatre Royal in the Haymarket, she 'appeared' with two of her 'subjects', the Chinese Commissioner Lin who prevented the spread of the opium trade, and his wife.

> To see you in clover comes Madame Tussaud
> Your model in waxwork she wishes to show,
> The King of the French and the Great Agitator [Daniel O'Connell]
> Kings, Princes and Ministers, all of them go
> To sit for their portraits to Madame Tussaud.

Marie's triumph in this instance had lain in procuring a magnificent set of ceremonial clothes as worn at the court of Peking. Another compliment of a sort came from the great showman Barnum who tried to buy the whole Exhibition and transport it to New York. Madame Tussaud and Sons, as the firm was now called, took a certain pleasure in rejecting this offer.

In 1845 John Paul Fischer,* the German artist, painted eighty-four-year-old Madame Tussaud seated at the entrance of her Exhibition. She was *still* entirely devoted to it, and 'Eyewitness' in Dickens's *All the Year Round* would reminisce: 'The present writer remembers her well, sitting at the entrance to her own show, and receiving the shillings that poured

---

* Paul Fischer arrived from Hanover in 1810 and became a court painter. He worked for Queen Charlotte and the Prince Regent and exhibited regularly at the Royal Academy. His water-colour portrait of Madame Tussaud survives in today's Exhibition.

into her Exchequer. She was evidently a person of marked ability and shrewd and strong character.' It is surprising that so old a lady could find time to supervise the box office as well as the studio, but she remained single-minded, and her sons had become a tremendous help. 'The Royal Family at Home' was produced in a new group, with portraiture by Francis Tussaud and costumes by Mrs Joseph Tussaud. The brothers got on well together, which was fortunate, although in one letter Francis refers to Joseph as his mother's 'favourite' because she had brought him up. Joseph lived at 88 Baker Street, Portman Square, and Francis bought a home nearby at 18 Salisbury Place. They had teenage families now, and as a kind of compliment to each other Joseph named *his* eldest son Francis Babbington, and Francis named *his* eldest son Joseph Randall. Among staff, these two were referred to as the *young* Mr Joseph and the *young* Mr Francis. Both grandsons were artistically gifted and worked in the studio from boyhood, as did her granddaughter Louisa. At the age of sixteen, Joseph Randall entered the Royal Academy School to train under the painter Westmacott and improve his techniques, with the idea of eventually taking over the studio. His cousin, Francis Babbington, was also talented but delicate.

In 1846 the Separate Room acquired fresh notoriety and the permanent name of Chamber of Horrors. Curiously enough, this new, attention-catching title came about through an attack on certain aspects of Madame Tussaud's Exhibition in *Punch*. She had advertised the special attraction of her season in a snobbish vein which delighted the public but annoyed the editor of *Punch*. Her words proved an alluring bait to class-conscious Victorians: 'A Magnificent Display of Court Dresses of surpassing richness, comprising 25 ladies' and Gentlemen's costumes intended to convey to the MIDDLE CLASSES an idea of the ROYAL SPLENDOUR; a most splendid novelty and calculated to display to young persons much necessary instruction.'

But this was the year after the repeal of the Corn Laws, of disastrous harvests and hunger and misery in England as well as in Ireland, and under the sarcastic heading of 'A Great Moral Lesson at Madame Tussaud's', *Punch* trounced her for announcing a lavish display in such language:

The collection should also include specimens of the Irish peasantry, the hand-loom weavers, and other starving portions of the population all in their characteristic tatters; and also the inmates of the various workhouses in the ignominious garb presented to them by the Poor Law. But this department of the

Exhibition should be contained in a separate Chamber of Horrors and half a guinea entrance fee should be charged for the benefit of the living originals.

Marie had never considered herself a social reformer; her energies had been entirely concentrated on catching the imagination of the public. She often donated special evenings to charities, but would many people be keen to spend half a guinea to view the degradation of poverty which lay in every back street? *Punch*'s indignant outburst was not written with the intention of helping Madame Tussaud's box office, but it actually did so, and further scolding merely inflated her publicity. There were, at the time, certain doctrinal disputes going on within the Church, and with her unfailing sense of newsworthiness, Marie immediately produced portraits of the leading clergy involved. *Punch*'s editor blew up afresh:

Madame Tussaud presents her grateful compliments to a discerning public, having had peculiar success with her CHAMBER OF HORRORS – a charming apartment cut off from the public room – in which are grouped together bloodshed and homicide in every variety – she has determined to set aside another nook in which the harmless eccentricities of various members of the Church may be duly commemorated. Madame Tussaud proposes to call this apartment 'Clerical Corner'.

These outbursts in *Punch* established the name of Chamber of Horrors as a household word. It appealed to the Victorian taste for the macabre while remaining respectable. The Exhibition was extremely fashionable. There had been other wax shows in the world but never anything like this. Cartoons by the famous Cruikshank and others appeared – 'I dreamt I slept at Madame Tussauds', and 'A Row Amongst the Figures', which depicted a popular song about a midnight political fracas among the 'waxy lot'.

Marie lived and died a French citizen, but in 1847 her two sons applied for British naturalization. One sponsor was Admiral Charles Napier, former MP for Marylebone who had his portrait in the Exhibition. As co-proprietors it appeared to be a natural step, especially when their father was angling for participation. The correspondence between father and sons continued, and although they firmly debarred him from any business dealings, the tone grows less hostile. 'Mon Père,' writes Francis, or 'Mon cher père'; never again is he coldly addressed as 'Monsieur'. When the old man considered moving into a smaller apartment Francis travelled to Paris, and eventually he and his brother agreed to pay half the rent of this new abode. Monsieur Tussaud remained healthy and he was looked after by a lady companion, one widow Bertrand who seems to have taken good care of her charge, for which the sons send her their thanks with phrased 'compliments' in the French manner.

At last Marie's health deteriorated. Strong people are often more resentful than others when teased by the twinges of old age. When her eyes and legs gave trouble this tiny old lady of eighty-six could not suffer her diminishing powers gladly. Then, far worse, she started to suffer from asthma. This terrible affliction, incomprehensible to those who do not know it, plagued her especially at night. The sons wrote that the damp London climate was to blame, but, of course, she had really worn herself to a shred. Yet Madame still came to the Exhibition nearly every day. Nothing else interested her, and the stream of silver shillings which grew into thousands of pounds gave her intense pleasure. She had been totally dedicated for so many years, and although the money did not interest her as such, it represented success.

Joseph Randall wrote of his grandmother:

I can see her now, very small and slight, and wearing a bandana handkerchief tied about her head after the manner of Frenchwomen in full dress 'to keep her hair tidy'. Her eyes were most vivacious, she was a great talker, full of anecdotes and blessed with a faultless memory. She was a Catholic, but during the greater part of her life, piety was not a characteristic. She was 'converted' at the end by a religious relative, and passed a deal of her time in prayer and meditation, but to the horror of her pious companion she generally used a large crucifix which had been placed in her room as a cap-stand. She used to say, 'Beware, my children, of the three black crows – the doctor, the lawyer and the priest.'

In March 1848, the barricades went up in Paris yet again and the abdicating Louis Philippe fled to England, where the hospitality of Queen Victoria never failed to be shown to ill-used sovereigns. Carrying the unlikely pseudonym of Mr and Mrs William Smith, the last Bourbon king and his consort stepped on the quay at Newhaven. Meanwhile in France the provisional government tried to reduce unemployment by directing the hungry into national workshops where jobs were invented at small wages. This created still more rage, and bigger and better barricades went up in the streets, paving stones were pulled up and used with overturned carriages to seal off whole areas. On 14 March 1848 Francis wrote to his father:

I feel most anxious; the new scene in Paris must affect you considerably and at your age the nerves cannot stand such upsets. I do hope that these disturbances have not affected you too seriously. . . . At least I am glad to know that your district is calm. I feel angry for after such a crisis how could it go differently. I pity the poor workers, they behaved so honourably during all this scrap and they will have to suffer plenty of injustice before things get better. They will need philosophy. May God protect them in their peril. Do write us immediately. . . . My mother is getting weaker and her asthma gives her no chance of resting at night.

Paris remained in a state of frenzy and dictatorial powers were accorded to the respected Republican General Cavaignac who took action and brought the capital under control in three bloody days. Between 23 and 26 June, 5000 insurgents were shot dead in the streets of Paris! There were 15000 arrests and 4000 deportations. In England, Louis Philippe remarked blandly: 'The Republic is lucky. It can fire on the people!'

Much of the fiercest fighting had occurred in the faubourg du Temple, and on 29 June the Tussaud sons wrote yet more anxiously to their father:

Mon cher père. I hope that this letter will get an immediate answer after what has passed in that *terrible* Paris. We are wondering about you and hoping that you have escaped in that city of demons. Can one believe that beautiful France can produce such ogres? If you need anything let us know. I am so afraid that all this can do you real harm, so do write us immediately. . . . Oh, how splendid that General Cavaignac could deliver Paris from the hell which that lovely capital nearly became – and France also. May the Eternal Being watch over him. Adieu. Write by return. *Vos très chers fils*

J. and F. Tussaud.

On 5 September the last surviving letter was penned by Francis to 'Mon cher Père'. It announces that in a few days his brother Joseph will arrive in Paris to discuss matters in general, and Francis stresses the pleasure that Joseph will get from chatting face to face. This letter ends: '*Je vous serre la main. Votre fils*. F. Tussaud.'

So the story ended on a happy note, for on 12 December Monsieur Tussaud became extremely ill and sent for a lawyer to rewrite his will. He had run through his wife's inheritance and it was perhaps tactful not to mention her or their sons when there was so little to leave! But the family surely approved his legacy of 5000 francs to Madame Bertrand together with any possessions she might care to take. 'This is the free expression of my last wish,' dictated the old man, and then unable to sign because of blindness, the lawyer and witness took the necessary steps to make the will valid. Four days later on 18 December he died and the funeral took place in the church of St Elizabeth, rue du Temple. He had never departed from the district where he met Marie.

Sixteen months later, in April 1850, Madame Tussaud was looking forward to her eighty-ninth birthday, but her weakness increased. Joseph and Francis visited her every day. A cluster of completely English grand-children was growing up in London and she liked to hear of their doings. During the long nights when it was so hard to breathe, the strange panorama of her life fell into focus. She remembered herself a little German-speaking child of six leaving Berne, travelling down the moun-tain passes by stage-coach, arriving in Paris and discovering the wonder of Dr Curtius's studio; her first lessons in wax-modelling became vivid, and so did pride in her accomplishment. Alone through the dark hours in mid-Victorian London, she remembered the faces she had seen and touched and reproduced – Voltaire, Marie Antoinette, Louis XVI, sweet Madame Elizabeth. Could she believe in those eight years spent among vanished splendour of the Château de Versailles? And were the years of Revolution and Terror really true? She could see the faces of Marat and Danton and Robespierre and Fouquier-Tinville–the Princesse de Lamballe she chose to forget, and there were other moments better forgotten – not the chilling moments when it was expedient to take a mask of some criminal after execution, but others more horrible. There was the morning when the Queen of France went by with heart-piercing dignity on a tumbril; although Marie had fainted it was as if she had seen the proud figure. And there was Josephine, brave in prison, delicious and flirtatious out of prison, and Napoleon's face at the beginning and again at the end. And marriage – well, at least that had given her two sons. She must forgive François for all the rest. And she thought of the four years touring in Ireland and the twenty-six years travelling England, and then the final incontestable success. She deserved her fortune. She had worked every yard of the way. And then perhaps she thought of Curtius – that strange unpredictable man pounding the table and declaiming with his revolution-ary friends – she had loved him dearly, but how curious was his judgment. She could not be very religious, it had never been her bent, not even when living in the household of Madame Elizabeth. But now that death drew near, Marie Tussaud cheerfully accepted the tenets of her faith. She would be buried in the churchyard of that Catholic chapel in Chelsea, which had become a centre for French *émigrés* after the Revolution. She was not a political *émigré* herself, but she had many friends among them.

On 15 April her sons saw that she was going to die. They stayed with her quietly. Marie Tussaud remained practical to the end. She knew that Joseph and Francis were there, and as she slipped away she wanted to give them some sound advice. Opening those dark beady eyes which had seen so much, she looked at her two sons. 'Do not quarrel,' she said, and then like a fluttering bird she was gone – a little bird that no one had ever known well. A secret person. An enigma.

When she lay there, light as a leaf and tiny, the ninety years of her past seemed incredible. Joseph and Francis, now bearded Victorian gentlemen in their fifties, found it difficult to realize all that she had casually related of the past was true. Even with her sons Marie had remained reticent. Always alert and vivacious and ready to throw an anecdote into the conversation, Madame Tussaud remained secretive about herself, about her emotions, about what life had done to her. The family knew that she had been brought up in Paris with Curtius who had taught her to model in wax, and that she had spent eight years at Versailles as art tutor to Madame Elizabeth and the Royal Family. Here was a woman who had spoken with Marie Antoinette, and curtsied to Louis XVI, who had modelled them 'by royal command' and touched their dead faces after execution. She had chatted with Robespierre and most of the revolutionaries, and taken the death-masks of some of those who had mounted the scaffold. Had she so wished she could have repeated the bawdy brilliance of Mirabeau's dinner-table conversation. She had known the Empress Josephine, spoken with Napoleon and recorded his face before victory and after defeat. In Europe there could scarcely be another woman with such memories.

Little Marie Grosholtz had become part of history, and yet of the scars on her own spirit, of her personal fears and triumphs, she said nothing and wrote nothing. The simplest diary describing ordinary life at Versailles would have held great interest, but her recording talent remained entirely visual. We will never know the personal impact made on her by Marie Antoinette.

And how deeply did Marie love François Tussaud, and why did she insist on separation? None of these human aspects would ever be revealed.

Her sons, looking down on the silent shell of Madame Tussaud, were moved by her courage. How she had slaved for them! Without children could she have been so dauntless? Without the impetus of affection could she have maintained her absolute dedication to the Exhibition? Even Joseph and Francis did not know. She remained an enigma to the end.

Epilogue

Madame Tussaud was buried in the churchyard of the Catholic chapel in Chelsea, where many French émigrés lay. When, fifty years later, the chapel was demolished, the coffins were removed and sealed in the crypt of the new church of St Mary's near by, and there her memorial tablet can be found.

Joseph and Francis carried on in her tradition. She had instilled into her sons the importance of spectacle, of quickly presenting personalities in the news and of keeping the show *educational*. Human beings *want* to learn and want their offspring to learn, and the visual pleasure of such learning would gladly be paid for. Joseph and Francis had, while working with their mother, turned into perfectionists.

The year after Marie died, 1851, saw the opening of the Great Exhibition under the patronage of the Prince Consort, in Paxton's vast glass house erected in Hyde Park – the Crystal Palace. London teemed with visitors and Madame Tussaud's opened a new attraction – the Hall of Kings – in a room said to be the largest in Europe. It measured 243 feet by 48 feet. This project had surely been discussed with Marie during her last months, for it bore her stamp. The new gallery, like Curtius's original Cabinet de Cire, combined wax portraits with sculpture and paintings. The monarchs and their consorts stood in authentic costumes, while on the walls hung paintings which included *Queen Victoria in Coronation Robes* by Hayter, *Prince Albert* by Patten, and a copy of Lawrence's famous *George IV*, *William IV* by Simpson, *George III* and *Queen Charlotte* by Reynolds, and *George II* by Hudson. The cost of the Hall of Kings had necessarily to be enormous, but the capital outlay was recouped within a year.

M

Illumination continued to improve and by 1860 500 lamps flooded an 'uninterrupted vista' of figures with light.

Most important of all, Joseph and Francis did not forget their mother's last injunction. They never quarrelled.

Joseph died in 1865 at the age of sixty-seven leaving only one daughter, Louisa. His wife, his eldest daughter and his only son, Francis Babbington, had predeceased him. The son, a talented artist, had died of consumption in Rome at the age of twenty-nine.

When Joseph had realized that Louisa was his only heir, he entered into a fresh deed of partnership with his brother Francis whereby his daughter (married to a Ph.D. named Kenny) and his nephew Joseph Randall (the eldest of Francis's three sons) should in due course inherit control of the Exhibition.

The inclusion of Louisa in the deed caused trouble later. She had no aptitude for modelling, but worked in the wardrobe and kept the ledgers, some of which survive. It would be too much to expect that every descendant of Marie Grosholtz should inherit her zeal and inordinate taste for hard work, and while Louisa no doubt took an interest in the costumes she produced, she was *not* dedicated to the Exhibition.

Some time after her father's death Louisa became the beloved of a French marquis, and departed to live in the south of France. Here she lived in a good deal of style, driving along the promenade at Nice in a carriage and pair. However, her way of life seems to have required more money than the Marquis de Leuville could provide, and in 1881 she insisted in withdrawing in cash her share of the Exhibition. This demand had to be complied with and the loss of capital put a severe financial strain on the rest of the family. A treasured Boucher painting which hung in the Exhibition had to be sold. In the end Louisa was able to marry her marquis, but her affair was always kept 'hush-hush' by the family, and Madame Tussaud must surely have turned in her grave at this granddaughter who, even if she did die a marquise, put pleasure before the family interest.

It was not often that Francis Tussaud's sons were caught napping, but this did occur on one occasion – when Dickens died in 1870. For some reason the great writer had never been modelled, and Joseph Randall worked all night on a portrait. Clay was modelled, the wax poured, the hair and eyes correctly selected, and within a remarkably short time there stood Dickens!

Proud of his status as modeller-in-chief, Joseph Randall would produce over the years a wonderful variety of figures, including the claimant in the famous Tichborne case, the assassinated Viceroy of India, Lord Mayo, the explorers Livingstone and Stanley. The marriage of Princess Louise to the Marquis of Lorne provided the opportunity for a charming group, and portrait figures of great ladies wearing new court dresses by Worth drew fantastic crowds. At the request of the Duchess of Teck (mother of Queen Mary), Joseph modelled a portrait of one Dinah Kitcher, 'the soldier's wife', a woman typical of her kind, who had accompanied her husband through many campaigns.

Amidst the substantial number of documents and deeds which exist in the archives of Madame Tussaud's there are few human revelations, but a fragmentary diary kept by Joseph Randall contains this entry: '16 November 1870. Having so far conquered the inclination to drunkenness as to refrain from exciting liquids as nearly as I can remember for seven weeks to the hour, I intend with my full strength of Will to fight against my next besetting sin, *Procrastination*.'

This was written by a talented artist when thirty-nine years old, a man of great culture, a respected senior member and partner of the family business, who became the father of thirteen children! Maybe the weaknesses of Madame Tussaud's husband, that charming old François, could make cracks in the iron constitution which she handed to her descendants. Can one imagine *her* procrastinating or needing alcoholic support during those arduous touring years!

When old Francis died in August 1873 his will was proved at 'under £40000'. After provision for widow and daughters, the residue of his estate went to his sons, Joseph Randall, Victor, and Francis Curtius.

Throughout the seventies and into the eighties the Exhibition continued to flourish at The Bazaar. New groups, special illuminations for the Prince of Wales's birthday, and additional features such as a series of tableaux entitled 'Fashions of the Day', drew the public. Foreign royalty and notables enjoyed seeing themselves in wax; the kings of Sweden and Norway, the Marquis and Marchioness Tseng of China, and the Prince and Princess of Hesse were among those delighted by the Exhibition.

During its fifty years at the corner of Baker Street, Madame Tussaud's became a London landmark, but problems eventually arose regarding renewal of the lease. Joseph Randall, Victor and Francis Curtius took a momentous step, deciding the Exhibition could afford to move and to build its own premises. They purchased a suitable site in Marylebone

Road; excavations began in 1882, and walls were going up through 1883. Madame Tussaud's flair for dramatic purchases had been inherited by her grandsons. They discovered that creditors were stripping a splendid mansion in Kensington built by the bankrupted company promoter, 'Baron Grant' – an extraordinary personage from central Europe who had made and lost fortunes in financial speculation. Leicester Square, his gift to the nation, remains a fitting memorial, and perhaps there is something a little sad in the disasters that befell so magnificent a financier. 'Baron Grant' had paid thousands of pounds for a vast marble staircase supported by caryatids to grace his town house. Joseph Randall, Victor and Francis Curtius offered £1000 and obtained the staircase for the heart of their edifice. Marie would have approved this bargain in the grand style.

Another acquisition which gave prestige was a set of ceiling panels originally painted by Sir James Thornhill, favourite artist of Queen Anne. He had painted the famous ceiling of Greenwich Hospital, and the panels purchased by the Tussauds added a superb quality to the first gallery. The opening of the new Exhibition coincided with the 150th anniversary year of Sir James Thornhill's death. People who had probably never heard of the painter before craned their necks and could then travel to Greenwich if they wished to see more.

A surveyor's report made just before the finishing touches had been completed confirms the lavishness which would have delighted Curtius and Marie. It beat all the mirrors and candelabra of the Boulevard du Temple. The building was 'highly enriched, with a bold cornice, and all construction of a most solid and substantial nature. Stone dormer windows were filled with handsome frames and glass and there was a balustrade in red concrete. Inside the lofty hall rose to a handsome iron and glass dome.' 'Baron Grant's' two-flight staircase had marble landings and the lower walls panelled in coloured marbles, while the upper portions and roof cornice were painted plaster picked out in gold. The upstairs halls were also very fine. Entering the first gallery from a marble landing, the bewitched visitor gazed upwards at the Thornhill paintings. The walls were covered in drapery (the Tussauds understood acoustics) and the platform for the orchestra was a special feature. After this came a lofty Grand Hall lit by two domes, the ceiling and cornice being in ornamental plaster. In all there were seven stunning halls, which included the two Napoleon Rooms, and the latest addition was at the far end of the building, a Conservatory of Flowers, with waxwork figures placed among them. Thus the public were given their money's worth in true Tussaud tradition.

Special care had been taken concerning fire precautions. Ever since she had seen the first gas lighting tried out in the Lyceum Theatre in 1803, Marie had visualized with terror some blaze destroying her precious wax figures. Now the Exhibition contained curiosities of museum quality. Beneath the thick oak which covered the floors lay what was considered to be a fireproof substance. Heating came by safe hot-water pipes and the main water was laid on to ten hydrants placed in positions capable of commanding both floors with hoses. Two full-time firemen were to be kept on watch. Press reports estimated the entire building had cost £80000.

The stupendous task of removing more than 400 figures and all other paraphernalia from The Bazaar at one end of Baker Street to the Marylebone Road at the other end took a week. The actual removal was carried out by William Whiteleys. There is a description of exhausted workers stretched out to sleep among sheeted wax figures awaiting pedestals in their new palace.

On 14th July 1884 (the anniversary of the fall of the Bastille) the Exhibition reopened in its new premises. Weary workers vanished and important guests took their places, to be regaled with champagne, ices, strawberries and cream. The Tussaud family received the Dukes of Somerset and Cleveland, a host of other peers including Lords Fortescue, Annesley, Cranbrook, son of Lord Salisbury the Prime Minister, and many Members of Parliament. This day marked the apotheosis of the Exhibition to which a little Frenchwoman had with some temerity given her name nearly eighty years before.

Press acclamation was universal, and imaginative embellishments such as the orchestra of ladies playing at intervals throughout the afternoon received much publicity. The press also reported with satisfaction that visitors exhausted by promenading and gazing could refresh themselves, not merely with tea and buns, but in a restaurant where beer, wine, chops and steak were served.

Joseph Randall continued to control the Exhibition until he found the burden too heavy for his failing strength. In 1885 he retired from his position. Although he had accepted his responsibilities and made such a success, his diary records a dismal succession of ailments: 'Infernal cold still on'; 'I am evidently suffering from great depression due to cold.'

With thirteen children his family responsibilities were heavy, though his wife, far from minding frequent pregnancies, is said to have wept when the time came that there could be no more babies!

His eldest son, John Theodore, had modelled his first portrait for the Exhibition at the age of fourteen – this was King Milan of Serbia. Now a forceful character of twenty-three, he stood ready to take over the business. Another son, Louis, and a nephew were completing their training as modellers. The Exhibition had become too large and complicated to continue as a family business. In 1888, a year in which 400000 passed through the turnstiles, Madame Tussaud's was registered as a limited company, five descendants of Marie Grosholtz being subscribers to the Articles of Association. John Theodore was appointed chief artist and manager. Unfortunately her great-grandsons had not heard the old lady's deathbed exhortation. They quarrelled. Louis disliked the inevitable restrictions when Madame Tussaud's ceased to be entirely a family business. He broke away to purchase a site on which he could create a new Exhibition completely under his own control. Litigation followed, after which Louis was obliged to abandon this plan, but he set up a wax gallery in Regent Street intended to rival both Madame Tussaud's in Marylebone Road and the Musée Grévin which was now established in Paris. His hopes were short-lived. Within a year the Regent Street Exhibition was consumed by fire. After this blow Louis continued to show in a small way in the provinces, but he never renewed any connection with the London Exhibition, to serve which his father had had him carefully trained.

Meanwhile John Theodore developed into a clever and extremely efficient martinet. He possessed a fiery temper and his five sisters who worked in the wardrobe and hair and colouring studios were said to tremble visibly whenever their brother entered with an expression of displeasure on his countenance.

In 1889 John Theodore married an artistic woman, skilled in needlework and embroidery. Of their ten children, only one son, Bernard, would choose a career as a modeller. When the 1914–18 war broke out, five of the six sons were old enough to join up and did so. Their mother had the audacity to bargain with her Maker that if her sons were spared she would go to Mass every day for three years, which meant cycling over very hilly country. All the boys came through unscathed.

John Theodore seems to have taken after his great-grandmother; he was a dynamo of energy with her inordinate capacity for hard work, and his journal often notes: 'spent night at the Exhibition'. Presumably a sofa bed existed for the Manager-Chief Modeller. During John Theodore's long reign he produced literally hundreds of portraits, was personally known to many famous people, and met many members of English and foreign royalty.

Unlike Madame Tussaud, who never took up a pen if she could help it, John Theodore enjoyed writing, and he produced many newspaper articles and two books. One, *The Romance of Madame Tussaud's*, was a history of the Exhibition; the other was about those French generals who had accompanied Napoleon into exile. He found it easy to get immersed in historical research; he was never still and his hobbies became numerous. John Theodore liked gardening, riding, driving, sketching and painting, and was deeply interested in mechanical engineering. His numerous inventions, some of which were patented, included a special kind of modelling clay for sculptors. It was lucky that he had inherited the tough fibre of Marie Grosholtz, for John Theodore would have to struggle through two world wars, and see his great-grandmother's monument burn to the ground.

In the nineties the Chamber of Horrors reached new pinnacles of fame. On Boxing Day 1891 a crowd of 31000 people blocked the streets to see the model of Mrs Pearcey, the murderess of the moment, in her reconstructed sitting room and kitchen, the actual furniture of which had been purchased by Madame Tussaud's! In addition to murderers, there were now ghoulish tableaux such as the famous series, 'The Story of a Crime', all arranged to chill the blood and depict a stern moral lesson.

John Theodore had a special genius in building up scenic tableaux. The earliest series represented the sporting tastes of the Victorian period – 'The Boat Race', 'Cricket Match at Lord's', 'Covert Shooting', 'Fishing', 'Yachting'. With his realistic modelling of the sportsmen in the appropriate outfits and with backgrounds by such artists as Bruce Smith, these tableaux became world-famous. When John Theodore's 'Death of Nelson' tableau was first shown at the Naval Exhibition of 1891, the heir to the throne, the Duke of Clarence, was heard to remark admiringly, 'Why it beats Tussaud's', not realizing who had created it.

In 1890, to celebrate the installation of electric light, there was a party for 200 guests to see the switch-on of this new form of instant illumination. John Theodore created for the occasion a dramatic tableau, 'The Execution of Mary Queen of Scots'.

By 1899 increasing demands for space caused the directors to order the demolition of various workshops and offices alongside the building so that a restaurant could be built. The old refreshment room became another gallery for those vivid tableaux which drew big crowds.

In 1900 a dining hall was opened: 'Much use has been made of fumigated [*sic*] oak, the central buffet being a splendid piece of work, and the comfortable chairs are covered with maroon morocco.' All was in the opulent taste of the day; in fact all was just as Marie Tussaud might have directed. The outmoded heating system of 1884 was replaced by the Atmospheric Steam Heating Company's very latest creation.

The new century rolled in, Queen Victoria died, and Edward VII splendidly performed his duties as King of England and First Gentleman of Europe. Madame Tussaud's hummed with activity – hummed with music too, for a variety of orchestras and bands now played throughout the afternoon and evening. In 1908 John Theodore, always toying with new inventions, installed an 'auxetophone' worked by electricity. This device gave reproductions of orchestras and the voices of great singers. For a time the notes of Tetrazzini, Melba, Patti and Caruso echoed through the galleries.*

Then, in 1909, another novelty was presented free of charge. Madame Tussaud's boasted of giving a 'practically continuous high-class cinematograph entertainment'. The north-wing dining room was converted into a theatre for 300 people to look at 'animated pictures of the highest order'. This wording might have been devised by Philipstal in that Lyceum Theatre of 1803 when he combined his Phantasmagoria with a show of wax portraits. In 1911 John Theodore's eldest son, John Edwin, came of age and began work in the Exhibition. Other sons, notably Bernard, also inherited talent for modelling. In 1913 the Napoleon Room was redecorated green and gold in perfect Empire style, the walls panelled to frame pictures, and screens erected for the display of small relics which John Theodore, fascinated by Napoleon, made a point of acquiring.

In June 1914 a complete rearrangement of all the galleries took place, and the Hall of Kings was transferred to a different area with models of King George V and Queen Mary under a vast canopy dominating all other monarchs, as was right and proper when England had the greatest Empire

* There are examples of the auxetophone, also known as the stentaphone, in the BBC sound archives – as an early form of relayed music.

During the night of 18 March 1925 Madame Tussaud's was almost completely destroyed by fire. Bernard Tussaud, great-great-grandson of Madame Tussaud, surveys the devastation. *Madame Tussaud's Archives*

Above: The Grand Hall, 1978. Madame Tussaud's last self-portrait, modelled when she was eighty-one, gazes down the pillared vista, reminiscent of the Assembly Rooms in which she used to show during her touring years, upon the Royal Group at the far end. *Madame Tussaud's Archives*

Above left: On the night of 9/10 September 1940 a German bomb destroyed the cinema, a mould store, and badly damaged the restaurant. The main exhibition was damaged by blast and dirt. King George VI and Queen Elizabeth honoured Madame Tussaud's with a visit to inspect the crater. *Madame Tussaud's Archives*

Left: After the fire of '25 the reconstructed building was opened in 1928. The décor of the Grand Hall, with its palms and draped walls, was typical of the period. Princess Elizabeth on her pony, modelled in 1930, was a great attraction for many years. *Madame Tussaud's Archives*

The sculptors' studio, Madame Tussaud's, Marylebone Road. During the first stages of making a wax portrait, the sculptor builds up the whole figure in clay on an armature, a steel and wire frame. *Madame Tussaud's Archives*

ever seen. *June 1914* – what a poignant moment for reorganization of royal figures when their world was about to crash!

John Theodore worked like a beaver throughout the First World War and so did his bevy of sisters. To keep pace with the progress of hostilities, he made a huge war map in high relief for the Central Hall. In those days before radio and television, people flocked to the lectures given in front of it. They longed to visualize the front where early, easy triumphs were expected! Then attendances diminished, but as the months passed the tide of people swept back – and not only to gaze at the war map. Now khaki became the dominant colour in the throng as troops from overseas as well as British soldiers came to see what their commanding generals looked like, and, above all, to get a peep at the enemy. The Kaiser was there already, of course; dressed up in uniform and a spiked helmet. This particular effigy was attacked and mutilated so often that it had to be removed for a time. It was not soldiers, however, who did the defacing, and so frequent were their complaints at not being able to get a look at the arch enemy, that Kaiser Bill with those villainous sovereigns who were his allies had to be returned to view, although kept in a special area, and any damage was quickly repaired.

As the terrible years rolled by, Madame Tussaud's became a meeting place for a brief hour of escapism. When the doors opened at eight every morning, there would always be soldiers waiting for admission, some straight from the trenches who had a few hours only to spend between trains on their home leave; they would stumble through the turnstiles and after a few minutes assuaging their curiosity, they would fling themselves down to sleep on the ottoman, or curl up on the floor. John Theodore gave orders that they were never to be disturbed. Five of his own six sons were serving in the armed forces.

In the cinema which had now become a feature of Madame Tussaud's, war films were shown. For the civilians the war lectures had to be increased to three a day and supplemented by the showing of war relics. For soldiers the gorgeous costumes on historic figures were of more interest. In Madame Tussaud's they could wander around to music in a diverting wonderland and forget that 'bleeding war'. A newspaper of 1917 described Madame Tussaud's as 'the most interesting and inexpensive entertainment in the Metropolis'. Thousands of weary soldiers found it the best place for a cup of tea and a nap.

The Chamber of Horrors gathered a number of new inmates – war did not stop murder, and the hangman's rope was in frequent use, but the troops had their fill of horror in the trenches and preferred a glimpse of royal ladies in court gowns.

John Theodore was sixty when the Armistice came. His sons returned unscathed, although one of them had been shot down in an early air battle and taken prisoner. Of the returned warriors only Bernard, the fifth son, wished to remain a modeller. The others entered various professions and occupations; one emigrated to Canada and one to Australia. Angelo, the youngest, would become a future director, but his talents lay in painting birds rather than modelling those faces which photography now made world-famous.

In 1919 John Theodore began writing his reminiscences for the *Evening News* and these articles were later published in book form under the title *The Romance of Madame Tussaud's*. In 1923 he celebrated his fifty years as a modeller, and that December his old Uncle Victor, grandson of Marie Tussaud, died, aged eighty-two. He had worked for the Exhibition all his life, mainly on publicity and public relations.

Early in 1925 a new Parliament group, a new Colonial group, and a series depicting 'Our National Sports' were presented. At the beginning of March the Royal Family were attired in new court dresses and an Assembly of Notable Women was announced. On 18 March the last visitor departed, the offices were locked up as usual and all staff went home. Shortly before midnight the two firemen on night duty noticed smoke and tried to use the hydrants themselves before telephoning for the fire brigade. Flames spread with terrifying rapidity, and by the time that every fire engine in London had been alerted and rushed with clanging bells to the scene, Madame Tussaud's had turned into a blaze that lit the whole night sky. The author's grandmother, returning from a dinner party, told her taxi to follow the fire engines streaming past Marble Arch. When she got out on the pavement to watch, a great stream of water from the hoses swept over her feet, and she never saw one satin slipper again. Everyone who had gone to bed within a mile of Marylebone Road rose up and dressed. Windows were flung open, the streets became packed. And the magnificent edifice of Madame Tussaud's burned to the ground. No life was lost and many historic moulds stored in the basements survived, but all that remained in the marvellous Napoleonic Rooms was the charred axle of the Waterloo coach; all the paintings and sculptures were gone, and of 467 models on display at the time only 171 were rescued, and most of these sustained heavy damage. The cause of the disaster was never exactly ascertained, but it was presumed to have occurred through a fault in the wiring of the electrical organ.

Bernard Tussaud arrived on the scene and has described his feelings: 'As I joined my father, white-faced and tense, who was directing operations, the position looked hopeless. All that remained of the work of my great-great-grandmother and her descendants was a pile of smoking rubble and twisted iron girders. It seemed as though Madame Tussaud's had vanished for ever in a holocaust of flame.'

But there was something of Marie Tussaud which could not vanish – her legacy of courage and tenacity. She herself had known reverses, shipwreck, and breakage. The shattered Tussauds felt for a time that they had nothing left except their talent, but then they sat down and assessed the position. They still owned the site and the shell of the 1884 building, and most of the moulds safely stored in the basement had, with certain valuable curiosities and relics, escaped damage. And the trained staff remained. Two of them had worked in the Exhibition for forty years, three for thirty years, two for twenty and one for fifteen. As messages of sympathy poured in from all over the world, the descendants of Madame Tussaud vowed that the Exhibition would emerge again on the London scene.

Refusing to lament over the blackened caryatids of 'Baron Grant's' staircase, the cinders which had been Thornhill's painted ceiling panels, the occasional glass eye that had gazed from a pink and white visage, the Tussauds, whose whole lives had been devoted to the Exhibition, spent the next year planning reconstruction, though the loss of Napoleon's battle carriage and his personal belongings and relics collected with passion over the years seemed very hard to bear. In the summer of 1926 a fresh company was formed, and rebuilding started. The new structure was to include a bigger cinema and a restaurant. Three hundred new wax figures were to be created, and Herbert Norris, well known as an artist and costume historian, was appointed to design and supervise. While it was impossible to reproduce the grandeurs of 1884 – 'Baron Grant's' marble staircase and the Thornhill painted ceilings must be forgotten – the modern building would have dignity of a different kind. There would be modern music and fox-trotting in the restaurant and a Würlitzer organ in the cinema. John Theodore and his son Bernard were appointed chief modellers, and four of John Theodore's sisters would continue to work in the wardrobe and studios. Madame Tussaud's last surviving grandson, Francis Curtius, lived to see the building nearing completion. He had been born in the year that the Exhibition settled in The Bazaar, and had been pushed in his pram up and down Baker Street, had heard the nursemaids talking of the amazing old lady, and he had since childhood worked in wax, specializing in the colouring of the heads. He had given up when the Exhibition ceased to be a family concern in 1889, and devoted himself to his other interests, chemistry and electricity. He was ninety-two when he died, beating his grandmother for longevity.

On 26 April 1928 the new edifice opened its doors. Many living subjects were invited to come and gaze at themselves. Sir Oliver Lodge, whose scientific and spiritualistic studies were exciting the world, found his likeness very exact. Eight thousand visitors poured through the doors that day. And the first film to be shown in the new cinema was a wonderful affair of vamps in the early Hollywood style entitled 'The Private Life of Helen of Troy'.

The Prince of Wales paid a visit incognito, and Queen Mary graciously expressed approval of the way in which her model was attired. She had in fact given Herbert Norris, the costume designer, permission to order a replica of one of her dresses from her own dressmaker, and sent a lady-in-waiting to demonstrate exactly how she wore her jewels.

In came the thirties. Madame Tussaud's took note of world doings. Effigies were so much more amusing than newspaper photographs. In 1933 the portrait of a German who was beginning to be taken seriously in England suffered smears of red paint and had a placard hung round its neck – 'Hitler the Mass Murderer'. Attendants carried the figure away to be cleaned, after which it was returned to its pedestal.

On the fifth anniversary of the Exhibition's reopening, journalists were invited to a banquet in the Grand Hall and then taken on a tour. The Silver Jubilee of King George V was marked by special exterior lighting. When King Edward VIII abdicated, Madame Tussaud's arranged for his radio speech to be relayed throughout the Exhibition. People crowded into the galleries and stood transfixed around the Royal Group listening to the King of England explaining that he could not live without Wallis Simpson as wife. When Mrs Simpson in wax joined the Exhibition she was placed on a dais near the Royal Group, wearing a red satin evening dress and 'ruby' jewellery. An attendant was posted discreetly nearby in case this expensive figure should receive the kind of attention vented on Hitler.

But no attempt to daub paint was made; the crowds just stared agog.

In 1937 a Coronation group of King George VI and Queen Elizabeth had to be set up. Television was beginning and Bernard Tussaud appeared on it for the first time. He demonstrated the modelling of the head of Neville Chamberlain. In May 1938 John Theodore celebrated his eightieth birthday. He had started working in wax at the age of five and never rested from his trade. His energy resembled that of his ancestress.

By now the Munich crisis loomed, but Madame Tussaud's continued to produce glamorous new portraits, amongst them Anna Neagle shown in her film role of Queen Victoria. That winter new up-to-date sound equipment was installed in the cinema.

When the Second World War was impending it was decided not to move any wax figures from Madame Tussaud's, but a number of historic moulds were sorted and taken to the country for safe storage. When hostilities broke out Hitler was placed with the group of 1914–18 enemy leaders, and Bernard Tussaud modelled a likeness of Goering. As in the Kaiser's day, people longed to know what their enemies *looked like*. But this war proved very different from the last when Madame Tussaud's had become a haven for tired soldiers between leave trains. The partial evacuation of Londoners, virtual disappearance of children, shortage of staff and, above all, the black-out caused attendances to fall drastically. The restaurant remained open, and the band played from 7 to 10 p.m. but such was the emptiness of the halls that it looked as if the great Exhibition might have to close.

Then, as sometimes happens when shock and excitement die away, the attendance figures rose. Adjusted to black-out conditions and desperately in need of entertainment, people remembered the refrain, 'Let's go to Madame Tussaud's'. When soldiers from overseas arrived, they always asked for Madame Tussaud's in their sightseeing tours of London.

During the first months of 1940 Bernard Tussaud and members of his studio staff were kept hard at work making portraits of war leaders, but these busy personages could seldom grant sittings. To supplement the information gleaned from photographs, Bernard and his staff were frequently to be seen (and recognized by the police!) stationed at vantage points in Downing Street and Whitehall waiting to observe and take notes. Medals and medal ribbons became extremely difficult to obtain. On applying to the appropriate source for a replica set of medals for General Gamelin, the Head of Wardrobe was crushingly informed that none of the General's forty-five decorations was available in replica. France had not yet fallen, so Bernard asked Cartier of Bond Street to apply for help in this matter to their Paris house. The correct selection of medals arrived and the General took his place decorated *comme il faut*.

On 22 July 1940, as the German army crashed through France, John Theodore Tussaud, great-grandson of Marie, celebrated his eighty-second birthday. He celebrated the occasion by modelling a portrait bust of Queen Mary in his own patented self-hardening clay. Within two months came the Battle of Britain, and on the night of 9/10 September a direct hit destroyed the cinema and damaged the restaurant. No lives were lost but the wall of a storeroom filled with moulds not yet evacuated to safety collapsed. The moulds, which were stacked up, toppled into the crater to be irretrievably smashed. Two hundred and ninety-five male heads and fifty-seven female heads were lost, many of them being of historic interest.

Dirt, rubble and broken glass kept the Exhibition closed for some weeks, but cheering messages arrived from all over the world, and King George VI and Queen Elizabeth honoured the crater with inspection! A further incendiary bomb landed on 23 September without causing much damage, and in December the Exhibition was open again. The Hall of Tableaux had received the worst effects of the blast and could not be reopened, but a constant stream of new personalities mounted their pedestals in the other halls. Troops now began to make a focal point of Madame Tussaud's – the fantasy, the accuracy, the sense of war perspective drew soldiers and civilians alike.

As the war continued, restrictions became increasingly stringent. Clothes rationing meant acute problems, for the small number of coupons allocated to Madame Tussaud's proved totally inadequate, and much of the large stock of pre-war materials in the wardrobe – velvets, satins and silver lace – were unsuitable for wartime personalities. Many of the 'subjects', Lord Mountbatten and Tommy Handley among them, provided some of their own clothing or helped out with coupons. Nearly all the new entries needed to be attired in uniform, and uniform materials were in particularly short supply. Soap rationing also caused some worry, for fine curd soap had always been used for washing wax faces and shampooing the hair. Now the staff had to make do with a small allocation of liquid soap.

On 13 October 1943 John Theodore died quietly in his sleep at his home in Croxley Green. This great-grandson of Madame Tussaud was perhaps the nearest to her in vision, drive and energy, and he had inherited her splendid constitution. Born in 1858, his life had been entirely devoted to her Exhibition, and even after the blow of that 1925 conflagration he remained at work for another eighteen years, so active in fact that no one could now believe that he had actually gone.

During the clearing of the cellars of John Theodore's home, a black tin box was discovered. When opened, it was found to contain the papers brought over from Paris after the death of old François Tussaud back in 1848. There were a number of legal documents relating to numerous unsuccessful property deals, several letters written by Curtius (such a good hand!), the inventory of his house at Ivry-sur-Seine, and the only letters ever seen written by Marie Tussaud – those she sent her husband from London, Scotland and Ireland in the years 1803 to 1804.

John Theodore left only a few thousand pounds. Like his great-grandmother he had worked with passion for the Exhibition and not to amass money.

Bernard, his son, carried on as Head Modeller, and Joan, one of his daughters, remained in charge of the wardrobe all through the difficult years. Perhaps the most acute of all shortages was that of hair, for it had always been obtained from the Balkans and the Balkans were now under enemy control.

For Christmas 1943, visitors rejoiced to see new models of the teenage Princesses Elizabeth and Margaret attired in blue gowns with silver trim made by Norman Hartnell and approved by the Queen – a little glamour was welcome after so many girls in uniform.

When peace came many new figures were needed for the Exhibition, but the pre-war stocks of modelling materials were practically exhausted and hardly any blue or grey glass eyes (which had originally been imported from Germany and Czechoslovakia) remained. It began to look as if only dark-eyed subjects could be portrayed! Eventually, to the relief of studio staff, a European family which specialized in glass-eye manufacture arrived to settle in London. Then, unexpectedly, the new National Health Service caused a crisis by allocating all available supplies of fine plaster for medical use. No moulds could be made without this substance and urgent representations had to be made pointing out the value of Madame Tussaud's to the nation as a dollar earner.

Restrictions eased and in 1949 a catalogue twice the size of pre-war catalogues was printed, the first since paper rationing had been introduced in 1942.

The centenary of Madame Tussaud's death in 1850 brought world-wide press comment, and many mentions on radio programmes. Radio personalities such as Jimmy Edwards, Joy Nichols and Dick Bentley were coming increasingly to the fore in the Exhibition, drawing in many visitors to see their favourite broadcasters 'in the wax'. Jimmy Edwards gave an extra-special sitting to Madame Tussaud's senior hair-insertion expert to make quite sure that his famous moustache was right.

The sudden death of King George VI in February 1952 necessitated a new Coronation group – the seventh in the history of the Exhibition. Bernard modelled the portraits of Queen Elizabeth and the Duke of Edinburgh, and it was decided to follow the theme used by Madame Tussaud for George IV's coronation, when a reproduction had been made of the throne room at Carlton House. For the new group, nineteen members of the staff were employed on a reproduction of the throne room at Buckingham Palace. Four tons of plaster, 1000 feet of timber and 600 feet of tubular scaffolding were needed. The original manufacturers of the throne-room carpet were traced, and it was discovered that the loom cards had survived. Permission was obtained for a length of the Tudor Rose pattern carpet to be woven, and two crystal chandeliers, copies of those in the palace, were ordered. In the wardrobe Madame Tussaud's great-great-granddaughter Joan completed the Queen's coronation dress of white embroidered with gold and her crimson velvet ermine-trimmed state robe. Norman Hartnell, the royal dress designer, delivered the Queen Mother's turquoise dress and Princess Margaret's pink one. The press had a preview of the £10000 tableau, but the Queen's white and gold dress was not put on until the actual Coronation day.

Visitors thronged London all through that summer and Madame Tussaud's remained packed. In November Beatrice 'Birdie' Tussaud died, aged seventy-eight. She was the last of John Theodore's sisters who had worked with that formidable genius in the Exhibition. She had spent her life in the colouring and hair-insertion studio and although she had not imparted her skills to anyone in the family, she had trained a first-class successor. Bernard and his sister Joan were now the only members of the Tussaud family working for the studios and wardrobe.

Attack on the wax figures remained a hazard; one of the most unexpected took place in February 1954 when a thirty-year-old draughtsman, in protest against the government's educational policy, smashed with a hammer Sir Winston Churchill's head and those of three other political figures. The damage cost £1000 to repair.

Gradually the bombed site was cleared and redeveloped. A full-scale Planetarium, with equipment imported from West Germany, was opened in 1958 by the Duke of Edinburgh to great press acclamation. How Marie would have revelled in this most appealing of all educational projects!

Joan Tussaud retired from the wardrobe, but Bernard worked on as Modeller-in-Chief. His brother Angelo joined the board in 1959 and under a new Managing Director fresh developments continued through the 1960s.

It was only now that the historic aspect of Madame Tussaud's began to receive serious attention. The archives which had survived fire and bombing were set in order, records scattered through many files were assembled and collated. The curious story of Marie Tussaud and her teacher Curtius emerged. Painstaking research in Paris, London, and the reference libraries of those provincial cities and towns visited by Madame Tussaud during her touring years, gradually revealed her story. Relics believed lost came to light when cupboards and lofts, long untouched, were cleaned out. Out of one dusty parcel fell the coronation robes of George IV and from another the robes of Napoleon and Josephine. These by good luck had not been on display at the time of the fire.

In September 1966 came a tremendous new project – 'The Battle of Trafalgar – as it happened', which gives

an accurate reproduction of the lower gun deck of the *Victory* where some forty sailors are serving four guns on the port side. Below on the orlop deck is the cockpit where Nelson died. Only Nelson is a portrait and only Nelson is in wax. The shafts of sunlight, the darkness of collision, the flash of gun fire, the smoke of black powder, the sounds of a wooden ship in water are reproduced.

Not only the eyes and ears are assailed but the nostrils can smell Stockholm tar and rope. This tremendous educational entertainment was opened by Admiral Sir Philip Vian, famed fighting sailor who as commander of H.M.S. *Cossack* had rescued British seamen from a German ship with the cry 'The Navy's here!'.

Fresh ideas can aid old skills. A new surface technique was tried out on the portrait of Nelson and the first living subject to be modelled in this manner, which broke away from smooth texture, was Sir Francis Chichester.

N

In September 1967 Bernard Tussaud died at the age of seventy-one, and for the first time no member of the family remained active in the Exhibition. Bernard had been the great-great-grandson of Marie. His brother Angelo had retired from the board earlier in the year.

As in the past, death caused no halt in the progress of the Exhibition. In October a contemporary 'Exhibition within the Exhibition' was opened. Called 'Heroes Live', this was a constantly changing collection of portrait figures of men and women currently in the news. A variety of media was used for these figures, and there was a variety in their size. De Gaulle, for example, was nearly twice life-size modelled in concrete, while Brigitte Bardot was in wax in the classical tradition. This, together with the use of sound, projection and lighting effects, made 'Heroes Live' an entirely new concept, which was praised by Dr Roy Strong in an article published in the *Spectator*.

Madame Tussaud's always had a diverse appeal – historic and popular. While the Beatles used a picture of their wax models to illustrate the sleeve of a record, the bust of Marat and the death-head of Fouquier-Tinville, both the work of Marie's own hands, were loaned to the Royal Academy for its 1968 exhibition, 'France in the Eighteenth Century'. Marat's bust was placed beneath David's painting of the death scene, and it was easy to imagine little Marie Grosholtz proud to help a great artist with her life-like model. David wanted an exact reproduction of Marat's assassination – Marie gave it to him, and to generations to come.

1969, which had a record number of visitors, marked the completion of 200 years of public showing, for Curtius, who had started his modelling career in Paris under the Prince de Conti's patronage, opened his first permanent public Exhibition in 1770.

For the first time another permanent Exhibition was now launched. Holland was the country chosen, and on 25 September 1970 'Madame Tussaud in Amsterdam' opened its doors in the heart of the city.

Meanwhile the London interior was reconstructed. A pillared Grand Hall, based on the design of the nineteenth-century Assembly Rooms which had been Marie's favourite venue, was completed. Her last wax self-portrait was placed looking down the brilliantly lit *coup d'œil* so often emphasized. Visitors could move at their own pace among the waxen figures; only an orchestra to accompany the promenade was lacking.

In 1973 Wookey Hole Caves and an adjacent paper mill in Somerset were purchased. This was the start of a programme of expansion embracing a variety of family entertainment outside London. The former paper mill transformed so that it could house moulds and relics. Visitors can look over 'Madame Tussaud's Store Room' there. In London, modern studios, more convenient if less picturesque, have replaced the old ones, but tradition is not forgotten and in 1975 a conservatory resembling that attached to the 1884 building was built.

The educational aspect stressed by the founder continues. The naughtiest and most inattentive child could hardly experience the noises and smells of the Battle of Trafalgar, rush past the famous people of today and glance for a minute at the kings and queens of history, without learning *something*. And no youngster has ever left the Planetarium without receiving a wondrous impression of our starry universe.

Of course, the Exhibition must change with the times, but the pattern of all that Marie Tussaud learnt in the Boulevard du Temple and during nearly thirty years of touring and her last years in London remains. It is quite extraordinary how often she is mentioned as a person. The working staff continually find themselves saying: 'I like that, it's Madame Tussaud', or 'I don't think that quite comes off. It's all right in itself, but it's not Madame Tussaud'.

The stamp of her personality endures. One difference exists, however, and the old lady would certainly approve. It just would *not* be possible for her to sit in person at the box office counting the money brought in, for more than two million visitors a year now pass through her Exhibition.

Perhaps the most touching tribute to Madame Tussaud's comes from a nineteenth-century Exhibition attendant who only signs himself 'L.B.' He knew the founder and her sons personally, and his recollections of the family history, painstakingly written down over a hundred years ago and preserved in the archives, reads: 'There is no more that I can tell but what is already known. The exhibition as far as I can judge is improving yearly, and I trust that it may flourish for centuries to come.'

Appendix 1: Inventory of 20 Boulevard du Temple

To give an idea of the enormous number of pictures, mirrors, chandeliers, and pieces of furniture collected by Curtius in his two houses and left to Marie on his death, the following is an extract from the eight-page inventory of No. 20 Boulevard du Temple. It is surprising to note in the inventory that no rooms in this Paris house seem to have been set aside as studios. Almost every room contained *some* wax figures and modelling material, and one has to presume that work was carried out in many corners. The fourteen-page inventory of the house at Ivry-sur-Seine gives the impression that not only had Curtius an eye for paintings, but he found the collection of furniture and *bric-à-brac* irresistible. Every room of this private country residence, as well as those of his large Paris house-cum-Exhibition, must have been overflowing. Had Marie managed to transport the contents of the houses she inherited to England, doubtless many treasures, as well as her own chairs from Versailles, would have reached her London Exhibition. This translation of one of the closely written pages of the inventory of No. 20 Boulevard du Temple in the autumn of 1794 gives an idea of the Main Gallery:

In a room on the ground floor giving on to the Boulevard, known under the designation of the Cabinet of Figures, the evidence is as follows: a large looking-glass in its frame adorned and decorated with crystal; another glass in two panels, in its frame of carved and gilded wood; another glass set in its panel of wood, another little glass in its frame of gilded beading; a glazed pottery stove with its copper flues; two little writing tables; two bench-seats stuffed with straw; another bench in Utrecht velvet; a velvet-covered dog-kennel; a square cashier's table covered in waxed cloth; three chairs with straw seats, a stool in

Utrecht velvet; two branched wall-chandeliers and three copper candle-holders with crystal pendants; three lamps, each with three lights; three console tables in carved and gilded wood with marble tops; a clock in its case decorated with gilded copper; a barometer in its dial-case; two pairs of curtains in cotton material; two curtains in red serge; two pairs of large curtains in green taffeta; eight small muslin curtains; thirty-six pictures representing various subjects, painted in oils in their gold frames; 114 others, glazed in their gold frames; two more looking-glasses set in their panels decorated with gold mouldings; sixteen busts in their cases, each with three glass sides; nineteen other cases with glass panels, containing animals; twenty-nine other similar ones containing various objects; four more small tables; four side-tables three with copper gallery; another little table and two chairs stuffed with straw; a large mirror in the antique style, with its borders and capitals in glass with ornament of gilded wood; three large copper candlesticks; two tin candlesticks; one guitar; an Egyptian mummy in its case of painted wood; two cane chairs; four Argand lamps,* each with a single light; a small dressing-table; two pieces of glass not set in panels or frames; twenty-eight figures of large size, each clothed in its costume; ten other figures to the waist, also clothed; three other figures recumbent on beds; sixteen heads; an infant in its little chair with seat stuffed with straw, clothed; another little child, naked; two lanterns and two lamps; two flower-vases in blue glass; two large pictures painted on canvas; two more figures, one large-size, the other a bust, in their case with a glazed frame; and various other occasional objects.

* The name 'Argand lamp' was applied to a lamp and gas-burner invented by Aimé Argand (1755–1803). In France it was known as a *quinquet*.

Appendix 2: The 1803 Biographical Catalogue

Seventy pages of the 1803 catalogue are devoted to the lives of Bonaparte, Carrier, Hébert, Marat, Mirabeau, Charlotte Corday, Robespierre, Frederick the Great, Benjamin Franklin, General Kléber, the Princesse de Lamballe and numerous others whose names are now forgotten. These sketches must have been dictated, or at least scrutinized, by Madame Tussaud, and they provide a guide to the opinions she voiced openly in this year when Napoleon was only beginning his conquests. He gets a good wigging for 'ambitiously planning' the invasion of England, and the 'overthrow of her people, their laws and their liberties'; Josephine has only one paragraph which calls her a 'woman possessed of great abilities of mind and body', but hints that her connection with Barras may not have been 'of the most honourable nature'. Carrier has the longest biography of all, and it presents his own defence for drowning and shooting, which is not uninteresting. Civil wars have always been noted 'for the reprisals made by one party upon another; and there never was a civil war during which the revolters perpetrated so many horrors, cruelties, murders, and massacres as in that of *La Vendée*'. Charlotte Corday gets a eulogy. Marat is 'the enemy of the whole human race', and Robespierre 'affords a memorable instance of the effects of sudden elevation in debasing the human mind by making it ferocious. . . . He affected to be called a *Sans-Culotte*, but his clothes were always chosen with taste and his hair was constantly dressed and powdered with a precision that bordered on foppery'.

There is a short note on Madame de St Amaranthe, widow of a colonel of the Life Guards killed in the Tuileries: 'Robespierre in the height of

BIOGRAPHICAL

SKETCHES

OF

THE CHARACTERS

Composing the Cabinet

OF

Composition Figures,

Executed by

The Celebrated Curtius of Paris,

AND HIS SUCCESSOR.

Accurately selected from all available Sources of Information.

EDINBURGH:

PRINTED FOR THE PROPRIETORS,

By Denovan and Company,

LAWN-MARKET.

1803.

MARAT.

THIS man, from the very beginning of the Revolution, evinced the most barbarous intentions. It was he, who, at an early period of it, and ere any blood had yet been shed, uttered the execrable sentiment,—" That three hundred thousand heads must " be struck off, before liberty could be established!" This bloody sentiment, regarded at that time as a prophecy, actually contributed to the assassinations that ensued.

IF not the adviser, he was at least the apologist for the massacres of September. On that, and on every other occasion, where there was the least prospect of danger, he disappeared; and is said to have taken refuge in a subterraneous apartment, where he carefully secluded himself, until his party had prevailed.

HIS disinterestedness, joined to his sufferings, had endeared him to the Parisians; for he lived in poverty, and was actually tried for his life before one of the tribunals, by which he was acquitted.

F

BY turns the tool of Danton and Robespierre, he lived, as it were, the enemy of the whole human race, and died the victim of a woman's vengeance.

IT is not to be denied, that Marat possessed some abilities, although they were disfigured by presumption, and obscured by passion. Previously to the Revolution, he passed through Switzerland to France, and resided for some time in England. He even distinguished himself as a man of letters, and acquired the reputation of considerable scientific attainments.

Title page and extract from Madame Tussaud's Catalogue for her Exhibition in Edinburgh, May 1803. The educational aspect of the Exhibition is already emphasised. *Victoria and Albert Museum, London*

his glory became enamoured of the lady's beauty, and importuned her to become his mistress, but, on meeting with a refusal, he ordered her head to be struck off by the guillotine.' Madame du Barry, 'elevated by accident from a brothel to a partnership in the throne', is suitable castigated, and the details of the end of the Princesse de Lamballe were certainly known to Madame Tussaud, for she mentions the perpetration of 'a thousand barbarous and indelicate acts'.

The paragraphs entitled 'The Late Royal Family of France' explain how Curtius managed to keep this group until it was shown in the Trianon after the outbreak of the Revolution, and subsequently how Marie was able to bring it to England:

The history of this unfortunate family is so well-known as to require no comment. The full length Portraits of the King, Queen, Princess Royal and Dauphin were taken by royal authority, to be sent as a present to the late Tippo Sultan a short time before the breaking out of the Revolution; the likenesses are equal to nature, and do much honour to Curtius. The commotion which took place in Paris prevented the King from putting his intention into effect – and the Portraits remained concealed in the possession of Curtius and his successor until they were privately conveyed to this country.

The catalogue ends with three items: the shirt which Henry IV of France had been wearing when he was assassinated; 'the best conserved Egyptian Mummy ever seen in Europe'; and 'A model of the Original Guillotine, upon a scale of three inches to a square foot, accurately measured from that by which many thousand celebrated characters suffered in the Place de Grève at Paris'.

O

Appendix 3: Madame Tussaud's touring years (1802-35)

Surviving press reports, posters, handbills, and catalogues give a remarkably comprehensive picture of Madame Tussaud's Exhibition during her long years of touring. Listed below are visits on which there is documentary information. Madame Tussaud seems to have taken few holidays, and from 1802 until she finally settled in London, touring was her life.

Alnwick: 1827
Bath: 1814; 1815; 1824; 1831
Belfast: 1808
Birmingham: 1813; 1822; 1823; 1831
Blackburn: 1822
Bolton: 1821
Boston: 1819; 1825; 1826
Brighton: 1822
Bristol: 1814; 1823; 1831
Burton-on-Trent: 1830
Bury St Edmunds: 1825
Cambridge: 1818; 1824
Canterbury: 1818; 1833
Carlisle: 1828
Chelmsford: 1825
Cheltenham: 1823
Chester: 1822
Cirencester: 1824; 1832
Colchester: 1824; 1825
Coventry: 1823; 1831
Cork: 1805

Deal: 1818
Derby: 1819; 1830
Doncaster: 1826
Dover: 1833
Dublin: 1804
Duffield: 1830
Dumfries: 1828
Durham: 1827
Edinburgh: 1803; 1810; 1811; 1828
Gainsborough: 1826
Glasgow: 1803, 1804
Gloucester: 1823; 1832
Grantham: 1830
Greenock: 1804; 1808
Hull: 1812; 1826
Ipswich: 1818; 1825
Kidderminster: 1822
King's Lynn: 1819; 1825
Kilkenny: 1805
Leamington: 1831
Leeds: 1812; 1820; 1827

Leicester: 1830
Lincoln: 1819; 1826
Liverpool: 1813; 1821; 1829
London: 1802; 1803; 1809; 1816;
   1833; 1834; 1835
Louth: 1826
Maidstone: 1816; 1833
Manchester: 1812; 1813; 1820; 1821;
   1822; 1829
Newark: 1819; 1829
Newbury: 1816
Newcastle: 1811; 1827
Northampton: 1824
North Shields: 1811; 1812; 1827
Norwich: 1819; 1825
Nottingham: 1819; 1829
Oxford: 1824; 1832
Penrith: 1828
Peterborough: 1824
Plymouth: 1815

Portsmouth: 1815; 1830
Preston: 1822; 1828
Reading: 1816; 1832
Rochester: 1818
Salisbury: 1816
Sheffield: 1819; 1820; 1829
Shrewsbury: 1822; 1830
Stamford: 1824
Southampton: 1816
Stockton: 1827
Sunderland: 1827
Taunton: 1815
Wakefield: 1820
Warrington: 1822
Waterford: 1804
Worcester: 1814
Wigan: 1821
Yarmouth: 1825
York: 1812; 1826

Appendix 4: Chronology

1761   Anne Marie Grosholtz is born at Strasbourg, the posthumous daughter of Joseph Grosholtz, a soldier from Frankfurt, and Anna Maria Walder of Strasbourg. She is taken to Berne, where her mother acts as housekeeper to a German-born doctor and wax modeller, Philippe Guillaume Mathé Curtius.

1767   Marie is taken to Paris by her mother to join Dr Curtius, now established there as a successful wax modeller under the patronage of the Prince de Conti. Marie is taught wax modelling from a very early age.

1770   Curtius opens his first public wax exhibition in Paris.

1780   Marie, now a talented modeller in wax and working in Curtius's exhibition, is appointed art tutor to Madame Elizabeth, sister of Louis XVI. She goes to live at Versailles.

1789   Curtius calls Marie home to his house in the Boulevard du Temple in view of the political situation. On 12 July the mob seizes wax busts of Necker and the Duc d'Orléans from the exhibition. They are paraded through the streets, royal troops fire, and the first blood of the Revolution is shed. Curtius participates in the storming of the Bastille on 14 July.

1793   Louis XVI and Marie Antoinette are guillotined. Marie models their decapitated heads by command of the National Convention.

1794 Curtius dies at his country house at Ivry-sur-Seine, leaving Marie as his sole heiress. She continues to model and to manage the Exhibition in the Boulevard du Temple.

1795 Marie marries François Tussaud, a civil engineer from Macon.

1796 Marie's daughter is born, but dies in infancy.

1798 Marie's son Joseph is born.

1800 Marie's son Francis is born.

1802 After the Peace of Amiens, Marie decides to take her Exhibition to England, accompanied by her eldest son. She exhibits at the Lyceum Theatre, London.

1803 Marie takes her Exhibition to Scotland.

1804 Marie takes her Exhibition to Ireland. She decides not to return to her husband in Paris.

1808 Marie leaves Ireland for Scotland and England and starts twenty-six years of touring in both countries.

1835 Marie decides to settle permanently in London, with the Exhibition at The Bazaar, Baker Street/Portman Square.

1848 François Tussaud, Marie's husband, dies in Paris. They had not seen each other since her departure in 1802.

1850 Marie dies in London in her ninetieth year, leaving her Exhibition to her two sons, who in due course are succeeded by their descendants.

1884 Marie's grandsons move the Exhibition to a new, purpose-built building on the present site in Marylebone Road.

1889 Madame Tussaud's becomes a joint stock company but the family retain artistic direction and management.

1925 Madame Tussaud's Exhibition is almost entirely destroyed by fire. Rebuilding followed in 1926.

1928   The Exhibition reopens with the addition of a cinema.

1940   Enemy action destroys the cinema, and damages the rest of the Exhibition, but it reopens within a short time.

1953   With the accession of Queen Elizabeth II, Madame Tussaud's presents the seventh Coronation Group in its history.

1958   The London Planetarium, on the site of the war-destroyed cinema, is opened by the Duke of Edinburgh.

1966   The beginning of a major rebuilding and improvement plan to update the 1928 post-fire reconstruction: 'The Battle of Trafalgar – as it happened' with sound, light and special effects is opened.

1967   Bernard Tussaud dies. Sculptor and great-great-grandson of Madame Tussaud, he was the last of her descendants to be directly associated with the Exhibition. 'Heroes Live' opens.

1970   200th anniversary of the first public opening of Curtius's Cabinet de Cire in Paris. To mark the occasion, Admiral of the Fleet Earl Mountbatten of Burma presides over a dinner in the Grand Hall, to which all living subjects of wax portraits are invited. The only other genuine Madame Tussaud's in the world opens in Amsterdam.

1972   In London the new Grand Hall is completed, and new studios are built above the Exhibition.

1973   Wookey Hole Caves and Mill in Somerset are acquired at the start of an expansion programme embracing a variety of family entertainments outside London.

1975   The Conservatory opens, to be followed in 1979 by new tableaux.

1976   Tolgus Tin, Cornwall, is purchased.

1977   The Queen's Silver Jubilee Year. For the first time 2½ million visitors came to the Exhibition.

1978   The shareholders of Madame Tussaud's accept an offer made by S. Pearson & Son. As a result Madame Tussaud's becomes responsible for the operation of Chessington Zoo.

Select Bibliography

Abel, L. (Beffroy de Reigny). *Histoire de France pendant 3 mois du 15 mars jusqu'à 15 aôut.* Paris, 1789.

Alger, J. G. *Paris in 1789–1794.* London, 1902.

The Annual Register. British Library.

Anon. *A Collection of Modern Voyages. Vol. 3. Journal of a Tour in Ireland in 1804.* London, 1805.

Anon. *Chasseurs Nationaux de Paris. Projet de Formation de Six Compagnies de Chasseurs Nationaux.* Paris, 1789.

Auber. *Collection complète de Tableaux historiques de la Révolution.* Paris, 1802.

Audiffret, H. *Dictionnaire de la Conversations et de la Lecture.* Paris, 1833–51.

Bachaumont, L. Petit de. *Mémoires secrètes depuis 1762 jusqu'à nos Jours.* London, 1777–89.

Balteau, J. *Dictionnaire de la Biographie française.* Paris, 1833.

Bourbon, A. de (Mèves). *Dieu et Mon Droit.* London, 1876.

Bufferon, H. *Les Portraits des Robespierre.* Paris, 1910.

Brazier, N. *Chronique des Petits Théâtres de Paris.* Paris, 1883.

Cain, G. *Les Anciens Théâtres de Paris.* Paris, 1906.

Carr, J. *The Stranger in Ireland*. London, 1806.

Castelot, André. *Paris the Turbulent City*. London, 1963.

Dalrymple, Elliot G. *Journal of my Life during the French Revolution*. London, 1859.

Délécluze, E. J. *Louis David, son École et son Temps*. Paris, 1855.

Disher, M. Willson. *The Greatest Show on Earth*. London, 1937.

Dreyfous, N. *Les Arts et les Artistes pendant la Période révolutionnaire, 1789–1794*. Paris, 1906.

Dulaure, J. A. *Nouvelle Description des Curiosités de Paris 1785, 1787, 1791*. Paris.

Duval, G. *Souvenirs de la Terreur de 1788–1793*. Paris, 1841–2.

Furet, F., and Richet, D. *The French Revolution*. London, 1970.

Favrolles, M. de (Mme de Guénard). *Mémoires historiques de Jeanne Gomart de Vaubernier, Comtesse du Barry*. Paris, 1803.

Fleischmann, H. *La Guillotine en 1793*. Paris, 1908.
———. *Anecdotes Secrètes de la Révolution*. Paris, 1908.

Fournel, V. *Le vieux Paris, Fêtes, Jeux et Spectacles*. Paris, 1863.

Fournier, E. *Deux Mots d'Histoire sur les Figures de Cire: L'Illustration 22 mai*. Paris, 1852.

Gazette Nationale ou Le Moniteur Universel. Paris, 1789, 1793.

Ginisty, P. *Mémoires d'une Danseuse de Corde*. Paris, 1907.

Goncourt, E. and J. *La Société Française pendant la Révolution*. Paris, 1852.

Hué, F. *Les Dernières Années de Louis XVI*. Paris, 1814.

Hervé, F. *Madame Tussaud's Memoirs and Reminiscences of France*. London, 1838.

Jèze. *État ou Tableau de la Ville de Paris*. Paris, 1760.

Lebreton, G. *Essai historique sur la Sculpture en Cire*. Rouen, 1894.

Lefeuve, C. *Paris, Rue par Rue, Maison par Maison*. Paris, 1875.

Lenôtre, G. *Les Massacres de Septembre*. Paris, 1907.
———. *La Vie à Paris pendant la Révolution*. Paris, 1936.
———. *The Guillotine and Its Servants*. London, 1929.

L'Intermédiaire des Chercheurs et Curieux. 1877, 1900.

Lyceum Theatre: Cuttings, etc. 1781 to 1840, British Library.

Madame Royale (Dsse. d'Angoulême). *Royal Memories of the French Revolution*. London, 1823.

Mead. *London Interiors*. London, 1841–4.

Mercier, L. *Tableaux de Paris*. Paris, 1782.

Pernoud, G., and Flaissier, S. *The French Revolution*. London, 1962.

Pinkerton, P., and Ashworth, J. H. (eds). *The Reign of Terror. A Collection of Authentic Narratives written by Eyewitnesses of the Scenes*. London, 1899.

Pyke, E. J. *A Biographical Dictionary of Wax Modellers*. Oxford, 1973.

Reilly, D. R. *Portrait Waxes*. London, 1953.

Rénouvier. *Histoire de l'Art pendant la Révolution*. Paris, 1863.

Ryan, R. *The House of the Temple*. London, 1930.

Sellers, C. C. *Benjamin Franklin in Portraiture*. London, 1962.

Thiéry, L. V. *L'Almanach du Voyageur à Paris*. Paris, 1786.
———. *Guide des Amateurs et Étrangers*. Paris, 1787–8.

Tussaud, J. T. *The Romance of Madame Tussaud's*. London, 1919.

Vatel, C. *Histoire de Madame du Barry*. Versailles, 1883.

Vaulx, H. F. de. *Louis XVII*. Paris, 1928.

Williams, H. M. *Memoirs of the Reign of Robespierre*. London, 1795.

Watson, Elkanah. *Men and Times of the Revolution*. ed. W. C. Watson. New York, 1851.

LIBRARIES AND ARCHIVES

Bibliothèque Nationale, Paris; Bibliothèque Historique de la Ville de Paris; Archives de Paris; Minutier Central des Notaires des Archives Nationales, Paris; Archives de la Mairie d'Ivry-sur-Seine; Le Musée Carnavalet, Paris; Baptismal register, old St Peter's Church, Strasbourg; Baptismal register, Stockach parish church, West Germany; The British Library, London; India Office Library, London; John Rylands Library, Manchester; John Johnson Collection, New Bodleian Library, Oxford; Ashbridge Collection, Marylebone Public Library, London; Guildhall Library, London; Public libraries in the English, Scottish and Irish towns visited by Madame Tussaud during her travels; The Victoria and Albert Museum, London; Madame Tussaud's Archives, London.

Index